D0455454

LUDWIG II

THE MAD KING
OF BAVARIA

LUDWIG II
THE MAD KING
OF BAVARIA

BY
DESMOND CHAPMAN-HUSTON
AND EDITED BY
OSYTH LEESTON

DORSET PRESS
NEW YORK

PUBLISHER'S NOTE

Major Desmond Chapman-Huston died prior to the completion of this work. The final revision of the book was accomplished by Osyth Leeston.

Originally published as *Bavarian Fantasy*

This edition published by Dorset Press
a division of Marboro Books Corporation.
1990 Dorset Press

ISBN 0-88029-493-0

Printed in the United States of America

M 9 8 7 6

To
T. B.

. . . What matter who may hear me,
If I must miss thy fond, unlearned praise?
Helen Lady Dufferin

CONTENTS

Posterity cares nothing for discretion or reticence, and very little for veracity ; therefore tell all it is likely to want to know ; otherwise it will distort or invent.

Prelude

IT is my privilege to offer to Field-Marshal His Royal Highness the Crown Prince Rupprecht of Bavaria my sincere and deeply grateful thanks for his trust and kindness in placing at my disposal for the purposes of this biography the entire contents of the secret Archives of the Royal House of Wittelsbach. I was specially privileged to be granted this unique favour. Not only was I admitted to all the documents, diaries, memoranda and, most valuable of all, letters to and from King Ludwig II preserved in the secret House Archives, but given complete freedom to use them as I wished. The result is that this book is based entirely on first-hand material and owes little, if anything, to the mass of material published about the King. It contains nothing for which there is not concrete evidence.

Unfortunately it will be impossible for any future writer to enjoy the research privileges extended to me and which I deeply regret the advent of the Second World War prevented me using even more exhaustively. When the Munich Residenz was bombed in 1944 the secret House Archives were partially destroyed, including the catalogue ; everything salvaged was removed to Nymphenburg and Hohenschwangau.

That the secret Archives remained sealed for some fifty years after the death of Ludwig II had the inevitable result that most of the information published about him was fragmentary or conjectural. Unfortunately he was considered by many popular biographers good romantic material and the results were deplorable ; here, to the utmost possible extent, Ludwig writes his own life and reveals himself.

A few writers went to published Wagnerian sources for material, but little concrete evidence about the inner life of Ludwig was to be found at Bayreuth.

No one interested in music, Ludwig II, or Bavaria, can fail to be grateful to Mr. Ernest Newman for his truly monumental *Life of Richard Wagner* to which I am in a general sense indebted. Dr. Richard Sexan's biography of Duke Karl Theodor in Bavaria, the world-famous oculist who was the father of Queen Elizabeth of the Belgians, will shortly be published and will illuminate the period dealt with here.

Any romantic illusions concerning Ludwig II that I may have consciously or subconsciously derived from others were speedily shattered when I began studying the first-hand material, till then such a closely-guarded secret. Popular Bavarian illusions apart, there was little that was fairy-like about Ludwig or his destiny. The record is dark, tragic, pitiable, terrifying ; to try to romanticize it in order to tickle the ears of the groundlings would seem to me to be little short of literary prostitution.

Few men and, as far as I know, no Monarch has had such a detailed and fully documented biography as the one of Ludwig II that it has been given to me to compose, simply because it is largely written by his own hand. Normally all such revealing material would be destroyed.

Not long before his death some strange premonition of oncoming disaster caused Ludwig to demand the return of his intimate letters to Wagner, Paul of Taxis, Varicourt, Hornig, Hirschberg, Kainz, his beloved governess Sibylle von Meilhaus (Baroness von Leonrod), and others.

To us, Ludwig's immediate value is that he is a terrifying example of the prevalent evils of perpetual adolescence to which in contemporary life individuals and nations seem so prone.

Basically this is the personal history of a man ; Bavarian and European histories have been dealt with only where they impinge directly upon the King's personality and destiny. A full historic treatment would have deflected attention from a unique pathological case and made the book too long. Light is inevitably thrown on the few important events by which Ludwig II will be remembered in history, but on which, generally speaking, his influence was negative rather than positive.

Nevertheless, long before others did so, Ludwig II foresaw the danger of Prussianism dominating the German peoples and poisoning Europe, and, as far as he could,

never ceased to work for the freedom and independence of
Bavaria and the other self-governing German States ; he
disliked Napoleon III and admired, though he distrusted,
Bismarck ; yet, soon after the onset of the Franco-Prussian
War in 1870, his sympathies veered to France. Probably
he never fully realized the infamy of the Iron Chancellor
in deliberately bringing about the fatal contest at his own
chosen moment by means of the forged Ems telegram ;
because of an uncanny streak of intuition and native
shrewdness in his make-up, Ludwig knew quite well that
Bismarck tricked him into sponsoring the plan to make the
King of Prussia German Emperor, thus destroying the
wholesome balance of the German States and Peoples.
Ludwig's sensible suggestion that the Imperial Crown
should be worn alternately by the Heads of the Houses
of Hohenzollern and Wittelsbach was quite feasible, had
long historic precedent behind it in the Holy Roman
Empire, and had it been adopted, might possibly have
prevented two World Wars. Bismarck's explanation as to
why this course was not even seriously considered is a
perfect example of his political chicanery. By narrowing
the German Empire into a mere Hohenzollern family preserve he destroyed the political equipoise of Europe and
ruined the Hohenzollerns.

Geographically, historically and culturally the centre of
Europe, contiguous to Austria, Italy, France and Switzerland, close to and having historic ties with the Low
Countries, Bavaria had—indeed still has—centripetal,
cohesive and unifying forces, and powers of leadership far
more deep-seated, subtle and commanding than an out-
lying State, basically Slavonic, such as Prussia could possibly have. Those who anticipated disaster for Europe and
the deliberate and senseless destruction of Austria after the
First World War, and the crippling of Bavaria after the
Second, saw clearly and objectively. We may yet see Prussia
admittedly a mere province of the dropsical Soviet Empire.

Inclined by his nature towards Liberalism until his mental
powers began to deteriorate, Ludwig II disliked all forms
of repression. He inherited from his ancestors a liberalizing
tradition of love of art, architecture, the humanities and

music for which the ancient and illustrious Royal House
of Wittelsbach has long been world famous ; in addition,
from his grandfather and father he inherited a real interest
in letters, philosophy and, more particularly, science.
Although good Catholics, the Bavarian Rulers were one
and all wide-minded and tolerant, democratically keeping
on debatable subjects an open mind.   Ludwig II supported
Döllinger in his noble fight for intellectual and religious
freedom and, as Bavaria was the centre and stronghold of
that prolonged and bitter struggle, his Sovereign's overt
support, and his admiration and warm personal friendship
for his former tutor meant more to Döllinger than can now
be accurately estimated.   When judging Ludwig we must
therefore bear in mind his contribution to the fight for
religious and political freedom and toleration.   Ludwig
had a proper respect for the Holy See but, like all Liberal
Catholics, disliked and distrusted Vaticanism.

Whatever the final verdict of history on the Kingship of
Ludwig II, the cardinal, and in the long run probably the
most important, fact in his life is that he, in spite of immense
purblind opposition, rescued Wagner the man and the
musician.   He petted, praised and encouraged Wagner
personally, was humble towards his genius, bowed before
his greatness as a composer, consistently subsidized his
significant musical projects and (except Wilhelmina Planner
and Cosima von Bülow) did more than any living being to
foster the composer's vast creativeness and succour it for
the world.   Without Ludwig, Wagner, creatively speaking,
would in all probability have been maimed, possibly even
destroyed.

At this point I must crave the indulgence of being allowed
to obtrude a personal note.

I lived in Bavaria a great deal between 1927 and 1934
mainly for the purpose of collaborating with Daisy Princess
of Pless in the writing of her Memoirs [1] ; and, later, collaborating with Princess Pilar of Bavaria on a travel book [2]

---

[1] *Daisy Princess of Pless*, 1928, *From My Private Diary*, 1931, and *The Private Diaries of Daisy Princess of Pless*, 1873–1914 (Albemarle Library, 1950, London, John Murray).

[2] *Bavaria The Incomparable* (London, 1934, Cassell & Co.).

about her beloved and lovely country and, after that, working with her on our biography of her first cousin, King Alfonso XIII of Spain.[1]

In Munich I scoured the secret Archives for any scrap of material concerning Ludwig and Wagner and, while doing so, was told by Dr. Ignaz Hösl, Curator to the Crown Prince Rupprecht, that he understood there were unpublished documents at Wahnfried : I determined to see and, if it proved worth while, get permission to use this material. As there is a tenuous connection between the Wagner family and ours I several times went to Bayreuth to pay my respects to Frau Winifred Wagner, widow of Siegfried, the great composer's only son ; but there was nothing at Wahnfried suited to my purpose.

All I found in the Royal House Archives that could be described as an addition to our knowledge of Wagner was the detailed, vivid account of his last hours, death and funeral given in Chapter 13. Written at the time and on the spot for Ludwig II by von Bürkel, his Court Secretary, it takes us into the death-chamber in Venice, shows us once again Cosima's superb devotion and, at the same time, somehow humanizes and endears Wagner to us in a unique fashion. He could not exist without feminine inspiration and subservient devotion and, could he have known of Cosima's royal immolition, would not only have loved it, but have considered it supremely fitting.

While immersed in the task of collecting and sifting the Ludwig material for this book, I occupied a little chalet high above the town of Starnberg overlooking Starnberger See and Ammer See. In the centre of the Ludwig-Wagner country, it enjoyed a superb vista of the whole panorama of the Bavarian Alps from the Wendelstein (6,030 ft.) to the Zugspitze (9,725 ft.).

Ludwig II, who once loomed mightily in those regions, was gone ; the puissant House of Wittelsbach which reigned in Bavaria for over seven hundred years was temporarily in eclipse ; Hitler was posturing in the Royal town of

---

[1] *Don Alfonso XIII : a Study of Monarchy*, by H.R.H. Princess Pilar, of Bavaria and Major Desmond Chapman-Huston (London, 1931, John Murray).

Berchtesgaden in the shadow of the Watzmann. In Munich the quietude of night was sullied by the thud of marching feet, hysterical shrieks of 'Heil Hitler' and, where once Wagner's music inspired the multitude, the crapulent strains of the *Horst Wessel leid* and similar diuretic, outraged the waiting stars.

Then, after the Roehm blood-bath of June 1934, the attentions of Hitler's local myrmidons becoming really annoying, I decided to give up my mountain erie, but fortunately could not foresee that nearly twenty years would pass before circumstances allowed me to finish this book.

In addition to the Crown Prince Rupprecht, I have many people to thank for prolonged and generous help in preparing this biography. King Ludwig's first cousin, Prince Ludwig Ferdinand, who was of course the eldest son of Prince Adalbert ('the good uncle', who held the symbolic candle at Ludwig's baptism, and who played such a loyal and sympathetic part in the denouement of the tragedy), went on answering my questions until within a short time of his death. He and his consort (the Infanta Paz of Spain) were the last two surviving members of the Royal Family who knew Ludwig well, loved him, and who, in all circumstances, supported and championed him. Their children, Princess Pilar and Prince Adalbert,[1] have helped me continuously, but of course neither of them knew the King. As a serious historian well known in Germany and Spain, Prince Adalbert has been as invaluable as he has been indefatigable in the tedious work of clearing up obscure points and answering perplexing questions. I must, however, emphasize the fact that neither the Crown Prince Rupprecht, Prince or Princess Ludwig Ferdinand, Princess Pilar, Prince Adalbert, or any other member of the Bavarian Royal House, has seen a line of my manuscript, or is in any way responsible for anything I have written.

The late Dr. Hösl, already mentioned, was unfailing in his help and advice. To Baron Zu Rhein, Comptroller and Keeper of the Privy Purse to the Crown Prince

---

[1] In July 1952 the Prince became the first Ambassador of the West German Federal Republic to Spain, his mother's country.

Rupprecht, I appealed for help at every difficult point and his wide historic knowledge and sound advice were always mine to command. In particular he went to great trouble to have made for me photographs of unpublished Royal portraits in the possession of the Crown Prince.

Joseph H. O. Craven wrestled manfully with the obscurities of the Secret Diary and the technicalities of the post-mortem ; Frank Webb spent the autumn and winter of 1938 making a chronology and sorting and arranging material ; then they both went to war. Herbert Gurschner helped me to arrive as near as possible to correct translations of passages that are obscure in Ludwig's flamboyant German, but for more than six years he too was in the army and unavailable. My dear friend Edward Hutton had the patience and generosity to read the manuscript, and to encourage me by his approval and valuable suggestions.

D. C.-H.

LUDWIG II
THE MAD KING
OF BAVARIA

CHAPTER ONE

THE BOY : 1845–1854

IN Munich, the second highest capital in Europe, August is apt to be uncomfortably hot. Wise Müncheners who can afford to do so go to the mountains, and in the late summer of 1845 the lovely new city, largely created by the reigning King, Ludwig I,[1] was crowded with trippers, most of whom (except the North Germans) were welcome. In the Residenz, the imposing town palace of the Royal Family, all the blinds were down because the King, who had been on the throne some twenty years, and his consort Queen Thérèse were at Nymphenburg, the summer palace so charmingly situated in an artificially created park a few miles north-west of the capital. There, in the south-west wing built by Effner in the first decade of the eighteenth century, the Sovereigns occupied a suite of rooms on the ground floor. They stand now almost as they did then, bourgeois, gloomy, depressing, over-filled with a heavy mixture of indifferent Empire and tasteless Biedermeier furniture, as dismally early nineteenth-century German as anything could well be. True, they had been modernized by the King, who had established in a small dark room, reached through a little door in the bedroom panelling, a fearsome-looking metal bath with attendant horrors in the shape of many clumsy pipes, one of which suggested a large garden hose, by means of which His Bavarian Majesty presumably enjoyed something not too utterly unlike the delights of a shower-bath. The adjoining water-closet, if neither ample nor elegant, contained everything essential —except adequate light and ventilation.

Immediately above the King's rooms were those of his eldest son, the Crown Prince Maximilian [2] who, two years earlier at the sensible age of thirty-four, after sowing an agreeable quantity of wild oats, had married his cousin

---

[1] Born 1786 : succeeded 1825 : abdicated 1848 : died 1868.
[2] Born 1811 : succeeded 1848 : died 1864.

Marie, niece of King Friedrich Wilhelm III of Prussia. To bring a Prussian Protestant princess to Catholic Bavaria, and a Hohenzollern at that, was a risky proceeding. The marriage took place in October 1842 at Munich, and seven months later the Crown Princess had a miscarriage ; she was very ill indeed, and for fourteen days was not told what had happened.

For this reason the doctors and members of the Royal Family, assembled in the Crown Prince's apartment on Monday, August 25th, 1845, were in a state of even more acute anxiety than is normal on such occasions. The expectant mother, as her portrait by Josef Stieler in the Gallery of Beauties in the Munich Residenz shows, was at that time very lovely ; although not tall, she was extremely graceful, with blue-black hair, large blue eyes, lovely slender hands with tapering fingers, and a wistful charm inherited from her Hesse-Homburg mother rather than from her Hohenzollern father. One thing about the Crown Princess not apparently considered ominous, even by her doctors, was that she had a very small pelvis.

The apartment of the Crown Prince was in every way more cheerful than that of the King, his father, beneath. Being on the first floor it commanded westward the imposing vista composed of water-pieces, fountains, cascades and statues, some three miles long and flanked by splendid woodlands which make the park of Nymphenburg famous in a country of magnificent palaces, and which to English visitors recall Hampton Court. The bedroom of the Crown Princess is little changed to-day. If somewhat formal, it is spacious and sunny ; the walls covered with green silk tapestry with a satin stripe, all the decorations and furniture are Empire—Empire candelabra hold candles and the handsome green window hangings harmonize with the walls. The Empire double bed, standing in a slightly bowed recess in the wall facing the windows, is big enough for half a dozen expectant mothers as small and fragile-looking as the Crown Princess Marie. To the left of the bed stands a night-table of wood, inlaid and gilded, decorated by a short green silk curtain worn thin by the touch of many long-dead hands.

In the minds of the King and Crown Prince all sorts of happy omens clustered round the date : it was S. Ludwig's Day, and he was not only patron saint of Bavaria and France but of both Catholics and Protestants. The King, who was of a sanguine, mercurial disposition, waited impatiently for the arrival of what he hoped would be his first grandson in the male line, and direct heir to his throne. True, the Succession was not exactly in danger because he had three younger sons, Otto, Luitpold and Adalbert : but Otto, who, to his father's joy, had become King of Greece thirteen years earlier, was by that fact excluded from the Bavarian throne and, anyhow, never succeeded in begetting legitimate children. Luitpold, who had married an Austrian Archduchess, was therefore, at the moment, Heir Presumptive ; he had, as yet, only one son, seven months old, who was Heir Apparent. The sex of the expected baby therefore concerned Prince Luitpold and his family very closely ; should it turn out to be a boy, Prince Luitpold and his son would lose the second and third places in the order of the Succession and—if the boy grew up and married —might well be excluded from all possibility of ascending the Throne. The great question also concerned, though in a lesser degree, Luitpold's youngest brother Adalbert, then unmarried.

Believers in such matters may find it ominous that the King waited so anxiously for the child's birth, and welcoming it so joyously, was soon to deal his coming grandson an irreparable injury. Involuntarily, Uncle Luitpold was cast by fate to play the part of the wicked uncle, Uncle Adalbert, who held the symbolic candle at the baptism, that of the good uncle, never failing his nephew, impregnably loyal and faithful.

The King, Queen, and Crown Prince Maximilian, surrounded by their Royal guests and all the available members of the Royal Family and the Court, awaited the great event in the Empire salon adjoining the bedroom. There was no shade because the nearest trees were some three or four hundred yards away, and in the hot August sunshine and the clear mountain air every detail of the outside scene stamped itself on the memory. No sun, however, penetrated the bedroom ; the handsome curtains were drawn, the heavy shutters closed. A beam of light, a breath of air, might endanger the lives of both the mother and the expected child.

The Crown Princess had no great intellect or force of character and, as Bismarck noted later, but ' scanty interest in politics ' ; deeply affectionate, she was of orderly habits and all her life liked to keep somewhat spasmodically a record of events important to herself and her family. She had no feeling for historic moments or great happenings ; seeing all things from the domestic standpoint, she could as a rule be relied upon for accuracy. In 1842 she had started a Hauschronik or Family History and there recorded her elder son's birth ; like other entries, it was made some time subsequent to the event ; the handwriting is very neat and clear :

Ludwig Friedrich Wilhelm was born on Monday the 25th August at 12.30 at noon at Nymphenburg in the room which is above the bedroom in which King Max Josef I died. King Ludwig I who was present, was extremely happy to see his grandson . . . so happy that he embraced several persons of the Household ! One hundred and one guns were fired in Munich announcing the birth. Nymphenburg was decorated and illuminated. On Tuesday the 26th the ceremonial baptism took place at noon in the great hall, conducted by Archbishop Gubsattel. King Friedrich Wilhelm of Prussia and Queen Elisabeth had already arrived on the 25th . . . Adalbert, Max's youngest brother, held the candle of baptism. King Ludwig of Bavaria held the child ; the King of Prussia and the King of Greece were godfathers ; the latter and Papa were absent. For some days the child was called Otto. Then his grandfather asked that he should be called Ludwig because he was born on S. Ludwig's day, and the anniversary of his own birthday. So he was called Ludwig.

Characteristically, for she never was a woman who talked about herself, there is no mention by the Crown Princess of her feelings, whether the birth was difficult or easy or whether her simple heart was entirely filled with joy, or with joy mixed with foreboding.

Four days later the Crown Prince Maximilian sent to his wife's only brother, Prince Adalbert of Prussia, the following letter :

NYMPHENBURG, *August 29th, 1845.*

These lines will bring you the happy news that the Lord has blessed our dear Marie with a strong little boy on the birthday of my father, who is very happy indeed about it . . . About four o'clock in the morning the pains began, at six o'clock Marie told me, and only at half-past twelve in the night were they over, when the little one saw the light of this world. The moment when the child gave its first cry was wonderful. The good Marie suddenly forgot all her pains . . .

One of the many difficulties of attempting to write accurate history is that two people watching the same event will frequently give accounts diametrically opposed. The Crown Prince says his elder son was born at midnight and— at that hour—first ' saw the light of this world ' ! His wife says the birth was at twelve-thirty noon.

My friend and former collaborator [1] Prince Adalbert of Bavaria writes : ' Ludwig I, who was always very exact, says in his Notes that " he was present at Nymphenburg at his grandson's birth which took place at 0.20 hours by the Nymphenburg clock and at 0.30 hours by his own watch, this being the exact hour at which he himself was born ". It seems odd that, when describing such a happy event, the mother should have thought of recording the fact that her first son was born above the room in which his great-grandfather Maximilian I had died.'

Was it also an omen ?

Ludwig I had a weakness for writing rather conventional poetry, a sad predilection which he never succeeded in overcoming. Six days after his grandson's birth he composed some verses in the child's honour in which he said : ' Only the man who governs himself is fit to reign ; think always of that.' He kept this effusion in his desk until his

[1] *Through Four Revolutions* by H.R.H. Princess Ludwig Ferdinand of Bavaria, Infanta of Spain, set forth by her son Prince Adalbert of Bavaria and Major Desmond Chapman-Huston (London, 1938, John Murray). The Infanta gives many vivid pen pictures of Ludwig II.

grandson's nineteenth birthday, by which time the Kingly poet had long since proved by a personal escapade that a truism can be true.

From October to December 1845 the Crown Princess and the young Ludwig were at Hohenschwangau in the Bavarian mountains four or five miles from the Austrian frontier. Nearly twenty years earlier the Crown Prince Max, as was the way of members of his House, saw and fell in love with the ruins of this ancient Schloss which had once been the residence of his Guelf (or Welff) and Wittelsbach ancestors. It stands high overlooking the glorious twin mountain lakes, the Schwan See and Alp See, with their deep emerald-green waters. Legend-haunted, it was said that the ruins were on the site of the castle of the wandering minstrel and Crusader Tannhäuser, whose patron had been Duke Otto II of Bavaria. Maximilian at once bought and started rebuilding the castle, retaining its ancient name, Schloss Hohenschwangau—the castle of the High Country of the Swan. In due course it was lavishly decorated by contemporary Munich artists with vivid, realistic paintings and frescoes. Dedicated specially to the legend of Lohengrin, every wall, room and corridor, and almost every piece of its massive early-Victorian Gothic furniture, was meant to illustrate the greatest of German sagas. In this romantic atmosphere of legend and unreality—continuously obsessed by a dream-life that never had been and never could be—the young Ludwig spent not only the first months but the greater part of his life : wherever his mother looked she saw knights and swans and, always, water. The occult swan legend was Ludwig's cradle as it was to be his doom.

While the Crown Prince was re-creating in Bavaria on its old site the new castle of Tannhäuser, in Saxony Richard Wagner was working on his sketch for the *Meistersinger* and on his operatic re-creation of this ancient legend which was produced in Dresden with but moderate success about the time the Crown Princess and her two-months-old boy reached Hohenschwangau.

Had the Crown Prince and Crown Princess known of the musical event at Dresden they might have been mildly interested because the Saxon composer﹨was, after all, a German, and rumours of his alarming revolutionary political activities had not, as yet, become generally known in the Bavarian capital. But it would never have occurred to the proud parents that the opera and its creator could possibly have any connection with the Bavarian Royal baby quietly sucking milk from its foster-mother's breasts. Yet it was so : moreover, Wagner at the very time of young Ludwig's birth was working on the text for his next opera *Lohengrin*, the scenario and, to a lesser degree, the music of which were to obsess Ludwig for nearly two-thirds of his life.

When he was eight months old the boy met with his first piece of concrete ill fortune. His wet-nurse died of typhoid fever ; he had to be suddenly weaned, became ill, and there was great anxiety about his life. Current psychology would say that to this shock could be traced most, if not all, of the many evil things that befell him afterwards.

Ludwig I was, with justice, known as the most cultivated King in Europe. From his young manhood he loved and sought the society of poets, architects, painters, scientists and men of letters. Although naturally belonging to the Romantic period, he early in life developed an intense love for Greece and Italy, the twin cradles of classical western European civilization. He determined to turn electoral Munich from a cosy little bourgeois German town into a European Royal capital and, as a result of his artistic knowledge and predilections, and lavish expenditure from the Privy Purse, it was, until partially destroyed during the Second World War, a not unpleasing mixture of Italian and Greek architecture. At the age of twenty-four Ludwig I had married Thérèse of Saxe-Hildburghhausen, one of the most beautiful princesses in Europe, whom Döllinger, no indulgent judge, described as a ' model for all wives and mothers '. Feminine beauty appealed irresistibly to Ludwig I, and to such temperaments life can be one long age of indiscretion. When his grandson was born the King was almost sixty years of age and what, if not his last, was to prove his most flagrant amorous indiscretion

was close upon him. To understand how this happened
a backward glance at Bavarian history is necessary.

Although he owed his closed crown to Napoleon I,
Maximilian, the 1st King of Bavaria, was never completely
happy about the French alliance forced upon him by his
very able minister, Montgelas, whose ambition it was to
raise Bavaria to the rank of a first-class power and, gaining
for her the most influential position in South Germany,
counter-balance the rising ascendency of Prussia and the
continual encroachments of Austria. Under Montgelas's
skilful guidance Bavaria won a kingly crown and much else
from the Napoleonic connection, but the brand-new king
had to suffer the humiliation of consenting to a marriage
between his daughter Augusta and Napoleon's stepson
Eugene Beauharnais, a marriage which, although basically
dynastic and political, turned out to be extremely happy.

Influenced by the French Revolution through his contacts with Napoleon, Maximilian I granted his people an
admirable constitution in 1818 and ruled as a model
constitutional monarch.

His eldest son and successor, who became the second
King of Bavaria as Ludwig I, hated Napoleon, and disliked
and feared French political influences permeating his
country. Moreover, like nearly all the Wittelsbachs, he
was by temperament a Liberal and reformer, a munificent
patron of art and architecture, devoted to the advancement
of education and science. Munich owes its magnificent
collections of paintings and sculpture, and its famous
library, to the artistic perception, foresight and courage of
its Wittelsbach rulers. Generation after generation they
had to fight the unimaginative obtuseness of the majority
of the population.

By 1831 the opposition of Parliament to generous expenditure on beauty and things of the mind, the July revolution
in Paris and the fall of Charles X, combined with a wide-
spread spirit of European unrest, frightened Ludwig I and
engendered in him an uncharacteristic reaction.

When, in 1837, the Ultramontanes came into power in
Bavaria with Karl von Abel as Prime Minister, the Jesuits
began to obtain ascendency and, bit by bit, the Liberal

constitution of Maximilian I was whittled away. It had guaranteed equality before the law, universal liability to taxation, abolition of serfdom, security of life and property, equality of Catholics and Protestants, liberty of conscience and the Press. Under von Abel's Ministry the Protestants were harried and oppressed, a rigid censorship prevented free discussion of internal politics, and, for a time, reaction was everywhere triumphant.

In the autumn of 1846 it was announced that a famous Spanish dancer called Lola Montez was to appear in Munich. She was a brilliant publicist and, as was her custom, had her arrival prefaced by a blare of trumpets. She was the greatest dancer of the age, was of noble Spanish birth, was the wife of an English peer and had taken London by storm. Her pedigree—dare she upset the Monarchies of Europe by avowing it—would prove her a scion of both the French and Spanish Bourbons. Munich, ever romantic, was duly excited and impressed. There was not a word of truth in all these rumours save the one that she had taken London by storm. She had : her dancing was so bad that, three years earlier, she had been hissed off the stage of Her Majesty's Theatre. She danced twice in Munich where the unfriendly verdict of the London public was emphatically repeated. Much, too much, has been written about this audacious Irish adventuress who, because of the belatedly adolescent infatuation of an ageing Sovereign, was caught for an hour into the orbit of Bavarian history. She is important here solely because her brief reign as favourite of the second King of Bavaria directly affected the whole life of his grandson and Heir Presumptive. Stories about her forcing her way past the Residenz guard and entourage into the King's presence and there ripping open her bodice may be dismissed as incredible. There was no reason why she should do either. It was customary for the cultured Monarch of eclectic tastes to honour foreign artistes by visiting the theatre during their stay, and receiving them during or after the performance in the ante-room to the Royal Box. As Ludwig I loved their company this, as often as not, led to invitations to the Residenz. Lola claimed to be an artiste, undoubtedly she was unusually beautiful and, even if she could only prance about the stage, fascinatingly graceful. When the time came for unbaring bosoms Ludwig could see to that matter for himself—and did so without much delay, and, anyhow, Lola's dancing dresses left little to the imagination. Elderly men in love are always in a hurry. Once more Queen Thérèse shut her eyes ; beginning as a proud gesture of self-defence it had become a habit. Lola's ' Andalusian accent ' came from Limerick ; her blue blood from an Irish father who had risen from the ranks to a commission in the English Army ; but how could the King know this ? Nor, in reality, did he care : like everyone in love he wanted to be deceived.

The Montez became the King's acknowledged mistress. That she had great vitality is proved by the fact that she withstood a continuous bombardment of her lover's verses. Had she been clever and modest all might have been well ; but, although quick, responsive and resilient, she adored the limelight and was greedy, stupid and vain. A wanton of European reputation, who was said to have been the mistress of Liszt and Dumas, she insisted on being received by the Queen. She coaxed the King to have her portrait done by Stieler the Court painter and added to that of the Queen, the Crown Princess Marie, and the thirty-odd portraits of patrician Bavarian beauties the Sovereign had already had painted, and hung in the Gallery of Beauties in the Residenz. She outraged the Catholics by posing as an anti-clerical, and frightened the Government and the large conservative element amongst the nobility and people by posing as an ultra-Liberal. Certain ill-disposed persons said that, in reality, she was a spy in the pay of the extreme Ultramontane Party ; if so, their choice of an agent did little credit to the wisdom of the serpent with which they were popularily credited. The Ultramontanes cunningly rebutted the charge by putting it about that the dancer was a secret agent of the Revolutionary party then spreading its poisoned tentacles all over Europe.

The King spent most of his time at the house in the Barer Strasse that he had at once bought, furnished, and given to Lola. It was sufficiently commodious and digni-

fied to be for many years afterwards the Legation of His
Britannic Majesty. It was said that the ill-assorted lovers
read the Spanish classics together ; if so, it was indeed one
of love's miracles because Lola understood little more than
a few words of the great language of Cervantes. Perhaps
' together ' meant that she sat silent, listless and graceful,
while her Royal lover held forth. The listlessness is a safe
assumption, and Lola was grace personified. Also she had
those wide-open ingenuous-looking eyes that always seem
to behold the other person's soul—whether they had such
a thing or not.

To express at one and the same time his homage to Lola
and his disdain of all criticism the King settled two thousand
a year on her and created her Baroness Rosenthal. Only
Bavarian subjects could become Bavarian nobles. If not
a Spaniard, Lola was without doubt some sort of foreigner.
Yielding to her foolish importunities the King declared
she must be naturalized. As if to make the Church and
Monarchical Society angrier than they already were she
was also made by the infatuated King a Canoness of the
Order of S. Theresa—an honour custom rigorously reserved
for Bavarian Princesses, and ladies of the highest birth and
most exemplary life.

Lola then aspired to a political rôle, seeking to make and
unmake governments. Hurriedly following the example of
their Sovereign, climbers, time-servers, intriguers and mal-
contents paid her court and her house—not much more
than a stone's throw from the Residenz—became a fac-
tional and political rendezvous. To ' Eliza Gilbert ' or, as
Lord Ranelagh, one of her London ' protectors ' had known
her, ' Betty James ', Bavarian politics, like life itself, were
merely a stage play of which she was the heroine, with the
Monarch as her unpaid impresario. The Münchener,
with his Celtic inheritance, can be as excitable as any Latin
and just as ready to make a revolution. Yelling crowds,
demanding the favourite's banishment, surrounded the
Residenz itself.

Montez, however, was only the occasion, not the cause,
of the popular resentment against the von Abel régime.
In reality the clericals hated Lola and all her friends and

this unfortunately included the King. Abel (without con-
sulting the Monarch) published a memorandum against his
master's proposal to naturalize the foreign dancer and was
promptly dismissed. His successor, the Protestant Professor and historian, Ludwig von Maurer, and his colleagues
proved more accommodating and immediately granted the
coveted certificate. Then passions broke loose. Ultramontane professors led opposition riots by university
students. To ebullient youth any excuse for a mimic war
is welcome, and the students divided into factions for and
against the lovely dancer. Mobbed in the streets, Montez,
who never lacked physical courage, valiantly defended herself with a riding-whip before being forced to find sanctuary
in the Theatiner Church opposite the Residenz windows.
The Ultramontane professors were dismissed ; parliament
was dissolved ; the Ministry fell.

Lola Montez was now the ruler of Bavaria. The King
created her Countess of Landsfeld, but could not make her
a gentlewoman or endow her with tact and intelligence.
Kings are, of course, never without sycophants, and Prince
Ludwig von Gettingen-Wallerstein consented to try to form
a stable administration, and failed. His cabinet was faceti-
ously known as the ' Lolaministereum '—a name that later
on was to have evil connotations for Ludwig II and Wagner.

Then, rumours of revolution from all over Europe
stimulated in Munich fresh outbreaks in February against
Montez and her ' government ', and, yielding to popular
clamour, the King dismissed the ' Lolaministereum '.
Conceding too little too late, Ludwig I was made to feel
that he had lost the love and trust of his people and abdicated in favour of his eldest son, who ascended the throne
as Maximilian II.

Thus did an erotic adventuress enslave for some eighteen
months an old man, rule a foreign country for five hectic
months, and vicariously influence the character and destiny of
' the lonely King ', by then two years and eight months old.

The turmoil Lola caused in Munich was but one rever-
beration of the Revolutionary storm that spread like wild-
fire throughout Europe in 1848 : there was revolution in
Palermo ; revolution in Paris ; revolution in Vienna ;

revolution in Berlin; in Venice, in Hungary, Sicily, Verona, Prague. Louis Philippe abdicated and fled from the Tuileries to Queen Victoria's 'dear Claremont' in Surrey; the Crown Prince William of Prussia—afterwards to become first German Emperor—fled in undignified disguise to friendly London from rebel Berlin; the Austrian Court fled to Innsbruck; the Pope himself fled to Gaeta; Metternich—always wise and prudent—fled to safe and homely Brighton. Following the political upheavals in Berlin and Munich, and the fall of the 'Lolaministereum', Ludwig I had abdicated in March; the Emperor of Austria abdicated in December. Louis Philippe; Ludwig I; Ferdinand I. Two great thrones, and one lesser, hurriedly abandoned by their legitimate occupants within some ten months.

England alone escaped Revolution.

Thus it was that, largely because of his grandfather's infatuation for an inferior dancer, young Ludwig never knew himself as anything but the Crown Prince of Bavaria. The farcical comedy had its tragic implications. Being the second person in the Realm from the time he could remember had far-reaching consequences on Ludwig's character and career. It set him in a position of extreme isolation, unnatural restrictions, and undue prominence; it intensified the innate loneliness of his peculiar temperament. This loneliness, morbid as it was inevitable, was to some extent mitigated by the birth of his only brother Otto five weeks after Ludwig became Crown Prince. The proud mother, now Queen of Bavaria, thus recorded the event in her House Chronicle. The entry, clearly, was made some considerable time after the event:

> April 27 at 10 o'clock in the morning our second son Otto was born in Munich (Residenz) in the Hofgarten-zimmer. April 29 he was baptized by Archbishop Reisach . . . The birth of Otto was Max's first joy since he became King on the 21st of March. Until then he has had only difficulties . . . His names: Otto Wilhelm Luitpold Adalbert Waldemar. Otto spent his childhood at Hohenschwangau and Berchtesgaden; he was educated with Ludwig and they did everything together except

the lessons which they could not share because of the difference in their ages. Otto learned willingly and was diligent. He had the same governors and governesses as Ludwig.

Ludwig had a lifelong passion for flowers and his mother sent him some from Hohenschwangau, saying : ' I have found many beautiful flowers in the mountains ; I thought of you and how much you would like them. I also found some *deep blue* ones ! ' The boy had a curious innate passion for the colour blue, and his mother unwisely fostered a taste that he inherited from herself. He replied : ' Heartfelt thanks for your dear letter and the beautiful flowers which made me very happy . . . Otto is a good boy and I will be good also.' From the beginning to the end Ludwig loved Otto. Indeed, his only brother was his twin-soul ; and had he not himself for the first few days of his life been called Otto and not Ludwig ?

Early in life the young Crown Prince developed seemingly irrational likes and dislikes, especially hating places where he had suffered punishments or any form of humiliation.

Years later Fräulein Sibylle von Meilhaus, writing to Ludwig when he was over twenty, reminded him how when a child he liked to disguise himself as ' the young Prince ' ; and that ' from his earliest childhood he made drawings of such subjects as the Annunciation, Resurrection, Holy Sepulchre and similar subjects '. The good, pious lady added that these seemed to her ' like mysterious symbols of some high spirit '.

At Christmas 1852 Ludwig's grandfather wrote to his second son King Otto of Greece that he had given his seven-year-old grandson a replica in toy bricks of the Arch of Victory in Munich, adding : ' He loves building ; I was quite surprised to see excellent buildings in good taste made by him.'

Both Ludwig and Otto were pathologically introverted, living within and on themselves, self-consumingly. A fatal defect in Royalty, both boys were shy ; therefore, to try and overcome this, boys belonging to noble families were invited to play with the Crown Prince and his brother. In all their games Ludwig always wanted to be first.

King Max II had very rigorous ideas about education ; they were of course those of his caste and generation.   From the age of eight Ludwig was given regular lessons from tutors ; he started his formal education with Dean Reindl, who began administering religious instruction and lessons in writing just after he had completed his eighth year.   It is significant and revealing that one of the first tasks Ludwig set himself was to compose a birthday poem to the beloved woman friend who had been with him almost from baby-hood as his governess :

> Dear Meilhaus !
> Could I more than wish, could I give
> dearest Milau, how quietly and pure
> would all your days pass by,
> how happy this high feast would be !
> But as I have nothing better now
> take my thankfulness as gift.
> My heart is full of love for you
> and hopes that you will love it too.

In the earliest examples of Ludwig's writing, as in the latest, he would begin by writing neatly and well, then would suddenly get tired or bored, and end with a hurried scrawl more or less intelligible.   To have to decipher his secret diary, and the thirty or forty letters to Richard Hornig in the possession of the author, was a purgatorial ordeal.

Fräulein Meilhaus early noted Ludwig's innate faults and wisely did her utmost to minimize them, especially his incipient Royalism.   Once when he was with her in Füssen, the little town on the river Lech two miles from Hohenschwangau, he took a cheap blue and silver purse from a shop ; when she discovered this and reprimanded him he replied : ' But why have I done wrong ?   Why should it be a sin ?   One day I shall be King of this country, and all that belongs to my subjects belongs to me.'   On another occasion, at Berchtesgaden, he wanted to go first when he and Otto were about to enter a hot-house in the gardens.   Otto laughed, but Ludwig jumped at and ill-treated him.   When King Max heard this he punished Ludwig, who immediately took a life-long dislike to the

Royal residence at Berchtesgaden. Throughout life the smallest slight to his kingly dignity infuriated him and, at the end, dictated his last choice.

Michael Klass, Ludwig's first German mentor, was a man of ideas and had published a pamphlet outlining a system for improving the prevailing educational system of the German elementary schools ; although religion was for him, as for Dean Reindl, the fundamental aim of all education, yet he was not really narrow-minded ; he advocated such things as the production of open-air plays, and his whole outlook was relatively modern. He wanted children to be *healthy* and *Christian*. The following paragraph is a typical example of Klass's argument and at the same time interesting because, years later, Ludwig remembered it and paraphrased it in a letter to his cousin the Crown Prince Rudolf of Austria :

> The monarch is the Lord's Anointed ; but at the same time he is the father of his subjects. It is religion that keeps the masses of the people in order ; and it is religion that brings out all the love and the attachment of the people for their Sovereign just as it is religion that inspires the love of the Sovereign for his people ; religion is the eternal bond between them.

In May 1854 Count Theodor Basselet de La Rosee assumed duty as Governor to the two Princes, and the Queen recorded that Ludwig was very grieved when he had to part with Fräulein von Meilhaus.

The odds against Ludwig were piling up. First the death of his wet nurse ; next his elevation to the dangerous eminence of Crown Prince ; now the loss of the only woman he ever wholly and disinterestedly loved, one whose great heart and selfless devotion might have led him to find redemption from himself and his loneliness in normal feminine love and passion. As there was never between Ludwig and his mother the precious bond of complete mutual understanding and confidence, the evil consequences of losing his one intimate woman friend and companion were incalculable.

It says much for the innate psychological instinct of Fräulein Meilhaus, as well as for some inner beauty of his own temperament that, in spite of his plebeian readiness to take umbrage, Ludwig never once resented her admonitions or counsel and, in all his vicissitudes, remained her devoted and grateful friend. An insatiable hunger for love made him instantaneously responsive to its slightest, as well as to its deepest, manifestations. In after life his dire need made him see love even when it was not there.

As usual the Royal family spent that summer and autumn at Hohenschwangau and Berchtesgaden, during which time the two boys were under the scrutiny of their new Governor. La Rosee was not a wise or discerning choice, especially for Ludwig. Strict, old-fashioned and narrowly conventional and militaristic in his views, he considered that the two princes should only be allowed to associate with members of the nobility. He ordered all the servants to bow very reverently to the Crown Prince, whom he taught to respond correctly ' but not too deeply '. This was in direct contradiction to a wise convention of the Bavarian Royal House which ordained that no member was to be styled Royal Highness until the age of eighteen, and even after that the simpler style of Highness was to be preferred. La Rosee's insistence on Ludwig being always singled out as Crown Prince and accorded extra deference consolidated his pupil's incipient megalomania. Worse still, it was at once made clear to Ludwig's ultra-sensitive perception that La Rosee considered that his most urgent pedagogic task was to break his pupil's will. He succeeded only too well. The first bars of the cage in which Ludwig was stealthily being immured were soon immovably in place. He learned to fear. He had always feared his father : now he feared his military Governor.

By September the two boys were back in Munich at the Residenz and La Rosee reported to their mother as follows :

Most Gracious Queen :
    I am very happy indeed that I am in a position to be able to tell Your Majesty the best about the Royal Princes' physical health, as well as about their general behaviour. They both make good progress in their studies and in their play ; they are happy and conciliatory and so we all live in peace together. The wet weather

forced us to shorten our walks, and once we even had to limit ourselves to a walk under the Arcades . . . On my birthday the two Princes gave me a very nice picture of Hohenschwangau which pleased me very much indeed as I have just as many happy—as I have serious and important—recollections of it ; because it was there that *I had many a battle to fight with the Crown Prince* [1] until we established the existing relationship. The gift itself made me as happy as the charming way in which they presented it to me. I have to thank Your Majesty for your kindness, and pray Your Majesty to accept my most sincere thanks.

[1] The italics are the author's.

CHAPTER TWO

THE YOUNG CROWN PRINCE : 1855–1862

1855

EARLY in the year 1855 Ludwig and Otto were given a military instructor. The Queen recorded : ' Baron Emil von Wuelffen came as companion to the children. Ludwig learnt and comprehended very quickly, but did not like it so much as Otto.' After his abdication Ludwig I had acquired the castle of Leopoldskron, magnificently situated on a spur of the hills above Salzburg and in recent years owned by Max Reinhardt until, with all its contents, it was stolen from him by Goering. From there his grandfather wrote to Ludwig on the tenth anniversary of his birth : ' As you like churches the Cathedral here with its marble front would certainly please you very much.' La Rosee's birthday admonition was characteristic, and contained a second direct acknowledgment that Ludwig was already overtly struggling with inborn defects : La Rosee was fifty-four, a trained cavalryman and polished courtier, his pupil was ten :

LANGRIES, *22nd August, 1855.*

. . . Therefore try unceasingly to train your mind and body. If the evil tendencies come up again, suppress them : with a strong will you can achieve anything. Weakness is not dignified in a man—and that is what you want to become : a man who shall be the example to his people. Be kind and charming and you will win all hearts ; but be obedient. Because it was disobedience that brought man to misfortune. Honour your father and mother because, next to God, you have to thank them for all you have and all you are ; then God's blessing will always be with you . . .

With sincere love,
Ever yours faithfully,
LA ROSEE.

Soon after this von Wuelffen, a tutor who was only

19

twenty-seven, congratulated Ludwig on having learned how to thresh, presumably during the holidays which, as usual, were spent in the mountains at Berchtesgaden in the handsome Schloss formerly belonging to the Augustines. The ever-devoted Meilhaus was pleased to learn that her former pupil was having piano lessons.

In 1856 it was decided that Ludwig's education should proceed, as the Germans say, intensively. In future he would have to study alone because Otto was too young to keep in step. If the scheme drawn up for the Crown Prince's education was not perfect it was not for want of consultation and advice. Inevitably it recalls the plans made by the Prince Consort for the education of the future Edward VII of England, who was only four years Ludwig's senior.

A high Court official, a cabinet minister and a distinguished general each submitted a plan, the three schemes being eventually amalgamated and adopted. It was at first laid down that what a Bavarian boy had to learn in eight years at the High School the Prince should learn in five ! The main purpose of the system, it was stated, was to teach the Prince ' to think '. It was, however, wisely insisted that he should also learn a handicraft to counterbalance theory and to make him physically fit. Further consideration made it clear that to accomplish everything in five years would be too great a strain, so seven years were conceded for the fulfilment of the scheme.

The strenuous new system designed for the boy was based upon that adopted for the education of his cousin, the future Emperor Franz Josef of Austria, who was Ludwig's senior by nine years. All this cramming was to be completed by the time the Crown Prince entered his eighteenth year ; then he was to go to the University. Franz Josef only got up at six-thirty in the morning and lessons were finished by seven in the evening ; Ludwig had to get up at five-thirty, and worked until eight o'clock.

To the scheme certain general injunctions—for which La Rosee was responsible—were appended, and these give vital clues to the pupil's character and temperament. Like many pedagogues, La Rosee, in spite of having a certain amount of insight, sought to achieve two diametrically opposed results : he wanted Ludwig to have a strong will, yet strictly subordinate to his own. 'Be obedient.'

Most important of all is to try to develop the Prince's *self-confidence* without letting it grow into self-conceit. The Prince ought to *develop a strong courage to live; he is to be kept from brooding ; he must not linger over disagreeable impressions, but try to be less sensitive towards them.*[1] A sum of pocket-money is to be granted ; but the Prince is to give an account of how he spends it. Special care is to be taken to train the Prince's will because the strength of the will can be trained ; it is all the more necessary to emphasize this because ours is an age in which the imagination and the mind are fostered, but the will to act and live are neglected.

La Rosee's concluding paragraph might have been written by any Nazi demagogue of the nineteen-thirties. It is impossible to avoid concluding that Ludwig's precariously poised, over-sensitive brain and febrile imagination were overstrained from his earliest years.

There were, of course, mitigations : like Otto, Ludwig spent a good deal of time with his mother ; then what joy to build, to construct, and above all to play near or, better still, with water ; to recreate the more dramatic scenes from sacred or secular history ; to dress up ; these tastes were atavistic or congenital and never left him. On July 17th he wrote from Nymphenburg to his mother :

Near our little brook the Count and I built a little group of rocks and we conducted the hose, which Liebig gave me, through it. If we pour some water into the hose it runs out of the rocks and looks like a well, and this stands for the water which Moses struck out of the rock with the rod of Horeb. The Count cut the tablets of stone in wood and I wrote the Commandments on them.

Liebig was of course the great chemist for whom Ludwig, to his honour, cherished a life-long devotion.

The way a boy spends his pocket-money is revealing. Ludwig's monthly allowance was twelve gulden (say about one pound sterling). In five months of 1856, out of a total

[1] The italics are the author's.

income of sixty gulden he spent over fourteen on charity, three gulden fifty on presents for Otto (who would also have his share of the one gulden spent on sweets), and nearly thirteen on ' useful objects '. Apparently as a punishment for some boyish prank he was made to pay for a broken window. Occasionally he had to buy his own tools, garden seed, copybooks, toothbrushes and nailbrushes, and he regularly bought his own gloves ; almost every month he bought himself two pairs for which he paid the magnificent sum of about two shillings. He was by comparison extravagant when he gave about two shillings for his first walking-stick. In any Bavarian bourgeois family he would have been given bread with which to feed his pets, but Ludwig had to buy it to feed the stags in the park at Nymphenburg. In May he was taken on a visit to Fürstenried, a Royal Castle on the outskirts of Munich some six miles directly south from Nymphenburg on the route to Schloss Berg and Starnberg ; there, out of his own pocket, he bought bread to feed the fishes.

As in the bright spring sunshine of Bavaria Ludwig watched his own face and that of his beloved Otto reflected side by side amongst the silver fish in the large marble basin near the Schloss, did any lurking shadows of the future stream out of the sinister castle behind him and strike fear into his sensitive and foreboding soul ?

1857

In January, Ludwig thanked his uncle Adalbert of Prussia for a Christmas present of a riding-whip, said he had enjoyed his first year's riding very much, and was already allowed a big horse instead of a pony. He loved horses, looked upon them as dear, personal friends, and early in life became an excellent horseman and horsemaster, if never quite so brilliant as his cousin Elizabeth of Austria.

On the eve of the summer holidays La Rosee again reported to the Queen :

MUNICH, *August 8, 1857.*

. . . Tomorrow evening at five o'clock we shall move to Nymphenburg . . . Both the Royal Princes are

perfectly well and are very glad to get a little relief.
I submitted the Crown Prince to a little examination and
am satisfied with the result. It gave me fresh hope that
a good deal can still be done—which I had begun to
doubt. Only those who know the Crown Prince well are
in a position to see the noticeable changes in him. The
last Confession had an extraordinarily good effect ; never
before have I seen the Crown Prince in such a happy
and open mood as at that time. The wonderful weather
with rather a hot temperature still continues ; even
Prince Otto, who does not exactly adore cold water,
takes his bath with passion and does it as nicely as a little
frog. . . .

During the autumn, while the Court was as usual at
Berchtesgaden, a curious incident took place. Ludwig,
aged twelve, and Otto, aged nine, were playing together
in a lonely part of the Park. Ludwig pinioned his brother,
bound him hand and foot, gagged him, put a handkerchief
about his neck and was twisting it tightly round a piece of
stick used as a tourniquet when he was discovered. Remonstrated with he exclaimed :
'He is my vassal. It is none of your business.'
He got a sound thrashing from his father.
Ludwig, like all German youth of the period, was stuffed
full of Schiller, whom, like Lord Melbourne, he then, perhaps indeed always, placed before Goethe. About the
same time there appeared in his copybook the following
short essay :

. . . Vanity can also be the consequence of flattery.
If one is, from one's youth, surrounded by people who
do nothing but flatter, one very easily becomes vain and
when one grows older it is very hard to give it up. Very
often vanity is the cause of egotism which is very bad for
men because one thinks only of oneself and forgets one's
neighbours. The vain man might be said to have a
poisonous snake gnawing at his heart.

1859

Every country has its own brand of romanticism. Turning from an unsympathetic present it wallows in a largely

unknown past, or in an unknowable future. It is as difficult, perhaps as impossible, for one country to enter into the romanticism of another as it is for a twentieth-century generation nurtured in an atmosphere of science to acclaim, as did his contemporaries, the subjective posturing and exhibitionism of Byron. A century ago Germans were already turning away from classicism and Lessing, Goethe and Schiller, and following the brothers Schlegel who were blazing a trail for such lesser writers as Wakenroder, Hardenberg (Novalis), Tieck, and Schelling. These in due course led to the group of writers which Maximilian II gathered around him in Munich between 1852 and 1860. The most important of them, the versatile, prolific Paul Heyse, appealed especially to Maximilian because all his work displayed a passionate love for Italy.

Disgust with what they considered the bitter fruits of the French Revolution drove Germans to delve into their own swampy forest of legends of dark gods, peerless knights and spotless maidens, hideous dragons, and a whole Valhalla peopled with heroes, half-men, and fabulous animals. Anglo-Saxons in general find it almost impossible to understand the fascination this eerie Walpurgisland had—perhaps still has—for the Germanic peoples. It obsessed Ludwig II all his life. Finding in Wagner's art these old legends unified and given new esoteric meanings, he succumbed to them utterly. Unlike the English, the Germans have never yet been liberated from their past.

It is reasonably certain that it was Wagner's pseudo-artistic outpourings and their literary and dramatic expression that gripped and held Ludwig's perpetually adolescent mind and imagination and that, to him, the matchless music was largely secondary. In the theatre and opera house he mostly put seeing before hearing.

When in February *Lohengrin* was produced at the Court Theatre in Munich it was given a hostile reception ; there was such a tumult that the curtain was hurriedly lowered and the opera not repeated as announced. Fräulein Meilhaus was present and undoubtedly reported fully. There was much discussion of this extraordinary event in the Royal Family which made a deep and painful impression on Ludwig who, surrounded from babyhood by the frescoes in the Residenz and, more particularly, by the hard, brilliantly coloured illustrations of the Lohengrin and Tannhäuser legends on the walls of Hohenschwangau, was temperamentally an inevitable victim of the spell of the old German sagas. When the fourteenth anniversary of his birth arrived he was at Berchtesgaden, and wrote to Fräulein Meilhaus that amongst his presents was : ' a picture representing the Swan Knight after a painting in Hohenschwangau '. Schwind's large picture, which is in the dining-room, shows Lohengrin's farewell invocation to the Swan. The mysterious white bird wears a jewelled collar round its neck and, aloof, enigmatic and proud, floats on the stretch of the green-blue waters of the lovely little Schwan See that is within sight of the windows. In the picture the castle itself is partly shown to the right of the brilliantly clad group of figures surrounding Lohengrin.

Although, in general, Ludwig's preceptors were not altogether satisfied with his educational progress, they admitted that he had advanced very rapidly in French. He was studying the Louis XIV period and, already, Le Roi Soleil had obsessed him for life ; nor did he ever forget that his grandfather, Ludwig I, was a godson of Marie Antoinette whom, in later life, he came to worship as ' la sainte reine '.

It is odd that, in spite of continuous scrutiny, neither Ludwig's parents nor any of his governors or tutors—not even Meilhaus—ever seem to have recognized his insidious addiction to day-dreaming, or did anything to find a healing substitute. Everyone from La Rosee downwards seemed to be in league to encourage his most dangerous tendencies. He was given as birthday presents ' many beautiful things ' ; several pictures of Hohenschwangau and Berchtesgaden, portraits of saints, and cuff-links made of blue enamel, and busts of Goethe and Schiller. A week before his fourteenth birthday anniversary Ludwig had an unforgettable experience ; the Queen took both him and Otto to see the Passion play. The part of Christus was portrayed by Rupert Schauer, and from that moment Ludwig had a predilection for Oberammergau, its associations and surroundings.

The connections between the Wittelsbachs and the Hapsburgs have always been close. When Ludwig was in his ninth year his lovely first cousin once removed, Duchess Elizabeth, known in the family circle as Sisi, had married Franz Josef, Emperor of Austria and Apostolic King of Hungary. Although she was eight years his senior, from that moment Ludwig cherished for her a romantic and highly idealized devotion ; she became in his imagination almost the living incarnation of the dead Marie Antoinette. Elizabeth, having been very ill, was ordered to Madeira and Queen Victoria placed a ship at her disposal for the voyage. Accompanied by Franz Josef, she passed through Munich on her way to Antwerp where Leopold I of the Belgians went to pay his respects, although, as he wrote to Queen Victoria, ' it certainly increased his stupid cold '. This incident aroused keen interest throughout Europe, inflamed Ludwig's knightly ardour for Elizabeth, and aroused in him a penchant for Queen Victoria that was to find curious expression in the last year of his life.

Ludwig was now equal to writing, in admirable French, essays on German themes such as *La Construction de la Wartburg* and *La Guerre de la Wartburg*. These old legendary tales, and his facility in expressing them in the French tongue, combined to make on his whole being an impression as indelible as it was unfortunate. The association was potent in reinforcing everything that was visionary, baroque and darkly romantic in his unbalanced nature. Here France and her history became confluent with the Tannhäuser, Lohengrin and Wartburg myths, and lead directly to their concrete re-embodiment later on in his castles of Linderhof, Herren-Chiemsee and Neuschwanstein.

In those early essays most of Ludwig's capital letters were decorated with flourishes and the pages finished off with little ornamental colophons or tailpieces. In honour of France fleurs-de-lis or florid capitals frequently appeared as, a year or so earlier, fascinated by his own cypher, he began to make floridly ornamented and intertwined letter L's in his exercise books.

Unexpectedly, Ludwig was very good at Greek and, almost unnaturally, nearly always translated more than he was asked to do. This, if they were told about it, must have greatly pleased his father and grandfather. In his work his tutors still complained of erratic thinking and illogical sentences, neither of which seemed to be much influenced by his liking for mathematics or his love of Greek. Occasionally taken to the theatre, he adored such plays as Schiller's *Jungfrau von Orleans*. No boy's tastes in literature, drama, poetry or art can be other than a reflection of the current tastes of his environment and period, and at fourteen Ludwig's preferences were by no means despicable. The trouble was that, like so much that was going on in his wayward mind, his aesthetic tastes, instead of developing, became prematurely static.

1861

Produced in Paris in March under the unsympathetic and incompetent Pierre Dietsch, *Tannhäuser* had even worse fortune than when it was first given to the world in Dresden sixteen years earlier. Aided and abetted by Walewski, the cultured natural son of Napoleon I, the wayward, witty, unconventional Austrian Ambassadress in Paris, Pauline, Princess Richard Metternich, had aroused all fashionable Paris in its support, beating every big drum and indefatigably knocking at every door, promising or otherwise. Napoleon III contributed money and, for the great occasion, he and his lovely Consort were present. Although the Empress Eugénie never got to like Wagner, or to know enough about music to recognize the Napoleonic hymn *Partant pour la Syrie* when she heard it, she, with incomparable grace, applauded the performance. Nevertheless, the reception was so hostile that Wagner, in high dudgeon, withdrew his score from the Opera House authorities.

No good German could tolerate this slight on German culture. As a consolation Friedrich Grand Duke of Baden invited Wagner to Karlsruhe, thus terminating his political exile. In May *Lohengrin* was produced in Vienna, and the composer, seeing his opera for the first time, received a great ovation ; thus shamed into activity, productions of both *Tannhäuser* and *Lohengrin* were announced by the Court Theatre in Munich.

Then, in May, came the most significant spiritual and emotional event that Ludwig had so far experienced ; almost at the same time as the composer himself saw it, he saw *Lohengrin* for the first time. To say that day and night the Crown Prince was spied upon from his earliest years would perhaps be rather an extreme way of putting it ; but there is no doubt that he was continuously under surveillance. Throughout Nature all young things go to ground when they feel themselves scrutinized. During that summer of his ninth year when at Hohenschwangau, La Rosee had, as he told the Queen, ' many a battle to fight ' before he appeared to conquer his pupil ; appeared, because Ludwig had by then, once for all, learned the bitter lesson, fatal to any child, that secrecy and deceit were the only two effective weapons he possessed with which to preserve his inner life, fight invading seniors and a malevolent world. Ludwig, dangerously highly strung, excessively imaginative, pathologically sensitive and abnormally introspective, felt like a cornered wild animal. No doubt La Rosee and his carefully chosen subordinates meant everything for the best, but any young human animal is inevitably bound, subconsciously and consciously, to arm itself against the custodians of its cage. Being but one against many, open defiance is soon found to be unprofitable and secrecy and subterfuge are subconsciously resorted to. Stubborn, vain, sensitive natures like that of Ludwig are specially liable to indulge in this form of self-preservation. At this, to him, world-shaking first performance of *Lohengrin* he was accompanied by Count von Leinfelder, who took careful note of the boy's reactions and described them in detail. From that moment Lohengrin, as the peerless Knight of the Swan, became for Ludwig the personification of his own inward fight against sin and degradation.

Exactly three years later Ludwig was verbally to re-create this great moment in his young life for the composer himself.

Ludwig was now obsessed not only by the Nibelungenlied, but by the musical wizard who was seizing age-old moribund German legends and, like a god, re-endowing them with a semblance of glowing life. He at once procured and devoured Wagner's *Work of the Art of the Future*, and this illogical, diffuse, stilted and emotional farrago thenceforth became his Bible.

The Bavarian Royal House was closely allied by both blood and marriage to the Grand Ducal House of Hesse-Darmstadt. Ludwig III, the reigning Grand Duke, had married Mathilde, daughter of Ludwig I. He had no children, but his brother Karl, married to Elizabeth of Prussia, a sister of Queen Marie and therefore Ludwig's maternal aunt, had three sons and one daughter, Anna, who, two years Ludwig's senior, became one of his earliest and best women friends. She was of course sister-in-law to Princess Alice of Great Britain, to whom she was devoted.

All his life Ludwig was subject to dreams, and on June 5th, wrote :

> My dear Anna !
> How many sad things you had to go through since we last saw each other ! Who would have thought it then ! Since she died I have dreamt several times of Darmstadt and aunt Mathilde. Only last night I dreamt we had a very elaborate dinner in Darmstadt and everybody was afraid that aunt Mathilde might die, but she was quite happy with us at the table. Please do write to me soon and a long letter too. Professor Steininger gave me a book about the Holy Grail the other day and I enjoy reading it very much.

Meanwhile the educational machine ground relentlessly on. In spite of it—or perhaps because of it—Ludwig was prematurely developing idiosyncrasies. His handwriting became more and more personal, the signature in particular assuming its characteristic outline, the curly tail or flourish with which the last letter of the name always ended was about then given three flamboyant loops or circles ; in later years it was flamboyantly endowed with six or even seven.

The fact that, although it was never intended to take Ludwig far in mathematics, he liked and voluntarily pursued the subject, obtaining the maximum number of marks, seems to indicate that the logical and rationalistic sides of his temperament were already hopelessly divorced from the emotional and imaginative.

Within two months of having seen *Lohengrin*, and while

absorbing *Work of the Art of the Future*, Ludwig, of his own volition, wrote this revealing sentence :

> . . . to take as a model a real man who is good and energetic in every respect, and make him the guide. One should make it one's task and duty to follow this man and, in order to be able to do that, one must know *and understand* him thoroughly and study his whole life. By this means one is inspired to follow his footsteps as closely as possible until, at last, one is completely animated by him, and inspired by his whole way of life.

His instructors, oblivious of the significant implications behind the essay, and apparently still quite ignorant of the true bias of their pupil's mind, cursorily dismissed the paper with the single word ' rubbish '. Rubbish maybe—but not in the sense that they meant.

Although he never spoke or wrote the language well, Ludwig was by this time capable of English compositions on such obsessional themes as *The War on the Wartburg*, the *Nibelungen Nôt*, the characters of Napoleon I, of Mary Stuart and (much more objectively) of Elizabeth I of England. Moreover, he was also taught how to adopt a suitable style when writing letters to ladies, to friends, to Court and social personages, and to servants, and remained courteously punctilious about such matters all his life.

La Rosee now desired to make certain changes in the curriculum and submitted a memorandum on the subject to the King :

1. That the lessons in playing the piano may be stopped as His Royal Highness the Crown Prince *has neither talent for music nor does he like it* [1] and, after a course of five years' lessons *no result* has been achieved.
2. That the lessons in Greek may be stopped according to plan.
3. That, in accordance with the plan, instruction in the use of weapons (arms) may begin.

1862

It is always difficult to realize that the beautiful girl floating around the ballroom like a wisp of fragrant gos-

[1] The italics are the author's.

samer, or the youth diving superbly into the lucent green water, contain within their lovely shrines seeds of their own death. Ludwig was as handsome as a young marble Greek god from the chisel of Phidias himself, yet, since birth, his bad health had already been recorded at least a score of times by his mother or himself.

Ludwig wrote to Frau von Leonrod :

BERCHTESGADEN, *August 19th, 1862.*

. . . Because of my sore throat I am not allowed to make long excursions, I had also had to give up riding. According to the wish of my father a Berlin Doctor, whose name is Dr. Traute, examined me the other day in Axelmannstein. At the beginning it was rather frightening. I was conducted into a dark room and there he looked into my throat with a mirror, but he only found a slight enlargement of the larynx. Then he examined my chest, but it is also strong. He is a Jew and his looks are not very taking.

On the upper left-hand corner of the notepaper he had painted a cluster of that most characteristic Bavarian flower the vivid blue gentian.

On August twenty-fifth, when Ludwig celebrated the seventeenth anniversary of his birth, he made his first formal public appearance.

Although the Bavarians, and the Münchener in particular, are, as history proves, capable under provocation of great excesses, they are on the whole an amiable people whose violent outbreaks soon evaporate. Lola Montez apart, they always loved Ludwig I, who, undeterred by their opposition, made Munich one of the finest capitals in Europe, and a shrine of great art. Lola, who had long ceased to be to Ludwig anything more than a lovely dream, had died in poverty and the odour of extreme Protestant sanctity in New York just a year before. The Bavarians had forgotten and forgiven ; the old King himself had almost forgotten. Both he and Lola always insisted that their friendship was purely platonic which, as the King was sixty-two at the time, may possibly have been technically true.

As the seal of his country's reconciliation and gratitude

Ludwig I was now to see an equestrian statue of himself
unveiled in the Odeonsplatz, the very heart of Munich.
Designed by Widnmann, it is not much worse than similar
statues in other and larger capitals, except that for some
obscure reason the King is arrayed as if he had lived in the
Middle Ages.

The old King was of course the star of the occasion.
Facing the dais, on which he stood beside his son the reigning King, and his grandson the Crown Prince, was the
Residenz, begun early in the sixteenth century by his ancestor Duke Albrecht V, and completed by Leo von Klenze
to his own orders only a generation or so earlier. Klenze
had also designed for him the magnificent Ludwig Strasse
which, on his left, stretched away to the Siegestor—the
Arch of Victory.

The slim, beautiful stripling, his grandson, was clearly
destined by nature and education for a reign that would
more than do its part towards consolidating in Europe the
seven-hundred-years-old reigning House of Wittelsbach for
another seven hundred years or longer.

Human loneliness being enormously intensified by the
exalted eminence and isolation of a throne, kindly human
nature has always been indulgent towards the erotic lapses
of kings.

On the seventeenth anniversary of his birth in August
Ludwig was made by his father, the Grand Master, a Knight
of the ancient Wittelsbach Family Order of S. Hubertus,
and, at his installation, put on for the first time the knightly
habit that was to be his shroud. La Rosee seized the
opportunity to write :

> In addition to your patron saint, S. Ludwig of France,
> who exemplified all the virtues of a true knight during
> the Crusades, you have now got another model in
> S. Hubertus.

As usual, the Royal Family went off in the autumn to
Berchtesgaden and from there Ludwig wrote to Anna of
Hesse : ' the mountains send their gracious greetings ; I
hope soon to climb their king, the Watzmann '.[1]

[1] 8,901 ft.

The year ended on a note to Anna, half regretful, half pleased :

MUNICH, *December 28th, 1862.*

. . . I do not think that I will be allowed to dance very much next year because to-day my throat is again rather swollen.   But I may go to the Theatre, and I like that much more than all the balls.

CHAPTER THREE

PAUL: THE FIRST ROMANTIC FRIENDSHIP: 1863

EIGHTEEN-SIXTY-THREE was the most important year in the early life of Ludwig.

In August, being eighteen, he officially came of age. In preparation for this important event he was given, not as yet a formal Household, but a personal adjutant, two Orderly Officers or aides-de-camp, and several male domestics. He was also given a modest appanage and his own small suite of rooms, having a separate staircase with entrance from the Hofgarten, was prepared and re-decorated for him on the top floor of the north-east corner of the Residenz immediately above those of his parents in the Hofgartenzimmer.

Richard Wagner on his long odyssey to fame had fled from Dresden to Vienna—which, as it turned out, was nearer to Munich than he guessed ; his poem *Der Ring des Nibelungen* was published in the Austrian capital, and his opera *Tristan und Isolde* given no less than seventy-seven rehearsals there without, however, being produced.

Nor was 1863 unimportant for the world.

Lincoln abolished slavery in the United States ; the Prince known in history as King Edward VII of England married Princess Alexandra of Denmark ; Alexandra's brother George was elected King of Greece in succession to Bavarian Otto who, with his unpopular consort Amalie of Oldenburg, had fled from Athens and retired to Bamberg in the previous autumn, their Throne being offered to and refused by Queen Victoria's second son, the young Duke of Edinburgh. Maximilian, younger brother of the Emperor Franz Josef of Austria, assumed his tragic Mexican crown.

Ludwig's two greatest women friends were still his cousin Anna of Hesse-Darmstadt and his dear governess Meilhaus who had lately become the wife of Baron von Leonrod, a cavalry general. To these two all (or nearly all) of the confidences of his earlier years were vouchsafed. In January he wrote to Anna :

> Last Tuesday we were present at *Antigone* which I liked very much. Real beauty is there. The other day I got R. Wagner's *Opera und Drama* from Count La Rosee ; the first part is about the opera and essence of the music, the second about dramatic poetry, and the third about the Art Work of the Future.

In March he told Anna that he was reading Goethe's *Faust*, and that making a drawing of Lohengrin's farewell occupied much of his time. He then related an incident that is evidence of how everything to do with insanity fascinated him :

> Just imagine, yesterday a madman wanted to see mother. He was already at her door when somebody asked him what he wanted ; ' That has nothing to do with you,' said he. And when he was advised to go first to Countess Dumoulin he said : ' Where does that woman live ? ' Then father ordered gendarmes and they took him to the Police. He is from Prussia and seems to be mad. They let him go.

Within a few days Anna, who genuinely loved him, contributed unwittingly another rivet to the cage of Romanticism in which he was gradually and steadily being immured for life :

> . . . You will be interested to learn that they are going to give here a performance of your favourite opera *Lohengrin*. It is the first time for many years. I am very glad because I have only a vague impression left . . . What an awful thing about the madman ! Did you see him ?

Ludwig early took to letter-writing as an outlet for his pent-up emotions ; the day he received her letter he replied to Anna quoting a long passage from the libretto of *Lohengrin*, from which he was afterwards to quote often in the secret diary.

In April he received from his father, the Grand Master, the accolade as a Knight of S. George and wrote to his old governess :

> How well I remember having as a child played with

Max Gietl at being knighted; once your blue veil
served as my knightly cloak. . . . I saw *Marie Stuart*;
Frau von Balyowski, who is acting here, again rendered
the part excellently.

Ludwig now confided to Frau von Leonrod an account
of his first recorded friendship. It was a momentous—perhaps the most momentous—and revealing event in the early
part of his personal life. Under its swelling glow his inmost
confidence was given to the devoted woman who was a
second mother to him:

> Knowing your good heart, which takes such a lively
> interest in everything I do, I feel I ought to tell you that
> I have found a true and faithful friend whose only friend
> I am; it is my cousin Karl, the son of Duke Max. He
> is hated and misunderstood by almost everybody; but
> I know him better, and know that he has a good heart
> and soul. Oh, it is so beautiful to have a true and be-
> loved friend to whom one can cling in the storms of life
> and with whom one can share everything!

Nevertheless, cousin Karl who, in the family circle,
rejoiced in the delightful nickname, Gackl, was not to be
clung to for long; his successor was already round the
corner.

In the middle of May Ludwig wrote to Anna:

> Saw the opera *Little Red Riding Hood* by Boüldieu . . .
> How beautiful is the grotto above the lake and the little
> shell-carriage drawn by four swans in Little Red Cap's
> dream! . . . saw *Don Carlos* . . . Moy has now become
> my Adjutant, First Lieutenant Sauer and Lieutenant
> Taxis have been appointed Orderly Officers; both seem
> to be very agreeable. I am studying the Tell Saga by
> Hausser.

At the end of the month:

> . . . The Schiller statue is so beautiful that every time
> we pass it I cannot help taking off my hat! . . . I
> very much hope to go to Hohenschwangau because it is
> there that I would like to come of age.

Anna, of course in all good faith, continued to encourage his inherent tendency to day-dreaming and fantasy :

DARMSTADT, *May 27th, 1863.*

. . . This letter is the *first* I write out of all my birthday letters of thanks. You see that I shall have lots to do in the near future ; but it is not everybody that will get such long ones as *you* do ! *A propos,* it interests me very much that you are reading about the Tell Saga now ! I cannot quite give up the idea that it is real history and not mere saga . . . I should think to see Switzerland would also interest you very much.

Love from your faithful cousin,

ANNA.

A day later Frau von Leonrod wrote to him from her married home at Ansbach :

. . . Often in my thoughts I shall accompany you on your beautiful walks, where I have so often been with you in reality, and listening to your childish phantasy. The more you read Shakespeare, my dear Crown Prince, the more you try to understand his great mind, the more truth and beauty will you draw from him. *There* is an elemental power in that spirit which makes him new and true to all times.

To this Ludwig replied :

NYMPHENBURG, *June 24th, 1863.*

. . . You thought that I was reading the *Nibelungenlied.* I have known it for some time and am very fond of it . . . The book I mentioned was *Die Nibelungen* which is a treatment of the historical side of the saga. I still read a great deal of Shakespeare ; what wonderful works ! The other day I got the new trilogy of R. Wagner : *Der Ring des Nibelungen*—just published ! I hope that Wagner may be able to compose the music for it—as he intends to do. I also possess Wagner's *Tristan und Isolde* . . . Shortly I shall begin the history of Philosophy which, I imagine, is very interesting. And now I am beginning to read *Troilus and Cressida* by Shakespeare. *Romeo and Juliet* I read in English.

In July he told Anna that he had again been to a performance of *Wilhelm Tell*, 'one of his best beloved plays'. The future King was now in fact romantically in love with the stalwart Republican !

A week or two later he gave Frau von Leonrod a glimpse of how they spent their time at Hohenschwangau :

> *July 23rd, 1863.*
>
> . . . We arrived here a week ago . . . When I go fishing I always read, and I find reading and fishing go very well together. *Wonderful* is Wagner's trilogy *Der Ring des Nibelungen* ! I shall finish it to-day. At three o'clock we have our midday meal. Otto is just playing the Pilgrims' Chorus from *Tannhäuser* !

It was to Frau von Leonrod he uncovered his heart just before the eighteenth anniversary of his birth.

> HOHENSCHWANGAU, *August 19th, 1863.*
>
> How quickly these eighteen years have passed away. My childhood's reminiscences are so vivid before mine eyes—all those beautiful days which we spent together.

Then, much against his will, he had to go to Munich, 'fortunately only for two days', because of the visit of his cousin the King of Prussia. The journey took nearly seven hours by the hot, dusty, ill-made roads. Back at Hohenschwangau he thus described for Anna what was, unknown to either of them, an historic moment :

> In the evening we had tea in the Amalienburg, a little Schloss in the park of Nymphenburg. There the Gentlemen of the King of Prussia were presented to me. They were Minister Bismarck who, I think, is very interesting, and Prince Hohenlohe . . .

Prince Kraft of Hohenlohe-Ingelfringen, who was at the time General-Adjutant to the Prussian King, afterwards recorded his impressions of the occasion :

> The young Crown Prince was then eighteen years of age and everybody admired his brilliance, his physical skill and his courage. He rode and drove extraordinarily well and had understanding and talent for Art and Science. We were told that some time ago he drove with his mother —as he often does—in his pony carriage, himself riding

postilion. On their way home the Queen was frightened because they drove so quickly ; but the Prince only said that it was beautiful. When they arrived at the Schloss (Nymphenburg) the Prince leant forward, gripped the two horses by their heads and so mastered them—the bridles had broken and the horses had run away.

Writing years later after mature consideration, Bismarck described how he saw the event[1] :

On our way from Gastein to Baden-Baden we visited Munich. King Max had already started for Frankfurt, having deputed his wife to receive the guests. I do not think that Queen Marie, with her retiring disposition and her scanty interest in politics, had any very active influence on King Wilhelm or on the decisions of which he was then full. At the regular meals which we took during our stay at Nymphenburg on August 16 and 17 the Crown Prince, afterwards Ludwig II, sat opposite his mother, and next to me. It seemed to me that his thoughts were far away from the table, and only now and again did he remember his intention to talk to me ; our conversation did not go beyond the ordinary Court subjects. But even so, I thought I recognized in his remarks a talent, a vivacity, and a good sense realized in his future career. In the pauses of the conversation he looked past his mother to the ceiling, now and again hastily emptying his champagne glass, the filling of which was, as it seemed to me by his mother's directions, somewhat slowly performed ; thus it happened that the Prince very often held his glass over his shoulder, behind him, where it was hesitatingly refilled. Neither then, nor later, did he overstep the bounds of moderation in drinking, but I had the feeling that his surroundings bored him, and that the champagne aided the play of his independent fancy. He made a sympathetic impression on me, although I must confess, with some vexation, that my efforts towards a pleasant conversation with him at table were unsuccessful. That was the only time I met King Ludwig face to face . . .

During the three days Ludwig had been in Munich in mid-September for the official visit of his great-uncle and

[1] Bismarck, Otto 1st Prince von (1815–1898) : *Reflections and Reminiscences* (London, 1898).

godfather King Friedrich Wilhelm IV of Prussia (whose Christian names he bore), he had what was for him a unique experience. That it was as strange and exciting as it was unique proves how narrow were his personal contacts, how poor and meagre his social life and surroundings, and emphasizes his isolation and loneliness. Back in the familiarities of Berchtesgaden, he felt impelled to confide in someone, and wrote to cousin Anna :

> Before leaving Munich I went for a walk in the town, for the first time quite alone, as I am now of age.

True, Queen Victoria recorded in her journal that, on the day of her succession, she was, by her own will, alone for the first time in her life ; but she was a girl, and that was sixteen years earlier. No understanding of what afterwards befell Ludwig is possible unless it be remembered that until after his eighteenth birthday he had never been allowed to go for a walk by himself !

Only one note to Ludwig from his cousin and first friend Duke Karl Theodor (Gackl) of Bavaria (who afterwards became world famous as an oculist) has been preserved. Written probably for Ludwig's birthday in August of this year, it is valuable as evidence of a normal and healthy influence which, unfortunately, did not prevail as, on Gackl's side, the friendship never flourished :

> . . . Only with a firm character, firmness of will and moral courage, can one hope with some success to cope with these disastrous times. The solution of such a task is, and always will be, difficult ; but one must not despair.

On Wednesday, September the second, Ludwig wrote to Frau von Leonrod from Hohenschwangau : ' It is already 11 o'clock at night. Friday at 10 o'clock we leave for Munich.'

Having told her only a few weeks earlier that he had discovered ' a true and faithful friend ' in Duke Karl Theodor, he now confided to her the momentous news that Paul of Taxis had already usurped Gackl's place in his impetuous heart. In love and friendship propinquity is everything—especially in Royal circles : Paul was now attached to Ludwig's person ; Gackl inconveniently resident at Posenhoven on Lake Starnberg. It would not be unfair to say that Ludwig seldom gave his friendships time to grow. Like all introspectives he had the childish habit of dragging them up by the roots to see if they had any. To his confidential news Frau von Leonrod replied :

ANSBACH, *September 22nd, 1863.*
. . . I heard lots of nice things about Prince Taxis ; he is said to be very talented and well educated. I am very glad indeed that Your Royal Highness has found a friend in him. Youth must stick to youth.

The Thurn and Taxis family, owners of a dull, grandiose palace in Regensburg and other castles and large properties elsewhere, is amongst the first of the Mediatized families of the continent. From the beginning of the seventeenth century they had been Hereditary Postmasters-General to the Empire, and became Princes of the Empire in 1695. Their monopoly of carrying the mails brought them great wealth, and the blue and white mail-cart bearing their coat-of-arms was a familiar sight in Bavaria and Austria as late as 1850. The family has always been, and still is, jealous of the right of its members to marry into Reigning Houses, and to regard themselves as the equals of Emperors and Kings. The status accorded to them, as to many other Austrian and German lesser Princely Houses by the Congress of Vienna in 1815, may nowadays seem to others a little démodé—but never to themselves.

Maximilian, head of the House of Thurn and Taxis in 1863, was born in 1802 and appears to have been somewhat uxorious. He married twice and had fourteen children ; the first three included his heir, the Hereditary Prince, and were, as the *Almanach de Gotha* baldly puts it, ' out of the first bed ' ; the last eleven ' out of the second bed '. The Hereditary Prince—also called Maximilian—had married in 1858 Duchess Hélène in Bavaria, elder sister of the lovely and, when she chose, fascinating Empress Elizabeth of Austria. As is well known, Hélène had been destined by her match-making mother for the Imperial Throne of

Austria-Hungary, but when the young Franz Josef first caught sight of Elizabeth he forgot not only Hélène but every other woman, and, with occasional lapses, remained her faithful friend and ardent admirer for life. Hélène consoled herself for the baroque magnificence of Schönbrunn by the cosier and much safer consequence of Regensburg. As things turned out, she made the better bargain of the two. We are seldom told what happens to the lady whom Prince Charming passes by in favour of her younger sister. In this instance she lived long and, we may presume, happily, bore two sons and two daughters, and her descendants, if they have never in the regal sense ruled in Regensburg, at least remain snugly and safely there to this day.

Of the Hereditary Prince Maximilian's eleven step-brothers and step-sisters, fortunately we are only concerned with the fate of Paul. Two years senior to his second cousin, the Crown Prince Ludwig, he seemed an ideal aide-de-camp for the Heir Apparent, as indeed in many ways he was. A thorough search in the Regensburg archives of the Taxis family failed to unearth a trace of Paul. Not a letter : not a memorandum : not even a portrait. Why? However, there are other sources of information available and we know that he was good-looking, charming, and as disinterested as are most human beings. His letters reveal the man ; not profound, not perhaps even particularly clever, he was—apart from his affaires de cœur—as honest as the day, and he fell for a time under that peculiar, almost uncanny spell that Ludwig seemed to be able to cast at will over both men and women. Like all spells it was evanescent, unhealthy—and very potent while it lasted. Paul is important for two reasons : he was Ludwig's first really congenial friend and, on the whole, his influence on Ludwig was better and less unwholesome than that of any of his successors. If Ludwig's favourites had all been like Paul, and if Ludwig himself could have exercised even a reasonable amount of circumspection, he might well have lived a happier and less frustrated life.

All Paul's letters breathe a warm devotion ; they are all about Ludwig and his needs, the writer, by the innate virtue of an unselfish nature, keeping himself and his wants in the

background, while by no means disregarding them excessively. Their sycophancy, so distasteful nowadays, was
characteristic of all intercourse with Royalty in Germany
until the fall of Wilhelm II and is to be found in even such
iconoclasts as Bismarck.

As an illustration of the uniform pattern of his emotional
masculine friendships, Ludwig's relationships with Paul of
Thurn and Taxis demand study. Although we have no
record of their having met before Paul was appointed one
of his two Orderly Officers, it is pretty certain that they
must have been at least acquaintances from childhood.
The fact that the Hereditary Prince, his brother, had married the sister of Elizabeth of Austria would alone have given
Paul a good footing in the Bavarian Royal Family. Maximilian II, it is plain, took endless care to obtain for his two
sons the right tutors and companions. He had the whole
Bavarian nobility to choose from, and when First Lieutenant
Sauer and Second Lieutenant Prince Paul of Thurn and
Taxis received the coveted posts closest to the person of the
eighteen-year-old Crown Prince we may be certain that it
was only after much thought and meticulous scrutiny.

During the customary stay of the Royal Family in their
lovely old mountain castle of Berchtesgaden Paul was the
only aide-de-camp in-waiting. Judging from his first mention of Paul to Anna in the middle of May, Ludwig, before
then, knew Paul very little—but, when it suited him, he
could be disingenuous about his romantic friendships.
Alone together at Berchtesgaden for more than three weeks,
they had ample and favourable opportunities of becoming
intimate. There was little state maintained and no ceremonial or public duties to be performed. Both young
men were romantically-minded, idealistic, adored Nature,
mountain scenery and the open air. All his life when
Ludwig loved anyone he bore them away to one of his many
mountain eries. On such occasions he purported to cast
aside all rank, conventions and reserves and, by the overpowering exuberance of his friendship, often defeated his
own ends. As their subsequent correspondence proves, he
revealed himself to Paul from the start of their intimacy as
' a young wild little brain '.

Although all the members of the Bavarian Royal Family might not care much for Court, Official or Society life in Munich, every one of them loved the country, the mountains, and country life, and enjoyed a delightfully informal and friendly relationship with the Bavarian farmers and peasants. These people, living for a thousand years on one of the great historic highways of Europe, are uniquely attractive; accustomed to the presence in their midst of princes and high personages, they have developed cosmopolitan courtesy and good manners without having abated one iota of their native independence. Ludwig had in a notable degree the family gift of establishing those warm and friendly relations with peasants, and enjoyed exercising it throughout his life.

One day he and Paul were out on a mountain climb and in one of the loveliest valleys of the stately Watzmann they paused to look at a wood mill. Ludwig, in particular, was attracted by a handsome young woodworker whose good looks were generally admired in the locality. The month was September, the weather mild and perfect and, as is the custom—the lad would be working almost naked—the brief leather shorts concealing but little of his muscular legs, the torso exposed to light, sun and air, the head also bare. One may be sure that Ludwig and Paul talked to him, perhaps sharing with their new-found friend their sandwiches as well as their smiles.

Ludwig never forgot what would have been to any ordinary youth but a trifling incident and, later, sought to have his peasant immortalized in a work of art. Peasants and kings were always encountered together in fairy and folk tales—so why not now?

The contact, brief though it was, consolidated Ludwig's secret and unquenchable hope that amongst the mountains he would one day find the unspoiled, perfect, peasant friend of his quest. It is, however, a measure of his fantasy-fixation that his inner vision saw not the hefty, sweaty, suntanned woodworker, but the palid, wraith-like Lohengrin, Knight of the Swan.

Was Paul already sufficiently an initiate to be able to recognize and measure the full implications of the incident

on the foothills of the Watzmann which a few weeks earlier
Ludwig had rapturously described to Anna of Hesse as
' king of the mountains ' ?

By the first of October the Royal Family was back in
Munich for the Winter Season, and Ludwig took his second
walk alone in the beautiful city that he was to learn to hate.
He told Anna :

MUNICH, 3rd October, 1863.

After dinner (on the 2nd) I went to see Prince Taxis.
I only got to know him properly in Berchtesgaden and
have grown very fond of him.

The first use Ludwig made of his new-found freedom had
fundamental implications ; the second occasion on which
he went out alone was equally significant, he made his way
to the door of his new friend and aide-de-camp.   The apartment was situated in 82 Türken Strasse, and Paul had undoubtedly taken it to be near the Residenz, because as a
member of the Crown Prince's personal staff it would be
no longer convenient for him to live in barracks.   There
was no room for him or anyone else in the new suite then
being prepared for Ludwig in the Residenz which, apart
from a pantry and a dark, ugly bathroom, only contained
four or five moderately sized rooms.

Four weeks later Ludwig again wrote to Anna a letter
which makes clear that, as hinted earlier, he had already
begun to live his night life :

HOHENSCHWANGAU, November 10th, 1863.

Don't forget, dear Anna, your cousin Ludwig, who hates
to leave Hohenschwangau.   Written at 11.30 in the night
. . . The night is gone.   I dreamt our beloved castle
was being besieged by Napoleon in the most wonderful
moonshine ; we were all frightened.   And when I woke
up the whole landscape was changed into a beautiful
winter garment—which has a charm quite its own.

Heartfelt greetings to you all,_
from your loving cousin,
LUDWIG.

Ludwig does not tell Anna that, in his obsessive way, he
had already decided that he must have Paul of Taxis all

to himself. Paul's first letter to Ludwig is undated but obviously belongs to the beginning of November of this year (1863), and was most probably written from Türken Strasse. It makes it plain that in their intimacy, as was inevitable, it was Ludwig who took the initiative; the word ' our ' in line *eight* is crossed out and ' your ' substituted :

My Most Honoured Crown Prince !

A thousand heartfelt thanks for the last lines from Hohenschwangau, which partly made me very happy, and partly rather upset me.

May you not have asked too much, and may you not have spoilt our whole affair ? That was my first thought. For God's sake do remember how easily you might spoil my present position by asking too much and pressing the fulfilment of your wish too much. In the highest quarters it might easily be thought that I do not want to stay, or that I am not content in my present position, which certainly is not the case. And considering my youth and short military career it is a very great favour to have been promoted to this post. Even if it takes longer than one at first thought—though not ten or twenty years— one must never lose hope. And one must be enough of a man not to show to others every movement of one's heart caused by a disappointment, or an unfulfilled wish, nor should one embitter one's own life and that of our fellow creatures by doing so.

Take care of yourself for me, and don't worry too much because there is nothing worse for your health than always brooding upon yourself instead of being impressed by beautiful Nature. Therefore, once more : head up. Look forward to the future and think that God—if it pleases Him—will bring us together sooner or later.

But that's enough moralizing for to-day . . .

During the day, and especially in the evenings, I also miss very much your kind Berchtesgaden visits ; and how often I would like to be near you in order to calm you and prevent you getting in too intense and passionate a state of excitement about our affair . . .

On October 7th Ludwig wrote Frau von Leonrod from Hohenschwangau :

I was very sorry to be separated from Prince Taxis, of

whom I have really grown very fond ; but I hope to see him all the more in Munich and enjoy his company.

Paul's next letter to Ludwig was from a country place near Regensburg belonging to his family :

DONAUSTAUF, *October 27, 1863.*

Most Honoured Crown Prince !

A thousand heartfelt thanks for the dear letter which reached me from the distant friend. I was very glad to see that there was a little more quietness in the young wild little brain, and that there is the good intention courageously to face the future . . .

Often, very often I think of you, especially in my daily prayers I remember you and pray to God that He make me worthy of the confidence which you have given to me.

During the long hours in the evening which I spend in my room how I would love to fly to you and have a chat with you, heartily and sincerely as we used to.

In finishing I would like to beg you insistently to stick with courage to the hope expressed by Geheimrat von Gietl and quietly watch how the things shape themselves.

Farewell, precious friend, and write soon to,

Your sincere and obedient,

PAUL.

Nothing is more attractive in Ludwig than his unfailingly chivalrous devotion to Frau von Leonrod :

MUNICH, *November 15th, 1863.*

(In town since the 12th.) Tomorrow I move into my new apartment (overlooking the Hofgarten and the Theatiner Kirche). Now that I am on the threshold of manhood I do not want to say goodbye to our old apartment without sending you heartfelt greetings from the rooms associated with so many happy memories of my childhood. If, in future, I should not be able to write to you so often, please do not think it is because I feel cold towards you. Let me assure you that I shall always foster with the same sincerity the feelings of gratefulness and faithful love which I bear for you in my heart. Poor Otto will feel very lonely now . . . I must finish because it is already getting very late.

Remember with love,

Your faithful friend,

LUDWIG.

Paul had returned to Regensburg for the silver wedding in January (1864) of his parents.   Meanwhile, jealousy was on the prowl.   The young Crown Prince had a favourite. Who is he?   No matter who: discredit him.   It was a foreshadowing of the sort of thing that was to follow Ludwig throughout his life ;   and from this early period can be traced his ever-increasing dislike and suspicion of the Court and Government officials.

Paul wrote to Ludwig :

REGENSBURG, *November 22, 1863.*

My Honoured Friend and High Patron !

. . . Please do be so good as to let me know the source which tells you that I am said to lead a frivolous life . . .

You have hardly given me your confidence, and already you see how everybody tries to bring me into disfavour with you . . .   I only ask you one thing : don't believe too much of the flattering speeches of others, but try to form your own opinion of those who are around you . . . If the conclusion that people are correct in their judgments about me, well, you have the right to judge me.

But you may be sure that I would not dare to use this free and sincere language if I hadn't a calm and pure conscience . . .

Please forgive me for writing to you in this way and, in asking you to lay me at the feet of Prince Otto,

I remain, in deepest admiration,

Yours sincerely and faithfully,

PRINCE PAUL TAXIS.

Now that he was of age Ludwig was entrusted with certain ceremonial duties.   Nevertheless, it was largely in appearance only that he was his own master.   His day was still mapped out for him from seven in the morning until seven, or even seven-thirty, in the evening.   During the summer La Rosee was asked to advise the King about the continuation of Ludwig's education.   Of all his mental activities Ludwig only mentioned enjoying Liebig's lectures.   Anna did not envy him :

BONN. *30th November, 1863.*

. . . Now you seem to throne it in splendid isolation

in Munich. But I do not envy you in the least for the official receptions which you have to attend : that is only the price you have to pay for the greater liberty which you now enjoy. Poor Otto must feel very lonely, living separated from you after you have been together all the time.

A day or two later, under the impression that he still cared for Karl Theodor, she tried to cheer him up by saying : ' By now Prince Taxis will have arrived and your heart will divide itself between the two friends.' Ludwig replied that Paul had not yet arrived ; told her he was ' sick of this eternal Schleswig-Holstein business in the papers ' ; and that Otto's favourite colour was pink.

Based presumably on something that had passed between them, Ludwig asked Paul to drop all formality—and not without reason. To anyone not a German it seems extra-ordinary that when writing to his Sovereign, cousin, master, and friend, a soldier should sign himself ' Prince Paul Taxis '. But that was the way of all the little petty German Courts, nor has this stiff and excessive formality perished with the Republican or Nazi Revolutions :

Paul's next letter is eminently sensible :

My Dear Ludwig !
I dare to address you thus as you have asked me to do so. A thousand thanks for your dear and impatiently expected letter which I received yesterday . . . I must confess that while saying goodbye to you at the station my eyes were wet, and that my thoughts have always been with you ever since. I often think of what you are doing and wonder whether you think of me . . . According to your wish I will tell you faithfully what the result of my conversation with Herr von Gietl . . . He is of the definite opinion that I shall come to you after the King's return from Italy . . . Please do write to me soon as I am always much happier when I know that you are happy, healthy, and living on good terms with yourself and your surroundings. I am convinced that you will use your independence in a reasonable way and that you will recognize and appreciate your high position in every respect . . . I always wear your chain and consider it

a symbol of the faith with which our friendship is bound together.

Your sincere and true friend,

PRINCE PAUL TAXIS.

This letter, which is undated, was probably written in December (1863) from Schloss Christiwitz in Bohemia. Unfortunately no letters between that one and April 1866 were returned to the secret Archives of the Royal House and, as has been noted, every scrap of evidence concerning Paul in their possession has been destroyed by the Thurn and Taxis family.

CHAPTER FOUR

WAGNER : 'THE GREAT FRIEND' : 1864

MAXIMILIAN II was hurriedly recalled to Munich from Italy in the middle of January owing to the state of excitement aroused throughout Bavaria by the Prussian ultimatum to Denmark on the Schleswig-Holstein question.

Three days after his father's return Ludwig wrote to Baroness von Leonrod :

MUNICH, *19 January, 1864.*

My new dressing-room is dark blue and my study light blue ; the bedroom and the corner room overlook the Theatiner Kirche, and the salon and study the Hofgarten ; in my study—which is the room I like best—there are carved on the walls ruins and castles from the neighbourhood of Hohenschwangau ; and there are pictures of the knights of the Swan (as they are painted on the walls of Hohenschwangau), reproductions of Schnorr's *Nibelungen* pictures, a portrait of Beethoven and one of Shakespeare . . .

At last I have been able to realize a plan which I have had in mind for some time, and that is to get a cup made with scenes from *Lohengrin* painted on it. Herr Rothmann does the pictures, but another hand must execute them on porcelain. There are to be four pictures : 1. Lohengrin's arrival at Antwerp. 2. Telramund's and Ortrud's revenge, and Elsa on the balcony. 3. The bride's chamber. 4. The revelation of Lohengrin's secret. I wrote to Berchtesgaden where I saw a young man in Ramsau who worked in a wood mill and who struck everybody by his beauty and heroic figure. I am getting him photographed by Malch and then he is going to be the model for Lohengrin.

PS. I forgot to mention a pair of cuff links : they are golden buttons with white enamel swans bearing a cross of sapphires.

A few days later he wrote Anna of Hesse :

> . . . The other night I had a very curious dream : I dreamt I jumped off the carriage on to the avenue leading up to Hohenschwangau, when we were on our way to Munich. I escaped into the thicket and then came into a far-away land where I rallied round me a troop of men with whom I wanted to go back to Hohenschwangau in order to live there—it was all very romantic . . .

Ludwig, however, had now to face the harsh realities of life. In quick succession the following bulletins reached him :

> Although His Majesty the King did not go out during the last few days he had fever yesterday which became worse towards the evening. This morning the fever is a little better, but it is not yet gone. The local disturbances are a catarrh of the nose, throat and trachea.
>
> MUNICH, *February 25, 1864.*
> His Majesty the King is better in every way.

Then, in deference to a strong contemporary convention that, in a palace, it must never be admitted that anyone was ever guilty of anything so disquieting and disturbing as dying, the Crown Prince was informed :

> *February 27, 1864.*
> The fever of His Majesty the King has completely gone and the catarrh is getting better.

These bulletins did not, however, deflect Ludwig's thoughts from his own private affairs.

Some little time before he had heard Albert Niemann in *Lohengrin* and immediately fell under the singer's spell. All his life Ludwig continued to indulge in the adolescent's habit of confusing the artist, actor or singer with the man— although he seems to have been able to avoid this bemusement as far as women were concerned. During his father's illness he caused his first scandal in Munich by never missing a chance of hearing Niemann sing ; and, worse still, by frequently granting him long private audiences at the Residenz. This was felt to be not only disrespectful towards his parents, but lacking in seriousness towards the Schleswig-Holstein question, daily becoming more acute.

A week after receiving the last reassuring bulletin about his father, Ludwig wrote Anna :

MUNICH, *March 7, 1864.*

Lately I have been reading a great deal of Goethe, and was so occupied with Niemann the singer that I really could not find time to write letters . . . How interesting is everything that Goethe wrote ! I am sick of this eternal Schleswig-Holstein business . . . *Please don't show this to anybody ! ! ! !* The other night I got somebody to throw lots of flowers to him, and I sent him a pair of cuff-links with swans and brilliants. Also a cross which gave him great pleasure. *Gardez silence ! Je vous supplie !* He wrote in my book :

No colours, no flowers,
No soul, no song !

' Him ' is, of course, Niemann ; he does not, however, tell Anna that one audience he granted the singer lasted forty-five minutes.

When Ludwig, an inexperienced youth of eighteen, wrote Anna of Hesse that he was sick of the eternal Schleswig-Holstein question in the newspapers he was not being guilty of political levity. Tradition has it that on his death-bed Hegel declared that : ' only one man understood him —and that even he didn't '. Palmerston is reputed to have stated that only one man in Europe understood the Schleswig-Holstein question, ' and he was a lunatic '. Although it has bedevilled European politics for over three-quarters of a century, has directly caused two minor wars and, indirectly, the First and Second World Wars and even now is only quiescent, there is fortunately no need to try and unravel the embroilments of the question here. It divided Germany, and neither Germany nor Europe then knew that Bismarck was, in reality, the sole arbiter of the crisis because, as he confessed years later in his *Reflections* : ' From the beginning I kept annexation steadily in my eyes.' Already that capacious but evil brain had decided that a policy of ' blood and iron ' was the only one by which

Prussia could become overlord of Germany, and, eventually, of all Europe. Disregarding the Prussian Landtag, and levying taxes without its consent, he relentlessly built up a Prussian Army. Schleswig-Holstein liquidated, he could then make Kiel into a great German commercial harbour and, eventually, the main base for a German Fleet. Great Britain would not much longer enjoy her long pre-eminence as the first Commercial and the first Naval power in the world. In order to achieve the meaner ambition of German hegemony, Bismarck deliberately destroyed the hegemony of Europe. His vision was limited to such meagre and temporary results as can be achieved by a policy of ' blood and iron '.

In 1863 the Emperor Franz Josef, as its Head, had summoned a meeting of the Germanic Confederation at Frankfurt-am-Main. Known in Germany as the Fürstentag, it was in all probability one of the most fate-filled European events of the nineteenth century. The Diet met in August to consider an Austrian plan for a reform of the Confederation.

From the time Frederick the Great raped Silesia from Maria-Theresa there had continued underground a bitter struggle to wrest Germanic leadership from Vienna and enthrone it in Berlin. Austria had long and, on the whole, successfully barred the gateway of the West against the Asiatic hordes, and now her pre-eminent right to this glorious leadership was soon to be openly contested by Bismarck.

Established in June 1815 by the ' Final Act ' of the Congress of Vienna, the Germanic Confederation might well have laid the foundations of a United Europe. Its main defects were the perpetual presidency of Austria and the unanimous vote necessary to change fundamental laws ; moreover, its central organ, the Federal Diet, became—like the United Nations—merely a party arena. All but four of the German States were represented at the Fürstentag, but the fourth was Prussia and her absence stultified the whole proceedings. A personal invitation signed by all present was taken to Berlin by the King of Saxony, but Bismarck threatened to resign if his Sovereign, Wilhelm I, accepted it. With Prussia success could have been achieved.

Even without her the assembly was a memorable and representative gathering.

During the autumn of 1863 it had become clear to a few discerning European observers that in Bismarck a new force had arisen in Europe. Had Wilhelm I been present at the Fürstentag there would have been the risk of Bismarck's ambiguous policy on the Schleswig-Holstein becoming exposed ; it might even have publicly emerged that, in order to attain Prussian supremacy, he was prepared to destroy, if necessary, every other State in Germany. His presence at the Fürstentag was the last appearance of Maximilian II on the international stage. It is doubtful if he, or indeed anyone else, recognized how momentous was the occasion, or what a great opportunity to consolidate and strengthen West European civilization was lost.

In the midst of all this turmoil King Max II died in Munich on Thursday the tenth of March after a seven days' illness. A conscientious and faithful servant and leader of his people, he had occupied the Bavarian throne for sixteen years. His chief claim to fame is that he was an enlightened and unfailing patron of science, law, history, art, music and medicine. Like all the Wittelsbachs before and after him he was a keen hunter and a good one. But he was physically delicate ; his portraits show him as a dyspeptic, he was a martyr to headaches, nervous and reserved. His early life had not been exemplary. He was said to have contracted syphilis on a visit to Hungary in youth ; and some time before his death it was even rumoured that he showed symptoms of mental disturbance. Rather narrow-minded and a martinet, his elder son may not in early life have actually disliked him ; but both he and Otto feared their father and, in Ludwig, fear almost automatically bred hostility.

We can follow the last illness of King Max hour by hour in the simple but vivid account entered later on in her House Chronicle by his perplexed and loving widow :

March 4, Friday : Max's last normal day.
   7, Monday : Max felt unwell ; swollen breast.
     Yesterday and to-day a talk with him about

Ludwig, Hohenschwangau, Branca, Orff,[1] etc.

March 9, Wednesday : at about half-past two last signature and work with Pfistermeister. From
3 o'clock onwards, worse. After 4 o'clock
four doctors. After my rest again to him at
4.30. He asked me to thank the Emperor of
Austria. 'And now finish with politics' he
said. After 8 o'clock a little better. Bulletin
issued. Theatre stopped. Family Tea ! In
the night, at half-past twelve, I first saw the
features of death and gave up all hope. After
4 o'clock in the morning he took the last
Sacrament and was given the last Anointing,
Reindl and I alone by his bed. Then a little
better. I rested for one and a half hours. At
half-past eight in the morning he saw the
children. From ten o'clock onwards worse
and worse—Gietl took all hope from me ! A
great deal alone with Max, and all during the
last hour ! The bells of the Cathedral rang ;
the sun shone gloriously into the room ; at
11.45 Max passed over quietly without a
great struggle. Beautiful, and somewhat surprised looking, he lay there ! The Archbishop
said the prayers and blessed his body. The
whole family present and Albrecht.[2]

Ludwig was *King* !

I felt that I was myself dead and had also
passed into the next world. Even if death
separates us our hearts cling together.

Two days later, while King Max II lay in state in the
Reiche Kapelle, the great notabilities of Bavaria assembled
in the two-storey high, elaborate Throne Room of the
Residenz. When they had all been placed according to
precedence Ludwig, in military uniform, accompanied by
the high officers of the Realm and his personal suite, passed
through the imposing State apartments into the Throne

---

[1] In a later entry the Queen wrote : ' In March (before Max died)
Baron Wilhelm Branca entered Otto's service and Orff became his
Governor. La Rosee remained with Ludwig.'

[2] Her first cousin, Prince Albrecht of Prussia.

Room, ascended the ten or twelve wide, semi-circular steps, stood before the high throne of Bavaria, and gazed steadily down on the solemn assembly. The high officers entitled to do so and the members of the Cabinet took up their appointed stations on the steps and around the throne. With twelve over-life-sized statues of his ancestors watching him, Ludwig took the oath to the Constitution and, as there is no Coronation ceremony in Bavaria, he was, in all due form, reigning King. The Prime Minister, von Schrenk, read the Speech from the Throne.

Condolences poured in and, wherever he may have absconded to in his private thoughts, Ludwig had not a moment he could call his own.

On Monday, March 14, King Max was buried in the Theatiner Kirche, overlooked by Ludwig's new bedroom and ante-rooms and, during the necessary ceremonials, the Court, aristocracy and populace collectively saw Ludwig for the first time. The Bavarians as a whole had practically never seen the Crown Prince and, when they now did so, went raving mad about him. As, with Otto by his side, he walked immediately behind his father's coffin as it was borne through the packed streets he made a profound impression. Indeed, neither before nor since, has any King on his Accession borne so unmistakably all the outward signs of Royalty. Eighteen and a half years old, over six feet three in height, with an excellent figure and bearing, Bismarck said that the only fault that could be found with his appearance at that time was that he was too thin ; his natural ivory pallor not only suited the occasion, but was a perfect contrast to the luxuriant blue-black curly hair and deep blue eyes.[1] The mouth, sweet and pensive, was a little too sensitive and beautiful for a man and a Sovereign. Ludwig bore himself with dignity and—thanks to practising on La Rosee—had by now acquired considerable facility in hiding his thoughts and feelings. During that walk,

[1] The Crown Prince Rupprecht told the writer that Ludwig's eyes were dark brown : painters have given him grey-brown, brown-grey and green-brown eyes ; they may have been hazel, but the evidence favours dark blue ; the Bavarian Royal Family as a whole have had blue eyes for many generations.

purposely lengthened by a detour—from the Residenz to the Church he challenged and won the sympathy and interest of watching Europe, and enthroned himself for ever in the hearts of his Bavarian people where, to this day, his position is secure.

An Austrian writer who was granted an audience about this time said :

> He was the most beautiful youth I have ever seen. His tall, slim figure was perfectly symmetric. His rich, slightly curling hair, and the few traces of a moustache, gave his head a similarity to those great antique works of art through which we have our first ideas of Hellenic manly strength. Even if he had been a beggar I would have noticed him. Nobody, old or young, rich or poor, could be left untouched by the charm which radiated from his personality. His voice was agreeable. The questions which he asked were clear and definite. The subjects of his conversation were well chosen and spiritual ; he expressed himself with ease and naturally. The enthusiasm with which he inspired me never diminished but, on the contrary, increased with the years.

Count Schack was a lawyer, poet, historian, author, diplomat and traveller and, as a Mecklenburger, unlikely to overpraise a Bavarian prince. As collector of the famous German pictures housed in the Schack Gallery in Munich he proved himself no mean connoisseur of beauty. He wrote that, during the lifetime of King Max, he had several times met Ludwig and

> . . . had received the best impressions of that beautiful boy. He had been severely educated by his Governor who, however, did not seem to have the gift of winning the affection of his pupil.

Three days after the funeral, writing to Frau von Leonrod about his father, Ludwig said :

> . . . he had only to stay in bed one day before he died ; I carry my heart to the Throne—a heart which beats for my people and which glows for their welfare—*all Bavarians may be assured of that.* I will do everything in my power to make my people happy ; their welfare,

their peace are the conditions of my own happiness . . .
In faithful love I remain, ever your grateful friend,
LUDWIG,
King of Bavaria.

It was the first personal letter he wrote after his Accession
and the first time he signed himself King in a private letter.
Within less than a month he assured her :

MUNICH, April 11, 1864.

. . . I shall never forget what you have done for me
in my childhood. The Hesses are staying in the Residenz.
Princess Alice, whom I did not know before, is charming
and shows great interest in art . . . Every day I grow
fonder of my profession. Count La Rosee is dying. It
would not only be a heavy blow to his family, but I also
should be very sorry, because he has been a dear friend
and adviser to me.

All his life Ludwig had the charming modesty to leave
his innumerable kind and generous actions unmentioned.
He does not say that one of his first regal acts was, not only
to promote La Rosee to the rank of Major-General, but to
announce his intention of retaining in his personal suite as
long as he lived the man who—in spite of his magnanimous
remarks to Frau von Leonrod—never really won his love.
About this time an English observer wrote :

The King sits with perfect ease on his horse, and for
a youth of his age he carries himself with an extreme
dignity, his beautiful eyes look straight ahead. Alas,
nobody, except perhaps an enthusiastic young girl, would
say that that beautiful young horseman looks very
militaristic—because he might have got his hair cut.

A close examination of Ludwig's early portraits proves
that he had straight hair. From a sculptor's standpoint
his head was too small for his long body and, like his father,
he had large ears. Ludwig's innate aesthetic sense told him
this and, early in life, to minimize these two defects, he wore
his splendid hair long and, like Charles Dickens, had it
waved. All his life he carried a hairdresser in his personal

suite, and if at times the effect seemed somewhat meretricious it was probably because of a new barber's lack of skill.

Soon after his Accession Ludwig visited Franconiá ; at the University of Würzburg, Felix Dahn, the historian and poet who was professor of Jurisprudence there, and a trained observer, said : ' I shall never forget the *schwärmerisch* look of that youth's blue eyes.' The delightful Karl August Peter Cornelius, poet—composer of exquisite perfection, recorded : ' His voice is very agreeable and full. His language pure and unpretentious German.'

Grandpapa Ludwig, who was in Algeria, wrote : ' In difficult times you succeed to the Throne too early. May God lead you in the right paths and may religion always be with you.' It does not seem to have occurred to the old gentleman that it was he and Lola Montez,[1] rather than the Deity, who not only made his grandson Crown Prince far ' too early ', but had disastrously shortened his apprenticeship to his regal duties by five years.

Alice Grand Duchess of Hesse, Queen Victoria's second daughter, wrote to her young host as soon as she got home to Darmstadt, and her letter shows that he had won his way into her warm, motherly heart :

> Before we said good-bye I promised to send you a little bust of myself, and the beautiful poem by Tennyson—*Idylls of the King*—a work which my precious father very much admired and which, after his death, the poet dedicated to his memory. I am sure that you will like it. You must study it quietly and attentively—there is deep poetic spirit in it which you are certain to appreciate . . .

But, as always, it is to Frau von Leonrod that Ludwig turned when he felt impelled to show his innermost feelings :

MUNICH, *April 27, 1864.*

. . . I intend to continue going out to Berg on Saturday afternoons in order to enjoy the quietness of the country-side. With innermost joy I was reminded of the beautiful days of my childhood ; I loved being there and I

---

[1] (1818–1861) so described on the simple stone that marks her grave in Greenwood Cemetery, New York.

recalled my first trip on the steamboat, and the happy games I used to play with the gardener's nice son, Peter. Do you remember ?

The Secretaries come in the morning from 8.30 to 9.30 or 10 o'clock . . . every day at 11 o'clock I see one Minister, then I have my second breakfast, and at 12 o'clock I usually give Audiences, or go for a walk or a drive. At four o'clock dinner, and at six o'clock one of the Secretaries comes alternately. After that Leinfelder [1] reads the papers to me which takes us until about nine o'clock. Then I have tea . . .

Almost before he had taken the oath to the Constitution Ludwig had made up his mind that the moment had at last arrived when he could summon to his side the man whom he had from his fifteenth year adopted as his affinity ; the composer of *Lohengrin*, whom he had cast to play the part of David to his Jonathan. In March, almost before his father's body was cold, he scanned the newspaper lists of visitors to the Bavarian capital in the hope of finding there the name of his hero. He confided to those close to him that he desired to invite Wagner to come at once to Munich and, by the middle of April, had despatched Pfistermeister, his principal private secretary, to Penzing near Vienna, where Wagner had recently been living with his latest mistress the daughter of a Vienna butcher. The composer was not there and Pfistermeister, who did not relish his mission, returned direct to Munich. But if he thought his young Sovereign could be put off he was mistaken : within three days he was again at Penzing investigating Wagner's apartment, which he found ' elegant but not luxurious ' ; he saw Mrasek, Wagner's factotum, who told him that his master ' had gone to Russia ' ! Detecting an evasion, he went to Dr. Uhl, Editor of the *Botschafter*, who told him that Wagner was, as usual, in financial difficulties, and had sought refuge with Frau Dr. Wille at Marienfeld, near Meilen, on Lake Zürich. Pfistermeister hurried back to Munich with the good news.

However, the death of Ludwig's aunt, Princess Luitpold,

[1] F. S. Leinfelder, Court Archivist, who afterwards was a determined enemy of Wagner.

and an attack of catarrh postponed the search for nine days ;
meanwhile he had not been idle. He composed a written
message to Wagner in which he confessed that, since first
seeing *Lohengrin*, he had been enchanted by his music, had
dreamt about him, read his books with intense pleasure,
and his greatest wish was to meet him. Yielding to his
innate urge to self-confession he went on to say—echoes of
Mozart and of his correspondents' own twenty-year-old
Rienzi—that he hated Italian music ; would like to know
how far the composition of the *Der Ring des Nibelungen* had
grown. This missive was accompanied by a photograph
of himself and, even more persuasively, by a gold ring set
with a ruby. While Ludwig was composing his letter in
Munich, Wagner, hiding from his creditors at Marienfeld
with Frau Wille, declared : ' Only a miracle can save me
now.'

On April 30th the harassed Pfistermeister—who disliked
taking part however vicariously in miracles—left Munich
for Lindau, the ' port of Bavaria ', where he passed the night.
Next morning he crossed Lake Constance, arrived at Zürich,
sought Frau Wille who told him in confidence that Wagner
had again fled before his latest financial earthquake, and
was in hiding provided for him by Karl Eckert, Kapellmeister of the Royal Court Theatre, in Stuttgart. Off poor
Pfistermeister started and, after several checks, at last ran
the fugitive to ground, handed him Ludwig's letter, ring
and photograph. The ' miracle ' had happened.

Pfistermeister asked : ' Do you want to go to Munich
and, if so, when ? '

' At once.'

There was no hesitation. Pfistermeister telegraphed to
his waiting Sovereign that Wagner would be in Munich
the following day. The mercurial composer, now once
again feeling himself on the crest of the wave, persuaded
von Gall, who had hitherto been rather tardy about advan-
ing money, to give him a sum on account of royalties for
projected performances of *Lohengrin* at the Stuttgart Court
Theatre.

Soon Wagner and Pfistermeister were seated together in
the train—Pfistermeister, we may be sure, paying both

fares ; at ten-thirty in the evening they arrived at Munich ; Wagner, with von Gall's advance in his pocket, put up at the Hotel Bayerischerhof, then, as now, one of the best in the city, and poor Pfistermeister, unwillingly metamorphosed into Mercury, hurried off to the Residenz to report to his impatient master. The King, who was already in bed, received him at once, and, neither hungry, tired, nor uncomfortable, kept his principal private secretary standing talking till midnight, and then ordered him to let Wagner know that he would receive him the following afternoon at two o'clock.

It is impossible to avoid speculating on the thoughts of these two as they each spent a restless, if not indeed a sleepless night, at last within less than a mile of one another. The King, three months short of nineteen, was incredibly romantic ; an inexperienced visionary ; Wagner was eighteen days short of being fifty-one and had lived, indeed overlived, every moment of his life. Did he not in *Mein Leben* describe himself as an ' incomprehensible young profligate ' ? In many ways as visionary, romantic and idealistic as Ludwig, he was a stony realist where his own interests and the interests of his art were concerned and, what is more, considered them identical. He had long dreamt of a Sovereign, preferably German, who would become his munificent patron, smooth out his every care and set him free for his destiny.

Was this the dream come true ?

By two o'clock, in the regulation evening coat and white tie, Wagner was in the ante-room at the Residenz. At two-fifteen he was received, and this, his first audience, lasted until three forty-five.

The big man with the little head and the little man with the big head instantly became bosom friends. Ludwig always fell in love at first sight. What did Wagner at that time really look like ? No Apollo certainly, yet the discerning critic intuitively felt as if standing on holy ground, indubitably in the presence of genius.

Was Ludwig disappointed with the appearance of his god ?

A small man with a long body, short legs, the great head

set sideways on the shoulders and protruding at the back over the collar in a manner uncomfortably suggestive of hunchbacks.   Did these defects, amounting in unfriendly eyes almost to deformity, put off this young Narcissus who was ever a lover of masculine beauty ?   Not in the least ; neither then, nor afterwards, did Ludwig ever see anything that he was determined not to see.

What did they talk about ?

Nothing ever stopped Wagner indulging in outpourings and, when he found himself in congenial company, Ludwig was, especially in his earlier years, almost as bad.   One wonders how either ever got a word in edgeways.   Ludwig must rid himself of the accumulated adolescent vapours of at least five years.   He started by embracing Wagner.   That was not, amongst Royalties, such a very unusual proceeding as it may appear.   Even now, such continental Sovereigns as are left, and French Republican generals, salute those whom they delight to honour with a chaste kiss on each cheek.   Perhaps, for once in a way, Wagner was tactful and more or less held his tongue.   After all, Ludwig was a King, and Wagner, in spite of his assertive and notorious radicalism and republicanism, was ever susceptible to the glamour of Royalty.   Moreover, the combined caterwaulings of his innumerable creditors scattered all over Europe no doubt engendered caution and, it has to be admitted, with Wagner caution and cunning were almost synonymous.   The emotional boy was as wax in his hands.   Wagner was an expert in bending women to his wishes, and there was over-much of the woman enshrined in this great big heroic-looking body.   Ludwig was enchanted.

He immediately directed Pfistermeister to order a portrait of Wagner and a bust to join the portraits of Shakespeare and Beethoven adorning his study : he cannot wait—he never could.   They parted—but only for a few hours. Ludwig adored flowers and perfumes, especially Chypre and the haunting odour of the Persian jasmine.   When Wagner had gone did the audience-chamber reek of snuff, and did Wagner's person and clothes emit its acrid scent ?

Wagner remained five days in Munich, then, succoured

by Ludwig with some thousands of florins with which to
pay his more pressing debts, he was reluctantly allowed to
go to Vienna—but only for three days. On the 13th he
was back ; on the 14th he accompanied the King to Lake
Starnberg. Ludwig of course stayed at the Schloss ; but
the wretched Pfistermeister had been kept at it and, on
Ludwig's behalf, had rented Count Pellet's lakeside house,
the Villa Seehaus near Percha, for the Master ; the new-
found friends were as nearly inseparable as both presumably
desired.

It was Whit-Saturday, May 14th, 1864, exactly two
months since the funeral of Max II, and nineteen days since
Pfistermeister set out on his search for Wagner.

Mid May on the banks of Lake Starnberg can be as
enchanting as any human being has a right to desire. For
the rest of his life May was to Ludwig ' the month of Rapture '. Enshrined here within range of the magnificence
of the Bavarian Alps were loveliness, luxury and peace, and
no artist who ever lived appreciated these three graces more
than Wagner, who indeed insisted that, for him, they were
not only necessities—but, because of his genius, his by right.
As for Ludwig, he was in his element although, in describing
it all so objectively to Frau von Leonrod, he is more than a
little disingenuous :

MUNICH, *May 29, 1864.*

. . . I stayed at Berg for twelve days : the long wonderful rides strengthened me enormously so that I feel
as well and as fresh as never before. I rode round the
Starnberger See to the Ammer See, Weissenburg, Partenkirchen, and once even to Hohenschwangau, where it is
beautiful just now . . . I came back here on Wednesday
and (for the first time) took part in the Corpus Christi
Procession. Soon I shall go to Kissingen, but only for a
few days in order to pay my respects to the exalted guests.
I shall start my tour round the country when the Court
mourning is over. As you probably know, I have now
appointed all the Court officials, Baron Moy has become
Master of Ceremonies . . . During my stay at Berg I
saw a good deal of R. Wagner who rented a house near
Starnberg. I see more and more clearly that my expectations in him will not be disappointed but, on the

contrary, excelled.   He is happy with me having at last
found the undisturbed quietness for which he was longing.
Oh, he is a great and noble spirit—unfortunately not
nearly so much appreciated as he deserves.

Wagner himself could not have expressed the last sentiment more perfectly.   Throughout his whole career he felt
himself to be ' a great and noble spirit not nearly as much
appreciated as he deserved '.   Ludwig could not too often
say that to the composer personally—and of course to the
world, because, oddly enough, the proletariat always
listens attentively to anything said by a King.

Fully to understand the relationships between Ludwig and
Wagner it must be grasped that from the outset they were,
on the King's side, idealistic, sincere and candid ; and, on
the composer's, realistic, histrionic and equivocal.   Apart
from his music, to which he ever remained incorruptibly
single-minded, it was not in Wagner's nature to be anything
but greedy, ungrateful and—to put it mildly—disingenuous.
Three days *before* Ludwig wrote assuring Frau von Leonrod
that the composer ' is happy with me having at last found
the undisturbed quietness for which he was longing ', Wagner,
already surfeited by being twelve days alone with Ludwig,
was longing for feminine society, and was intriguing to have
his ' undisturbed quietness ' invaded.

It is impossible to give the twelve-hundred-word letter [1]
Wagner wrote to Frau Wille from Starnberg on May 26, or
the long postscript to it he sent her a few days later, but one
or two quotations are unavoidable.   Already he was titivat-
ing the account of his early relations with Ludwig for the
benefit of history.   He untruthfully conveyed to this intimate woman friend at Marienfeld that, passing through
Munich on his way to Vienna he had to spend the night
there because he had missed the night train, that, next
morning he ' was hindered by a terrible sickness ' from continuing his journey, and that he could walk into the King's
presence without even the customary formality of asking for
an audience.

[1] Wagner's letters to Wesendonck, edited by Ashton Ellis (London,
1899, Grant Richards), p. 147.

Wagner wrote to Frau Wille :

26th May, 1864.

I pulled myself sufficiently together to visit the young
King after midday.   At once all was clear and appointed :
the curtain was drawn up.   After a few days I pursued
my journey to Vienna . . .   I came back with my
servants, a married couple, and my faithful hound to my
new last home, where, borne by the divinest love, I now
enjoy the wondrous fortune we gave birth to in that
fever-night at Marienfeld . . .   In the year of the first
performance of my *Tannhäuser* (the work with which I
first entered my new and thorny path), in the month
(August) in which I felt impelled to such excessive pro-
ductivity that I sketched the *Lohengrin* and *Meistersinger*
at the same time, a mother bore my guardian angel . . .
in his 15th year the youth was attending his first performance of my *Lohengrin,* which took such hold of him
that he thenceforth drew his self-tuition from the study
of my works and writings, and has openly declared to his
entourage, as now to me, that *I* have been his sole true
teacher and bringer-up.

Then the King of Bavaria died—quite unexpectedly—
and my compassionate guardian angel—against all rules
of Fate—ascends a throne.   His earliest care a month
thereafter, is to send for me : while I am draining the
cup of sorrow to its lowest dregs with your merciful aid,
the envoy already is seeking me in my deserted home at
Penzing ; he must bring the King a pen, a pencil from me.
Ah ! at last a tie that brings with it no pains and tortures !
What it is for me, to have this glorious youth before me !

He is thoroughly aware who I am, and what I need :
not a word have I had to waste about my situation.   He
feels that a King's prerogative must assuredly suffice to
keep all common cares from me, to give me altogether to
my Muse, and procure me every means to produce my
works when and how I wish.   At present he mostly
resides in a little castle near to me ; in ten minutes the
carriage takes me there.   Daily he sends either once or
twice.   Then I fly as to a sweetheart.   'Tis a fascinating
interview.   This thirst for instruction, this comprehension,
this quiver and glow, I have never encountered in such
splendid unrestraint.   And then this charming care for
me, this winning chastity of heart, of every feature, when

he assures me of his happiness in possessing me : thus
do we often sit for hours together, lost in each other's
gaze.   If I would—so they tell me—the whole Court
might stand free to me : He would not understand me if
I asked for an ambitious rôle there.   So beautiful and
genuine is it all . . .   In time they all will like me ;
already the immediate entourage of the young King is
happy to know and find me thus, since each perceives
that my enormous influence on the Prince's mind can
only tend to good, to no one's harm . . .   Now you shall
see how it lasts, and how all prospers.   Have no
doubt ! . . .

Wagner could not exist without a woman in attendance
on whom to cast his burdens, emotional and financial.   If
she was at hand he smothered her with verbal outpourings ;
if at a distance, he wrote them.   A few days later he con-
cocted another effusion to Frau Wille in which he did not
disdain to vilify his wretched wife Minna and cast on her
unmerited odium as one of those possessing only ' the
animal instinct for discovering the useful for the mere day's
need '.   When, during that hateful first visit to Paris, they
were starving together, if, as has been hinted, Minna did not
actually sell her body to buy them food, she shouldered without an apparent qualm almost every other form of degradation.   Going out, she returned with bread, or the money to
buy it, and her husband did not meticulously inquire how
she came by it.   Now that a King had taken him by the
hand this is how he maligned the woman who spent her
youth and health for his needs :   He went on :

> . . . But when a *woman's* heart so forgets every instinct
> of love, that she judges the object of her love by this
> philistine standard of ethics, commiserates, and—exhorts,
> it can no longer be suffered.   My having so petted and
> spoilt my own wife by excessive indulgences, that at last
> she lost all power of rendering me a little justice, has
> become to me a nemesis.   The result has appeared . . .
> Where are you now, dear friend ?   Won't you write
> me once again ?   I'm quite lonely here : I lack a little
> company in the house ; perhaps I shall get Cornelius
> to come.   Shall I be able to do entirely without the
> ' womanly ' ?   With such a deep sigh I say No, that I

almost must wish it ! One glance at his dear picture helps again ! Ah, this adorable youth ! Of a truth he is all to me, world, wife and child !

Ludwig as ' world, wife and child ' was all very well on paper. He might indeed be of use in aiding the composer to conquer the world for his music—but that was all. Ludwig had all his life an inner need for solitude ; Wagner could not exist without an entourage. He therefore summoned to his side two favourite henchmen, Karl August Peter Cornelius and Hans von Bülow, telling Ludwig that they were essential to his professional work. Liszt, von Bülow's father-in-law, had long been Wagner's close friend, so it seemed natural enough that Cosima should accompany her husband ; with their two children she hastened to Munich where, eight days later, Hans joined her, and they all went to the Villa Seehaus. This invasion naturally shocked Ludwig : when explaining to him why he needed von Bülow, Wagner had not hinted that he also needed Bülow's wife.

As far as Ludwig was concerned the mystic honeymoon, so long prayed for, was already over. Wagner was so extraordinarily obtuse where the feelings of others were concerned that he had not an inkling of what was going on in Ludwig's mind. If Ludwig imagined that his passionate devotion, his undue abasement, and his unique munificence would secure to him the wholehearted friendship and undivided society of the man he had already christened ' The Great Friend ', he was sadly mistaken.

Even had Wagner been able for a few weeks to do without a ministering woman and an obsequious suite, there were external reasons why the Starnberg idyll could not have lasted very long.

Owing to his Leftist political activities, which poor Minna Wagner had always feared and opposed, Wagner was, as elsewhere, under suspicion in Bavaria long before he arrived. The Bavarians now saw their young Sovereign falling under the influence of a politician of extreme views who had been compelled to fly from Saxony where he had abused his position as Court Kapellmeister at Dresden, lost the friendship of King Friedrich August II and had, in consequence, spent fifteen years in exile in France and Switzerland. It was as a political firebrand that the Bavarians of that day saw Wagner, not, as the world does now, as a great musical genius. As for Pfistermeister, who by no means personally disliked Wagner, and the King's entourage and Ministerial advisers—in spite of the contrary assurances to Frau Wille—they looked upon the composer simply as a needy adventurer who was out to bleed financially and exploit their unpractical Sovereign ; and who can blame them when that was how many of Wagner's own intimate friends regarded him.

A charming, detached private house in Munich, in the Brienner Strasse, important enough to be known in continental fashion as the Hotel Gotham, was found for Wagner, and, in October, the King guaranteed the substantial purchase money. It had a large attractive garden and was almost opposite the house in Barer Strasse bought by Ludwig I for Lola Montez.

Was that a bad omen ?

In addition, Ludwig granted Wagner an annual allowance of eight thousand gulden (or florins), at that time equivalent to about four hundred pounds, worth at least four times as much as now. To meet immediate needs a year's allowance was paid in advance. Modest as the amounts involved may seem to-day, they looked to the Müncheners of 1864 enormous as, throughout Germany, and in Bavaria in particular, salaries have always been meagre.

Criticism was not diminished by Wagner loudly proclaiming his hunger for luxury, and there was so much gossip about the seraglio-like furnishings of his new house. Wagner never had any compunctions as to how he obtained money for useless show ; worse still, his taste in surroundings and in dress was execrable. He owed money for food, furniture, and rent and loans in every town or city in Europe in which he had resided, and some of it was not paid for years. As early as the end of June, Heinrich Esser, the well-known conductor, wrote to a friend :

> H.M. of Bavaria will soon understand that, with his modest means, he will not be in a position to satisfy the whirlpools of Wagner's mania for extravagance.

The Brienner Strasse house was decked out in coloured satins, silks, frills and lace, more suitable to the abode of a fashionable cocotte than to the workshop of a man of genius. The private rooms reeked of Attar of Roses and Wagner would empty a bottle of Rose de Bengale into his bath. Although mostly glossed over—especially in Germany—there was indeed in Wagner distinct evidence of effeminacy and bi-sexuality; he adored perfumes, voluptuous sights and sounds, luxurious couches, oriental profusion such as he imagined for the Venusburg scene in *Tannhäuser* : inspired by these, and stimulated by rich food and iced champagne, he could in his own peculiar lordling fashion call his soul his own. It was in such surroundings, on occasions dressed up as a woman, that he could conceive and create his masculine projections and ultra-athletic heroes. The little man, physically tough and emotionally gigantic, evolved or re-created from the old German primordial myths, men like gods and women like goddesses. Nothing human satisfied Wagner ; everything had to be heroic ; over life-sized ; colossal. It has to be admitted that too often, especially in his librettos and prose writing, Wagner's grandeur often became grandiose ; splendour mere tawdriness, gold only pinchbeck. Significantly in all this Ludwig II was almost exactly Wagner's counterpart, and that was, from first to last, the eternal bond between them. Ludwig, himself an artist without wings, would give to this fettered angel freedom to soar ; that, at a most critical phase in Wagner's career, he munificently did this for the composer is—as has been suggested—his chief claim to fame, and it is no ignoble one.

Wagner, like Ludwig, was in his own fashion a wayward, grown-up child. The difference was that whereas Wagner's mean physique hid a robust constitution, an indomitable will, an unalterable purpose—and genius ; Ludwig's magnificent torso concealed a weak, changeable will, fitful purposes and, although intuitional as an animal and very shrewd, a mediocre and steadily decaying brain. Where they were equal was in egotism and narcissism. Neither had any use for anything or any person that did not minister to their adolescent vanity, hunger for sympathy, comprehension and applause, and their exhibitionism, innate and incurable. Both were spiritual and emotional vampires, living only for themselves, battening on others.

After paying a visit to his grandfather at Aschaffenburg, Ludwig went on to Kissingen where he met his cousin Elizabeth of Austria and received the Tsaritza Marie, Consort of Alexander II, who hoped that the eligible young King would fall in love with her ten-year-old daughter, the Grand Duchess Marie Alexandrovna. Ludwig discussed the girlish Grand Duchess with grandpapa, who wrote :

ASCHAFFENBURG, *July 8, 1864.*

Dear Ludwig,

You know how fond I am of you ; I cannot therefore suppress my innermost wish to say that you ought not to tie yourself by a marriage. At your age one is far too young for matrimonial life and, considering that you grew up so very quickly, it is doubtful whether a marriage would be good for your health. If you give your promise to marry you deprive yourself of the liberty of seeing other Princesses. Later on many things appear differently from what they did in the beginning. You decide now about your happiness for life, therefore do not act quickly but keep a hand free.

I am convinced of this, beloved grandson, and wishing you everything that is best, I remain,

Your affectionate grandfather,

LUDWIG.

As a matter of fact, like some youths, Ludwig was quite unsusceptible where young girls were concerned, and clearly always preferred the maternal warmth of mature women. He developed a *schwärmerei* for the Tsaritza ; born Princess Marie of Hesse, she was twenty-one years his senior. Pfistermeister afterwards said it was the only passion for a woman that he ever noticed. At the time he remonstrated with Ludwig about what he considered a silly and undignified infatuation :

'But, Your Majesty, the Empress might well be your mother.'

To this Ludwig replied :

'Oh, I wish she were.'

Ludwig wrote to Frau von Leonrod :

HOHENSCHWANGAU, *August 1864.*

. . . (in Munich) R. Wagner came several times with two excellent pianists—the famous Herr von Bülow and Herr Klindworth. They played Wagner's own works, also some unpublished ones ; for instance, *Tristan und Isolde* and *Der Ring des Nibelungen* ; magnificent, incomparable creations which possibly excel Wagner's earlier works !

I only left Schwalbach on the 11th where I went in order to see once more the Empress of Russia. She is an extremely intelligent and charming lady . . .

A few days later he again wrote :

HOHENSCHWANGAU, *August 27, 1864.*

. . . To-night the King of Prussia is coming here for one day . . . I grow fonder and fonder of my profession . . . Perhaps you will be interested to know how I have decorated my bedroom here—in which, as you already know, scenes from Tasso's *Jerusalem Delivered* are painted. You probably remember that orange trees are painted on the blue ceiling which represents the sky ; in order to make it still more convincing that I am sleeping out of doors, I have had a fountain with real water put in the room, which looks very nice indeed ; they were able to do it without causing any dampness in the room. I also ordered an artificial moon,[1] and some more orange trees to be painted in order that the spectator might be still more beguiled . . .

In the beginning of October the Court returned to the Residenz, and Wagner moved into his new home. Ludwig signed an agreement concerning *Der Ring des Nibelungen* which he was very anxious to see completed. He undertook to advance Wagner thirty thousand florins, the score to be finished within three years.

Less than a week after Wagner took up residence in Munich an unpleasant article, accusing him, amongst other things, of overweening vanity, appeared in the *Ausburger Abendzeitung*, a widely read evening paper of good standing. It was the first shot in the Bavarian press campaign that

[1] Worked by some form of clock, the moon could wax and wane !

was soon to drive the composer from his long-sought, new-found sanctuary.

In the summer of 1849, just before he was banished from Dresden, Wagner had already presented to the Government a considered and quite feasible plan entitled : *A Project for the Organization of a German National Theatre for the Kingdom of Saxony*. Ludwig, under Wagner's burning enthusiasm, now wholeheartedly adopted the scheme for Munich. Gottfried Semper, the famous architect who designed Wellington's ugly funeral car, now in the crypt of St. Paul's Cathedral in London, had already prepared grandiose plans, and was immediately summoned by Ludwig.

CHAPTER FIVE

DISILLUSION : 1865

ROME, *January 5, 1865.*

. . . Don't overwork yourself, and be quiet in the evenings. It is very bad for you to work while you digest your food, and it is bad for the eyes too. Don't give up any Rights of the Crown. For a short time you will be praised for it—but the loss remains. How changeable the aura popularis is ! Your grandfather has had his lesson !

However well learnt by grandpapa, his lesson is, alas ! never really much use to his grandson ; moreover, his grandson was not working nearly as hard as he appears to have made out. As usual, Frau von Leonrod gets rather more of the real truth than does any other of Ludwig's correspondents :

MUNICH, *January 22, 1865.*

. . . I ordered a good many classical plays lately ; I generally study beforehand a detailed analysis of these wonderful blossoms of poetry, especially with regard to the characters, which I find most instructive and interesting. Oh, really, one of the greatest enjoyments of the mind is to be carried away by these wonderful works— and then, elevated and strengthened, one can face the realities of life again. On the whole, as far as is feasible, I live a rather retired life . . .

The trouble about escaping easily into an ideal world is that inevitably the return to reality becomes more and more difficult and, therefore, more infrequent. From the beginning of this year of 1865 Ludwig's dislike of leaving his dream-world became increasingly noticeable, and was without doubt encouraged by the first great blow—perhaps indeed the greatest blow—his self-esteem ever received.

He discovered that he was not the Great Friend's one and only passion.

75

It was on the same day that he wrote to Frau von Wille loudly asserting that his glorious young King was now his all in all, that Wagner also wrote to von Bülow's wife Cosima summoning her to Munich. Throughout his life Ludwig, who was magnificently generous, showered gifts on everyone whom he liked ; but never quite succeeded in giving himself. Wagner never gave anything to anyone because the artist, to create, must be self-sufficient. Ludwig's abortive creativeness was a prolonged struggle to reach that self-sufficiency which is the artist's only form of freedom. In the personal sense, only two women and one man were unfailingly loyal to Ludwig ; his Mother and Frau von Leonrod, and another Richard, as yet unknown. As far as Wagner was concerned the twelve days Elysium was over.

The medical specialists, as a result of their post-mortem twenty-one years later, were to declare that the first definite signs of deterioration in the King's mental health were traceable to the year 1865. Ludwig's brain was not of a calibre to withstand emotional shocks or prolonged strain.

From Wagner to Gudden everyone assumed, largely because of his uncontrollable emotionalism, that Ludwig II was a half-wit, whereas he had remarkably acute mental powers and a prodigious memory.

Cosima's prompt arrival in Munich in response to Wagner's appeal to join him immediately aroused gossip— Frau Hans Guido von Bülow was with child. Leinfelder, and those in the Royal entourage who wished to discredit, and, if possible, get rid of the composer, did not fail to inform their Sovereign that it was commonly believed that the child was Wagner's.

The immediate consequence of the scandal about Cosima and Wagner was that, when the *Flying Dutchman* was repeated in February, the King was not present ; worse still, when Wagner presented himself at the Residenz the next day he was not granted an audience, and Pfister-meister ' had to explain this and console him '. A week or so later *Tannhäuser* was given and, to the astonishment of all, and the delight of many, the King was again absent. A serious signed article by no less a personage than the honoured Oskar von Redwitz now appeared in the *Allgemeine Zeitung* saying that public opinion would be grateful for any sign that the music of Mozart or Beethoven aroused any interest in the Bavarian capital. Poet, former professor of aesthetics at Vienna, and at the time an elected member of the Bavarian Second Chamber, Redwitz gave a lead to that informed dignified section of the public which Ludwig could not dismiss as ' wretched, short-sighted people '. Wagner, who could no more control his pen than he could his tongue, unwisely replied to Redwitz.

April the tenth was for this curiously entangled little group a red-letter day. Wagner's first child by Cosima was born and given in Christian baptism the pagan name of Isolde. Ludwig, possibly as a sign of reconciliation, slighted his father's memory by renaming his steam launch *Maximilian* the *Tristan*. Perhaps Wagner, always somewhat eclectic about the origins and parentage of his heroes and heroines and a bit mixed about their ambiguous sexual relationships, had managed to convince his Kingly Friend that Tristan was, somehow, the begetter of Cosima's baby Isolde ! As both lived in a world of phantasmagoria that is not as impossible as it sounds.

Wagner was never a moment idle where his own interests were concerned. Having, as he thought, put the twenty-year-old King securely in his pocket, he now proceeded to try and pocket the Bavarian Government, and, not knowing what was good for it, the Bavarian Government objected. But, from his childhood's days when he staked the pension of his poverty-stricken mother in the gambling dens of Leipzig, Wagner was a gambler. Moreover, this ' Red Republican ', as he had been called, although a Leipzig-born German, seemed to misapprehend the Bavarian character as completely as did the Limerick-born Lola Montez. Aspiring to play a political rôle in Bavaria, Montez fell ; Wagner had tumbled into disgrace and exile because of his political activities in Saxony ; neither event served to warn him. At that moment the world was *couleur de rose* and Richard Wagner was on top of the world. Like all gamblers he never knew when to stop. Indeed, modesty could hardly be described as one of the composer's besetting

sins. He now confided to Frau Wille that he was working
hard to overthrow the Ministry of von der Pfordten and get
rid of Pfistermeister ! A week later Paul of Taxis warned
Pfistermeister that, owing to Wagner's intrigues, his position
had become uncertain : whatever his feelings towards
Pfistermeister, Ludwig still relied on his Prime Minister,
von der Pfordten, and told Frau von Leonrod that he ' comes
to appreciate him more and more and is happy to know that
the Portfolio is in such good hands '.

There were three things on which Ludwig was always
adamant : his kingly office, his kingly prerogatives, and
his royal dignity. It took Wagner years to learn that in
affairs of state he never had, and with one brief exception
never would have, any influence worth talking about.
Knowing this, and yet realizing how incurably interfering
he was by nature, von der Pfordten, with public opinion
strongly behind him, determined to get rid of this political
busybody who could not keep his itching fingers out of
politics, for which indeed he considered that he had a
heaven-born genius.

In March, Elizabeth of Austria was at her childhood's
home, Possenhofen on the banks of Lake Starnberg opposite
Berg, and from there wrote to her daughter Gisela, then
aged nine :

> . . . Yesterday the King paid me a long visit, and if
> grandmamma had not come in at last, he would probably
> still be here ! He is completely reconciled ; I was very
> nice, and he kissed my hands so many times that Aunt
> Sophie (who had watched us through the door) asked me
> afterwards whether I had any hand left. He was again
> wearing Austrian uniform and full of *chypre parfum* . . .

History knows of few such tragic groups as assembled in
the modest ducal drawing-room on that spring morning.
Elizabeth to be struck down by an assassin and die in the
street of a foreign city ; Sophie to be burned to death in a
foreign capital, and the young King to die before middle age
in tragic circumstances.

To another correspondent Elizabeth described how, overcome with laughter, she and Sophie watched the arrival of

Ludwig in his state coach with four horses, outriders, equerry and the rest. A slight rain was falling and Ludwig, who had just had his hair specially waved for the occasion, had an umbrella held over him from the carriage to the door lest a drop should fall on his head or full-dress Austrian uniform ; in order not to disturb a curl he carried his head-dress.

A great deal of nonsense has been written about Elizabeth and Ludwig : that she was the only woman he ever loved ; that, in the best romantic tradition, because he ' lost ' her he proposed marriage to her younger sister Sophie ; that he was swimming across Lake Starnberg—three miles wide and four hundred feet deep, to seek refuge with her from his persecutors when he was drowned—and so on. Elizabeth was eight years older than Ludwig : when she became Empress of Austria in 1854 he was playing with his toy bricks and, although he undoubtedly knew his lovely Wittelsbach cousin, his admiration for her then must have been that of a child for a grown-up. Their atavistic inheritance was too similar, they were both too egocentric and too alike ever to be really fond of one another. There used to stand in opposite corners on the imposing staircase of the Munich palace of her father Duke Maximilian Josef in the Ludwig Strasse two white marble busts, one of Elizabeth and one of Ludwig. Both done in early youth before sex definitely reveals itself, they were so alike that they might have been two brothers or two sisters !

If Ludwig never saw through Sisi she certainly saw through him. Indeed, Ludwig's overmastering obsession was to some extent shared by her own father who, when young, had developed a friendship for a professional zither-player of his own age, Johann Petzmacher. The lad's skill on this popular instrument so fascinated the Duke that he not only appointed him his musical tutor and attached him to his person, but took him everywhere, including a long tour together in Africa and Asia. Elizabeth may have seen through Ludwig, but she understood him as so many failed to do.

Another aspect of Ludwig was commented upon by Count Blome when writing to his Chief, Mensdorff, the

Austrian Foreign Minister, and he gives an extraordinary acute appreciation of Ludwig :

> If I judge the young Prince correctly I should say that Nature has endowed him with more imagination than brain and that, in his boyhood, his heart was more neglected than anything. He is full of exaggerated self-esteem and wilfulness, and a certain lack of consideration for others is noticeable. The King does not take advice for which he has not asked . . . Literary men and artists are received in audience more than any other class of the population . . . His Majesty's chief tastes lie in music and literature, and the former—because he has no real musical talent—more because of the words than because of the music itself. The poetry of *Lohengrin* and the other texts based on the old Teutonic sagas of Wagner's operas are the cause of his predilection for Wagner's music . . .

Blome's opinion, backed by La Rosee's considered verdict given to King Maximilian II four years earlier, when he asserted that the five-year course of lessons in piano-playing showed no result because the pupil ' has neither talent for music nor does he like it ', settles the controversy as to whether Ludwig did, or did not, really understand and love Wagner's music.

The confusing thing about so many ' facts ' concerning such an extreme chameleonic person as Ludwig is that one ascertained ' fact ' so often obscures, or even seems to cancel, others. If music was not the germinal, the elemental source of Ludwig's strange obsessional love for Wagner, what was ? The King's lonely attachments to Paul of Taxis and his successors are plain enough, being, within their forbidden limits, quite simple. Although, like many great artists, Wagner was bi-sexual—in the sense that he could, and did, attract women and men equally, there is not a scrap of evidence that he and Ludwig ever indulged in a homosexual relationship. Both were temperamental ; nevertheless Wagner was the only lasting, intense, really disinterested love of the King's life ; suffering all things, overlooking failures amounting to betrayals, forgiving all things and, in everything that mattered, faithful to the bitter end. Moreover faults apart, there must have been something heroic and splendid in the man who could arouse, abuse, and yet keep a love so imperishable in a great woman like Cosima von Bülow, and in a man so wayward as Ludwig.

It has, however, never become quite clear how far Wagner knew of, understood or sympathized with Ludwig's temperament which obviously he did not find repulsive. Thirty-two years older than the King, very much a man of the theatrical world and only too well acquainted with its most squalid elements ; if Wagner's eyes were shut to what was under his nose, they were deliberately shut.

I have not myself seen it, but Mr. Ernest Newman courteously informed me that amongst Wagner's papers at Wahnfried ' there is one in which he speaks of failing to understand how anyone can be homosexual '. If so, it is as disingenuous as anything the composer ever wrote. From history, and experience, he knew quite well. Not, of a certainty, from personal experience, because the assertion of Guy de Pourtalès that there was evidence of ' an invidious friendship between Wagner and Liszt ' can be dismissed. Speaking generally, Pourtalès is sometimes an unreliable witness who, like Emile Ludwig and others of their school, would sacrifice all verity for a nasty innuendo or a sensational paragraph. Wagner from the outset knew about Ludwig's emotional friendship for Paul of Taxis, and made use of it for his own ends ; like all Munich he knew of the sudden fancy for Albert Niemann. Even before the crown had settled firmly on Ludwig's brow there was gossip in the inner circles of Court Society, not only about the King's relationships with Paul, but about those with one of his own valets, Voelk ! It was in fact known already that he was infected with *nostalgie de la boue.*

Through her innumerable continental relatives and connections Queen Victoria liked to keep her observant eyes on what was happening in Europe. About 1863, at her request, a Bavarian Notable and family connection, Prince Clodwig of Hohenlohe-Schillingsfürst, began to send the Queen regular reports on political conditions in Germany.

Clodwig's Aunt, Princess Feodora of Hohenlohe-Langenburg, born at Leiningen, was of course the Queen's beloved half-sister and, at one time, Clodwig himself had seriously considered applying for a commission in the British Army. Writing on April 15 (1865) to the Queen, Hohenlohe, although, as his Reminiscences prove, a very acute and intelligent observer of history, showed himself as far as Ludwig was concerned by no means as clear-sighted as the Austrian diplomat Blome :

> . . . With regard to Bavaria I cannot help saying that we have the most charming Monarch who ever came before my eyes. His is a thoroughly noble and poetic nature. His Wesen is extremely captivating because one feels that his politeness is the direct expression of his gracious heart. In addition, he lacks neither brain nor character. I hope that the tasks which lie before him in his reign will not exceed his powers.

Meanwhile Ludwig's grandfather was more than ever disturbed about the trend of political affairs, and wrote :

> ROME, *April 30, 1865.*
>
> . . . Don't overwork yourself ; save yourself. Your grandfather is not talking for himself ; he is not on the Throne ; but he is speaking for the Monarchy ; his heart beats for Bavaria's welfare . . . Don't have "douce" illusions. You are full of good will, you have brains, but you have no experience—and of course can't expect to have it. The Progressive Party will only be content when—as in England—Parliament has all the power and the King none . . .

The performance of *Tristan* was not given until June ; it began at six o'clock, and Ludwig, who had come in from Berg, was present, surrounded by members of the Royal Family. Ludwig I (in mufti) sat beside his grandson in the Royal box, as did Uncle Luitpold, and his son Leopold now aged twenty, Uncle Adalbert and Duke Max were also there. Ludwig Schnorr von Carolsfeld, who created the title rôle, sang and acted the part to perfection ; it is indeed doubtful if his magnificent interpretation has ever since been equalled, much less excelled. Schnorr's wife, Malwina, inspired by her husband, sang Isolde worthily. Bülow conducted and, at the King's behest, after the Royalties had left it, Wagner bowed his acknowledgements from the Royal box, thus driving the Courtiers, and the ever-growing number of his enemies, frantic with rage. But, then, Wagner never was a diplomat. Ludwig, enraptured, immediately commanded a second, a third and a fourth performance. Then, direct from the final repetition, he returned by train to Berg. Still in a state of extreme exaltation, he went to Hohenschwangau and, from there, to one of his mountain hide-outs. By Monday (June 12) his emotion had not spent itself and on that day he wrote to Wagner :

> I am exhausted ; it has laid hold of me ; I burn with longing for a repetition of the first delight . . . Hail to the Creator ! I kneel before him . . . I beg of you not to abandon him who only has GOD to depend upon— you and GOD.
> Until death, and after death in that kingdom beyond,
> Your faithful,
> LUDWIG.

Why was Ludwig so obsessed by *Tristan* ?

It has been said that Wagner's music, surcharged as it is with passion, makes an urgent and irresistible appeal to the adolescent sexual type to which the King belonged. The opera is admittedly a masterpiece, a work of genius, but it requires no very profound insight to see that here Wagner reached out and gave full measure, magnificently illustrating the focal point of his artistic credo ; everything in excess ; or, to use his own phrase about the early relationship between Ludwig and himself : ' splendid unrestraint '.

From the first of June until the end of November, The Fairy King, as his infatuated subjects called him, was almost continuously away from his Capital. Now that he could travel by train from Starnberg to Munich, the little schloss on the east bank of the lake was found reasonably convenient for his excursions to the theatre, and Ministers could without undue trouble wait on him at Berg and present their reports. From this year dates the beginning of Ludwig's openly expressed dislike of Munich and Court life ; indeed, were it not for his devotion to the theatre, his loving subjects would seldom have had him in their midst ; he

increasingly hated being stared at by anyone, and never
accepted the adage that a cat may look at a king.

Throughout his life Ludwig's letters to his mother,
although in earlier years quite frequent, in striking contrast
to those written to Wagner and his men friends, seem
curiously objective. There was always a lot about ' the
beautiful landscape '. She frequently sent him flowers and,
in general, their main subject was flowers ; and he never
failed to send ' heartfelt greetings to Otto '. From now
onward Ludwig is continually making excursions in the
mountains and started building for his own occupation
little inaccessible living-huts where he could be alone and
unmolested. This ache to climb for rest to craggy heights
is general among Bavarians of both sexes ; in this, as in
much else, Ludwig was typical of his countrymen, only
being a King, he was free to indulge his impulses. There
was hardly a single extravagance of the King's that was not
typically Bavarian, or which could not be paralleled in
millions of his subjects. That was the fundamental reason
why Germans in general, and the Bavarians in particular,
took Ludwig to their hearts and keep him there to this day.
Like all the Wittelsbachs, Ludwig could live happily in a
palace, an inn or a peasant's hut. The Queen Mother
shared her elder son's love of isolation and had a modest
mountain retreat of her own. If she took little interest in
politics, music, art or literature, her maternal love and
patience were inexhaustible and, as fate closed in upon him,
Ludwig increasingly came to find this a source of consolation. Meanwhile their common love of nature and flowers
was their greatest bond. Ludwig had an incomparable
eye for a magnificent situation for a hut, a cot or a palace,
and would placidly put up with discomforts his suite found
repellent in order to picnic and sleep in some favourite spot.

On July 1st he wrote to his mother from Hohenschwangau:

> More than anything I like to be alone, occupy myself,
> and think of you, and of father whom I imagine I see
> everywhere here. I am glad about this because every
> tree reminds me of him.

Is this hallucination ? Gietl—who had unique oppor-

tunities of knowing—declared that as early as his fifteenth
year Ludwig was subject to hallucinations. In the beginning of August he was at Brunnenkopf. A day or two later
he wrote from the Halbammerhütte :

> At two o'clock I left the Brunnenkopf and went to
> Pürschling. I felt like an eagle in his lonely erie in the
> rocks.

During the summer Elizabeth of Austria was again taking
the cure at Kissingen, but as, at the time, Ludwig was full of
a projected Wagner programme—not to mention a certain
private preoccupation—he excused himself from waiting on
her. Elizabeth, as usual where Ludwig was concerned,
wrote with her tongue in her cheek :

KISSINGEN, 8th of July 1865.

Dear Cousin !
Let me assure you that I am sorry beyond words that
I have no chance of seeing you this summer. I understand only too well how much you need care and quietness after having been so ill last winter. The wonderful
air on our dear Starnberger See and the exercise in the
open air will certainly do you a lot of good ; your stay at
Berg must be a real recreation after all your troubles and
all the business. I am much touched that you sometimes
use my little riding-whip and think of me. I need not
tell you how vividly I am reminded of the many agreeable hours which I spent with you so happily last year.

August, his birthday month, was spent entirely at Hohenschwangau and, on the 18th, he wrote to Frau von Leonrod :

> . . . It was here that I spent my precious childhood's
> days, and now a world of wonderful memories rises before
> me ! I am happy ; and I am glad about the profession
> which God gave me ; now I am taking a rest from the
> most difficult business, and next winter I shall start afresh
> at my work. I intend to study very seriously and shall do
> everything within my power to make my dear people
> happy . . .

All that summer his inseparable companion (although
seldom mentioned in his letters) was Paul of Taxis. One
August day Ludwig dressed up Paul as Lohengrin and,
carrying a harp, got him to appear on the Schwan See in

a boat drawn by an imitation swan. ·Although the north-east shore of the exquisite little lake lies within the Royal demesne the incident became known and gave rise to much gossip, and caricatures appeared in the Munich press in which Ludwig himself was mistakenly represented as Lohengrin. As a matter of fact, whatever posturings of this sort he may have done indoors—Ludwig never appeared in public in such a guise. A few days after Paul did so Ludwig tried on the same costume in the bath at Hohen-schwangau and, on a subsequent occasion, in the blue grotto at Linderhof, but as he could neither sing nor play the harp, he must have been as unpersuasive as the property swan. Probably what really thrilled Ludwig was dressing up in Paul's clothes and these histrionics were doubtless inspired by the command performance—worthy of the Albert Hall in London at its worst—which took place in the lovely little Residenz Theatre in Munich in July. Wagner conducted bits and pieces from *Rheingold*, *Valkürie*, *Siegfried* and the *Meistersinger*, and Schnorr the magnificent sang for the last time.

Wagner paid a brief visit to Berg and from there on August 28 Ludwig wrote to Frau von Leonrod :

> . . . Unfortunately I had to spend my birthday in bed because I felt slightly unwell. I got the original score of R. Wagner's *Rheingold*, a Sonata by Mozart in his (Wagner's) handwriting, and a book about *Tristan and Isolde* by Franz Miller of Weimar . . . To-day the King of Prussia left . . . I read a great deal about the Greeks. What a wonderful people they were ! In many things the people of to-day ought to imitate the old Greeks ! . . . I admire and love the works of the immortal Briton whose works I intend to get translated by Bodenstedt—at any rate I intend to do much to promote that work.

Ludwig proved the genuineness of his love for ' the immortal Briton ' by encouraging Friedrich Martin von Bodenstedt to follow up his translation of the Sonnets and, helped financially, his complete translation of the plays appeared between 1866 and 1872.

Two other examples of Ludwig's artistic munificence belong to this period. He bought for several hundred pounds a score of Mozart's, and in a most charming letter he thanked von Wesendonck for relinquishing the original scores of *Das Rheingold* and *Die Valkürie*. Wagner had given them to Wesendonck in return for what Ludwig described as ' friendly asylum to the artist in his struggles with want and incredible sorrows '. It was, he adds, ' a veritable need to express to you, honoured Sir, my sincerest thanks since it is in part to your lively sympathy that we owe the immortal works created by Wagner in Switzerland '. Ludwig's request for the return of the scores was made at the behest of Wagner and is, literally, a brilliant example of the composer's extraordinary craftiness in managing to eat his cake and have it.

All November Ludwig was at Hohenschwangau and from there wrote to Frau von Leonrod : ' On my way to Partenkirchen it suddenly came into my head that I might go on to Switzerland, and I decided on the spot to do so.'

Later he continued the story :

HOHENSCHWANGAU, *November 30, 1865.*

. . . During the last days of October I made a little journey to Switzerland—in strictest incognito. I visited Lucerne, went by steamer across the Lake to Brunnen, where I spent the night. Then I made an excursion to the historically interesting Rütli, to the famous chapel of Tell (the paintings of which I intend to restore), and to the Hohle Gasse and Küssnacht. I spent a few days at Burglen in a little inn which is said to be on the site of Tell's house. I also went up to the famous Berner Oberland and spent a few days in the beautifully situated Interlaken and at Grindelwald. One can have no idea of its sublime beauty unless one has been there. There, in the presence of those wonderful colossi of ice, the Mönch, the Jungfrau and the Eiger, which shine so mysteriously in the moonlight, there beside the deep blue lake in the lovely world of the Alps, there in contemplating the wonderful beauties of nature, one comes to realize the holiness of mankind and the exalted sublimity of the creation ; the soul feels nearer to eternity, and feels the deep need of adoration and praise to Almighty God who, as loving Father, created us and takes care of us. Unfortunately the Swiss people are less idealistic than the landscape which surrounds them. They are religious and industrious but without anything eminent, and lack every enthusiasm.

I hear there are still the most curious rumours in the country about my relations to Wagner ; don't lend your ear to such gossip, I entreat you. People must always have something to talk about and they exaggerate everything. In Munich I shall continue to receive my Ministers regularly. On the 6th there is to be a performance of *Maria Stuart* . . . The theatre should be a place of education and not an institution for the amusement of a pleasure-seeking, frivolous crowd. Franz Liszt dedicated his last Oratorio, *St. Elizabeth*, to me. It is said to be a wonderful work.

The excursion to Switzerland was not so very sudden as Ludwig suggested. He did not confide to Frau von Leonrod that he had lately become interested in Emil Rohde, a young actor of considerable merit who was rapidly making a name for himself by his interpretations of such rôles as Don Carlos, Ferdinand, Max Piccolomini, and other Schiller heroes, in all of which he had greatly pleased the King. Rohde was frequently invited to recite for Ludwig during the early autumn, and it was after seeing him in the title rôle of *Wilhelm Tell* that Ludwig, accompanied by Rohde, set off incognito for Switzerland. One evening towards dusk the King and Rohde arrived at Schwyz from Lucerne. They stayed at an inn kept by one Ross, visited a bookseller's shop, the Tellplatz, the Tell chapel, and everything associated by legend with Tell. The forty-three portraits of Swiss peasants hanging in the Schwyz Town Hall fascinated the King although, like the Hampton Court beauties, it must be difficult to tell one from the other. Next day they left for Küssnacht. There was, of course, a sensational account of the visit in the local Swiss paper and, upon the Editor sending him a copy, Ludwig, taking the unusual course of personally thanking him, said that from childhood ' Tell had for him a singular attraction '.

The last act of Schiller's play with its romantic suggestions of the beauties of a pastoral Switzerland, picturesque peasant huts, and an idealistic peasantry dear to water-colour painters of the period, combined with the grace and charm of a romantic-looking young actor, and the forbidden delights of temporarily laying aside his Kingship, had so thrilled Ludwig's impulsive and wayward imagination that it had to be gratified whatever the risk or cost.

The reference to the ' most curious rumours ' about himself and Wagner in Ludwig's letter to Frau von Leonrod had to do with two incidents that aroused throughout Bavaria criticism tinged with anger. The relationship of Wagner and Frau von Bülow was now notorious. Although Ludwig seldom received Cosima it was rumoured that she continuously wrote to him and that jointly she and Wagner had acquired an uncanny influence over him. It was said that their demands for money became so excessive that Pfistermeister took the extraordinary course of proclaiming the fact and trying to shame the two harpies by openly sending forty thousand florins to Frau von Bülow in a sack. All this happened in November about the time Wagner joined the King at Hohenschwangau, bringing with him a small orchestra and conducting Beethoven, Gluck, Mozart and Mehul for Ludwig alone. In an excess of gratitude to Wagner, and anger at Pfistermeister and the Müncheners, when Wagner left the Castle Ludwig ordered a four-horse, semi-state carriage with postilions and himself saw his guest off at Füssen station. The press and public became even more incensed with Wagner and, recalling Montez, the comic papers nicknamed him—sinister implication—Lolus, the masculine of Lola !

Events were now coming rapidly to a crisis.

Schrenk [1] resigned for purely political reasons and was succeeded as Prime Minister by von der Pfordten who, at a Council of Ministers immediately assembled at his home, threatened to resign unless Ludwig parted with Wagner. Ludwig personally informed ' the Great Friend ' of this hateful development—and the composer was forced to leave Munich. Throughout Bavaria the anger against Wagner had steadily grown all through the spring, until, in April, public opinion was temporarily deflected by the threat of the Austro-Prussian War.

[1] Baron Karl von Schrenk auf Notzing (1806–1884).

Wagner, who so far had never managed to stay put any-where for any length of time, wandering off on another stage of his long odyssey found a shelter, if not a home and resting-place, at Triebschen near Lucerne where he remained in exile for the next six years.

Ludwig wrote to Frau von Leonrod :

MUNICH, *December 21st, 1865.*

. . . It made me very sorry that I had to send away Wagner temporarily ; but under the existing circumstances it was necessary for me to act like that . . . It is a great pity that I cannot find time to do very much for myself in Munich . . . and I really ought to take the air . . . I am longing for the summer ! The Theatre is a real refreshment after the rush of the day . . .

There was no truth in the oft-repeated legend of the sack of florins which was the usual intuitive and melodramatic embodiment of undoubted facts by the mob. Ludwig's income from the Privy Purse was only about three hundred thousand florins a year. Between May 1864, when they first met, and December the tenth 1865, when he was banished from Bavaria, Wagner received for himself per-sonally, or for his works, forty thousand florins—just over one-eleventh of the King's modest private income for the period.

CHAPTER SIX

EXIT PAUL : ENTER SOPHIE : 1866

O N New Year's Day from his villa at Nice, Ludwig I wrote to his grandson :

January 1st, 1866.

. . . Yesterday I saw in the *Allgemeine Zeitung* that one Party wants you to give your permission to pull down the old walls of Nürnberg. Neither your father nor your grandfather would *ever* have consented to that. Nürnberg is *unique*, but without the walls it will lose the character which makes it so ; they are a *necessary* part of the town.

Apart from the many political perplexities caused by the Austro-Prussian War, which were of such moment not only to Bavaria but to the whole of Germany, Ludwig had his own more immediate anxieties. The Bavarian press and public continued to be thoroughly incensed against Wagner. Blome wrote to Mensdorff : ' the young King continues to live his indolent life and only receives Bülow the pianist '. Whether by accident or design, Bülow had opened a letter from Wagner to Cosima which was of such a nature that he could no longer pretend to keep his eyes shut. This belated ' discovery ' was to involve Ludwig in endless vexation and compel him to face a situation he had for months instinctively dreaded and evaded.

For some unknown reason Ludwig had quarrelled with Paul who appears to have been out of favour for some considerable time. Probably the earlier charges of his enemies, asserting that he was ' living a frivolous life ', had been revived, and with greater force because there was more, and later, evidence. Paul had yet to learn—as had all his successors—that Ludwig could not, and would not, tolerate a divided allegiance. However, during the last week of April there was a letter of reconciliation from Ludwig, and Paul wrote him, undoubtedly from Munich, the first of a series of extraordinary letters that are surely unique as exchanged between one adult man and another. They must be given in full because, as pathological documents, from them we get a truer and more accurate reflection of Ludwig's psychology than from any other source. Moreover, they throw new light on the vital part Paul played as intermediary between Ludwig and Wagner during a fate-filled year. Ludwig, as was inevitable, had taken the initiative in ending the quarrel ; he was never vindictive, and could be magnanimous. They met ; mutually melted ; confessed and communed in the most romantic, lover-like fashion. Paul, unfortunately, does not always head or date his letters, but it is pretty certain that he was back in his own apartment or flat in the nearby Türken Strasse. He was almost continually received by Ludwig in his latest toy, the Winter Garden he had caused to be constructed on the roof of the palace adjoining his own top-floor suite, and which was entered by a door from his study. As he never used the spacious suite known as the Hofgartenzimmer, formerly occupied by his parents on the first floor, or any of the state apartments, it was in his own top-floor apartment and in the Winter Garden that he spent much of his time and received and entertained his intimate friends.

It was in these unreal and to him romantic surroundings that Ludwig and Paul again met after their separation. They separated for a few hours regretfully and reluctantly and, as was to become his custom, Ludwig sent by hand a letter for Paul to receive and read just before he fell asleep. Paul immediately replied, the Royal footman—perhaps Voelk—being presumably kept waiting or sent down the long and nowadays somewhat sordid street to a beer-house for a litre of beer, and told to return. How Ludwig and Paul hoped to avoid gossip and scandal in such a small city as Munich is incomprehensible.

If to Anglo-American readers Paul's letters to Ludwig are what a private critic has truly called ' masterpieces of Baroque sycophancy ', they do not in that respect greatly outdo the letters addressed to Ludwig by Bismarck himself. Sycophancy towards Royalty and rank is a German trait ; and even Hitler demanded, and received from high and low, that worship of a God demanded by the Roman Emperors.

Paul of Taxis wrote to Ludwig :

April 29.   Sunday.

My Dear Exalted Friend !

Happy am I to be allowed to call you so after so long
a time.   Your lines which I have just received are balsam
after all I have had to suffer during our first unhappy
separation.   I am happy.   Fulfil my wish that I may
call myself by the highest name of ' friend ', and do let
me assure you that you have found in me the most
faithful and devoted friend who would rather lose his life
and everything he possesses than you and your friendship.
Forgive me if my letter is rather muddled, but your letter
has put me in such a state of happiness that I hardly
know what I am doing.   May God's blessings be upon
our friendship and may He let it last for ever.

This is the deepest wish of your sincerely and faithfully
devoted friend

PAUL.

The next evening they again met, the reconciliation was
complete, and, before going to sleep, Paul wrote :

April 30, 1866.   [Monday.]

My Dear Beloved, Exalted Friend !

With the greatest pleasure I fulfil your wish by letting
you know this very night that, by our conversation this
evening, I feel more closely bound to you than ever before.
After my sincere confession I recognized in you the
righteous and magnanimous friend !   I cannot express
in words how happy I am in our renewed friendship.
How different our relationship is now ;   it was a friendship of two young men who were just entering upon life ;
now it is a relationship of man to man.

I also shall be happy now, and feel life worth living
knowing that I may live for you, and realizing that I
am dear to you, and always shall be.   With my most
sacred word of honour I promise you faith and eternal
friendship and there shall be no cause whatever for
blaming me or my life.   I will have no higher thought
than you.   You are everything for me.

Dear Ludwig—I may call you so—how often have I
thought of that beautiful but all too short time at Berchtesgaden—they went past all too soon—the beautiful days

of Aranjuez [1]—and how magnificent their repetition was now !

May God give His blessing so that no power on earth may ever separate us.   You can build on me as on a rock. I will never disappoint you.   Pour out your heart to me ; I will share your sorrows and your joy ; everything that I may do for you becomes rapture and delight.

Oh, how much I have to tell you ; but I know you are longing for a few lines from me. I promise to send you as soon as possible a better picture of myself, only let me know whether you want it in mufti or in uniform.

Thanks a thousand times for your letter, your magnanimous pardon.

Once more my most sacred promise never to make a *faux pas* such as the earlier one.   Also I enter into the month of May with the happiest sentiments and a light heart—the month of May is correctly described as the month of rapture.   Remember me in your prayers as I always remember you and press you to my heart in thought.

Until death your faithful friend,

PAUL.

Paul appears to have kept a diary in the most approved romantic fashion.   Like everything else concerning him it has been destroyed.

Saturday [*May 5th*].

Dear and Beloved Ludwig !

I am just finishing my diary with the thought of the beautiful hours which we spent together that evening a week ago which made me the happiest man on earth . . . and I recalled the days of the past week, revelled in the happiest and most rapturous memory, pressed you in thought close to my heart, and so tried to overcome the sadness of being alone to-day.   Then your dear letter was brought to me—balsam, heavenly balsam ! for my heart.

A thousand thousand thanks for it !   The reason why the dearest friend seemed to be sad is because, at the end of the wonderful symphony which impressed me extremely, I saw you getting up and leaving the box whereupon your

[1] This refers to Schiller's *Don Carlos*, the scene of which is the Jardin de la Isla of the Royal palace of Aranjuez, thirty miles south of Madrid.

last words after dinner came back to my mind : ' When shall we see each other again ? ' Tears came to my eyes when I saw you leaving. Oh, Ludwig, Ludwig, I am devoted to you !

I couldn't stand the people around me ; I sat still, and, in my thought I was with you. I had to go home ; I knew that I would hear from you ! How my heart beat when, as I passed the Residenz, I saw a light in your window.

But now I am calm and shall sleep quietly and shall be with you in my dreams.

Thank you for your sympathy ; if ever I should suffer be sure that I will pour out my heart to you and tell you everything.

Farewell, dearest friend ; how I would love to go on writing but I must hasten to send off these lines in order that you also may be able to rest quietly.

Farewell, my dear Ludwig, I salute you from the depth of my soul.

For ever your true friend,
PAUL.

The next day he indites another rhapsody :

May the 6th, 1866. [*Sunday.*]

Beloved Ludwig !

A thousand thanks for the newspaper and your dear letter. You ask, dear friend, how I have spent the day. Heaven knows that I spent it lonely in spite of the many diversions . . .

The next day (May 7th) (Monday) :

Beloved Ludwig !

I also exclaim : this day has gone ; and how happy were the hours I spent with you. I was near you. I saw you. I was with you. How my heart beat when I saw your carriage coming along ; how happy I was to run up to the band and order them to play the National Anthem ; but what was the music compared with the feelings of your faithful Paul !

Oh, Ludwig, you could not have made me happier than by calling me to your side.

You ask w h ether I thought of you—you know that you

are my only thought . . . that your image is always
before mine eyes !

That endless dinner really lasted from 5.30 until 9
o'clock.   Immediately afterwards I ran home, sat down
at the piano and expressed my innermost feelings by
playing and singing—each note was to speak to you !

After I finished writing my diary I looked through the
books which I had ordered for you and which arrived
during my absence.   While I was reading the bell suddenly rang.   My heart rejoiced ; . . . your dear letter
was brought to me and I hurried to my desk in order to
thank you.   By your lines you have given me the most
divine end of this day, you have delighted me anew.
Oh, my most beloved friend !   I also shall dream sweetly
of you.   You shall appear in my dreams, your gracious
face, your beautiful dear eyes shall look at me.   Oh, I
shall be wonderfully happy !   Farewell, dear friend, sleep
well, dream sweetly and think of your loving Paul.

Once more a thousand thanks for the wonderful present.
I will always think of you in love.

Farewell, dear Ludwig, I embrace you and press you to
my faithful heart.

For ever your faithful

PAUL.

The friends of course met officially and ceremoniously in
the daytime and, when doing so, derived a strange satisfaction from the knowledge that there existed between them
recondite, irrevocable ties.   They not only met openly and
in secret, but like gushing schoolgirls continued to write to
each other daily, intertwining their initials and sending one
another crosses for kisses and coupling their Christian names
like hobbledehoys in love.   On May 8th Paul's rapture
was almost hysterical :

No pen could write, no words could express the
happiness in which I revel now that I see you and may
go with you to your door !

As we walked arm in arm I felt so well, so indescribably
well !

You may be sure that I shall count the minutes until
I come to you tomorrow, see you, and be near you !
How long to-day will seem to be.   Certainly, dear friend,
I will bring you my mother's letter to-morrow.   I have

no secrets about her, nothing that you also may not know.

Immediately after I left you I went back to the Theatre, said goodbye to my brother and went home, where I thought of you and was together with you in my thoughts !

I have just been reading Wagner's biography which interests me extremely ; a thousand thanks for it. Suddenly the bell rings, I pray, and receive your dear letter . . . How well this language suits me.

Yes, dear friend, it is a tie of some exalted kind that holds us together ; it is not an everyday friendship, it is a higher power that brought us together and that binds us ! To-morrow I shall go myself to see about the books which you ordered so that I may be able to fulfil that wish of yours.

But unfortunately it is already late and you are waiting for my letter. I close this letter ; have sweet dreams, I salute you faithfully and lovingly,

For ever yours faithfully,

PAUL

PauLudwig

This was the last time that the writer signed himself Paul. The friendship had now reached such a state of exaltation, the two protagonists were so bemused with their mutual hysteria that, for the time being, they cease to exist as normal human beings, and Ludwig—as was his custom—bestowed upon Paul a new name : to the Fairy King unreality was always transcendent.

But the rapture of individuals, however urgent and important to themselves, never yet caused the world to stand still a moment. Isolation from the common lot, however much desired, is unattainable.

Just to show his critical subjects that, even if they had forced him to banish Wagner the friend, they would never succeed in dividing him from Wagner the composer, Ludwig commanded a special performance of *Lohengrin* on May 22nd in honour of the fifty-third anniversary of the Great Friend's birthday. Amidst the storm of criticism aroused by this order Ludwig, in spite of the flatterers close to his person, was not without honest and disinterested critics. On May 12th Thérèse Frau von Gasser wrote him a letter

showing that, even then, there were German admirers of
Wagner's music who perceived that the idol had feet of
clay :

MUNICH, May 12, 1866.

. . . In Wagner's Oper und Drama I read everything he
says about music with intense interest, because I belong
to the great number of people who admire his music and
poetry and who follow his work with unfailing interest.
But his book has not satisfied me.   It is quite proper that
he should write about his work, make it better understood by the masses, and prove that he is aiming at a new
system.   But why criticize his living and dead colleagues
in order to make his own creations perfect?   It made
me feel very uncomfortable to find him blaming others
in order to be himself praised.   It is small and vain.
That Wagner does not even leave to the beloved
Beethoven all his honour is heart-rending.   Surely, there
can be more than one perfect musical creation . . .
Why does Wagner want us to dislike others because we
like him?   I cannot see that there is less feeling (Gemüt)
in the operas of Meyerbeer, Mozart, Haydn, Beethoven
and so on than in Tannhäuser and Lohengrin, both of which
I like very much.   Of course, Italian music is chiefly for
the ear, but in spite of that one can feel it very deeply—
certainly while it is being heard.   Wagner's criticisms
of all other music is, in my opinion, unjustified because,
in other ways, that music is just as high and valuable
as is his.   It is very immodest of Wagner not to let the
dead rest in peace but to try to diminish their fame.

As long as he lived Wagner, as far as was humanly possible, rightly insisted on personally supervising all productions of his operas and, preferably, establishing a tradition
by conducting the earliest performances himself.   Ludwig
—who should have known better—was now flouting this
essentially legitimate condition ; Schnorr von Carolsfeld's
widow Malwina, wrote an admirable letter to the King on
this subject.   Honest and outspoken (when divested of the
inevitable Royal verbiage of the period), it is entirely to the
point about both the political and artistic implications of
the situation, making it quite clear that, although only a
little over two years on the throne, the discerning were

already beginning to lose faith in, and admiration for, their young King.

During the Seven Weeks War it seemed intolerable to all true and loyal Bavarians that while Germans were fighting Germans the Bavarian Monarch was secretly rushing off to Switzerland in chase of a mythical Wilhelm Tell, and concentrating on honouring Wagner in Munich which had cast him out as an undesirable only six months previously. A few weeks after Malwina Schnorr wrote' her letter, which, however ambiguous its inspiration, was timely and courageous, Königrätz (Sadowa) was fought, Austria and Bavaria were defeated and humiliated and Prussia achieved an ambitious aggrandisement which, lasting a brief half-century, was to result in her downfall and that of Germany in 1919.

MUNICH, *May 21, 1866.*

Most Gracious Master and King !
Your Majesty !
. . . August Master, it cannot be unknown to you what the whole German people—not to speak of your own—expected from your youthful and flamelike enthusiasm ! The high hopes which were fostered by everybody—oh, Your Majesty, you are in danger of losing them ! God may prevent that—and yourself—because it is still within your own power. Will Your Majesty please forgive me for taking the liberty of offering a most humble opinion of how this could be done ? Though the terrible battles which threaten to destroy our precious German Fatherland cause the deepest anxiety to all your people, everybody here is embittered and full of ill-will because you, my August Master, only think of the performances of Wagner's operas. Oh, do let my beseeching supplication find its way to your heart and conquer your burning desire to enjoy the masterpieces of the dear friend during these sad times ! Do it not only for your own—but, more particularly, for his sake. Certainly Your Majesty would help him, of whom you are, and to whom you want to be light and life, much more if you would postpone the performances for some months. You know yourself how little he agrees for the moment with them. Believe me, Your Majesty, such a resolution on your side would cause infinite satisfaction and great jubilation. It is to be hoped

that the troubles will be at an end by the autumn of this year ; and then Richard may without any danger return. He himself is *indispensable*, for the performances ; *without him* we shall only be able to achieve imperfect work— and that is just the contrary to Your Majesty's wishes.   I beseech Your Majesty not to reject my humble supplica- tion—the spirit of my husband speaks to you through me —do not close your heart to him ! Examine my words and motives, which are as pure as your own, and, believe me, if you listen to my words you will act rightly in every direction.

Nobody knows anything of the step I have dared to take.   Keep it as a secret and make *everybody* and *him* happy by a free resolution . . .

It has been said that at that moment Malwina and Wagner were having an *affaire de cœur* and that the letter was inspired, if not dictated, by the Great Friend himself.

Almost on top of this emotional appeal Ludwig received through Queen Olga of Würtemberg a message from the Tsaritza who :

. . . wishes from the bottom of her heart that you may recognize your Royal duties and fulfil them with faithful devotion.   In saying this to you she remembers you with the same motherly love as if you were her own son.

Two days after this Elizabeth of Austria wrote to her mother :

I hear the King is away again.   I wish he would care a little more about his duties, especially now when times are so bad.

' I hear the King is away again ' !

On the morning of May 23rd, accompanied only by Paul and attended only by Voelk (at that time his favourite personal servant), Ludwig left Berg for his customary ride after having heard the Report of the Minister whose turn it was to be received.   They cut across country to the railway station at Biessenhofen and there took train for Lindau. Crossing Lake Constance on the little steamer which does the journey twice daily, some of the passengers thought they recognized the King, but Voelk told them they were mis- taken, his master was the Count von Berg.   Soon Ludwig and Paul were staying together at Wagner's villa at Triebschen on Lake Lucerne and once again Ludwig and Wagner were deep in the discussion of Semper's plans for a Bavarian National Theatre and Opera House.

The Austro-Prussian War, in which the fate of Bavaria was involved, could wait.

That villa at Triebschen has since become world-famous. It was Wagner's refuge for the six productive years of 1866 to 1872. In its garden Ludwig and Wagner sat dreaming great dreams and envisaging great plans. There, with Wagner and Paul beside him, Ludwig, just halfway through his life, was at his best. To construct great musical dramas was enchanting ; to construct great dramas and, at the same time, to erect great buildings was perfection ! Ludwig reluctantly returned with Paul to his capital. Later, in that garden of dreams sat Nietzsche on the day the *Siegfried Idyll* was first performed ; within the villa were composed or finished *Die Meistersinger, Siegfried* and *Götterdämmerung*. There, seventy-two years later, the great Toscanini broke a life-long rule never to conduct in the open air by conducting a memorable Wagner Concert in the garden.

Ludwig reluctantly met the Chambers and speaking of ' the Great German Fatherland ' said, somewhat belatedly, that he hoped civil war would be averted from Germany. But his visit to Wagner had of course leaked out and made his people angry. To his chagrin Ludwig was for the first time in his life received coldly and with every sign of dis-approval by the populace : as an expression of his anger at such disloyalty he dismissed the Prefect of Police and retired in high dudgeon to Berg.

Three entries in Clodwig Hohenlohe's diary of this period give a picture of Ludwig's odd combination of prescience and irresponsibility and briefly summarizes the situation. Dining with the King in the Winter Garden on April 11, Hohenlohe expressed apprehension regarding Prussia's pro-posal to set up a Parliament, and doubted her being con-tented with supremacy in North Germany. To this Ludwig replied : ' Just now, yes ; but, presently, she will want more.'

From Clodwig von Hohenlohe's diary :

June 3 [1866].

So long as the King is encouraged in his caprices by the sycophancy of the Court and Government officials, so long will he continue to regard himself as a demigod who can do what he pleases and for whose pleasure the rest of the world—at any rate Bavaria—was created.

June 16 [1866].

The King sees no one. He is staying with Taxis and the groom Voelk on Rosen-insel and lets off fireworks. Even the members of the Upper House who were to deliver the address to him were not received—a case unparalleled in the Constitutional life of Bavaria.

Meanwhile much was going on behind the scenes.

Because the German temperament is such that it demands a scapegoat the Bavarians were inclined to believe that Wagner was responsible for all their misfortunes.

On May the thirty-first, while it seemed as if civil war was going to sweep through Germany, Ludwig, looking as they said like a young god, sought to appease his good Müncheners by walking through the streets in the Corpus Christi procession. Even while he was doing so these same good Müncheners were discussing an article against Cosima which appeared that day in *Volksbote*; signed by no less a person than Zander the editor, it rudely used the French form of Cosima's name instead of the German:

It is hardly a year since the well-known Madame Hans de Bülow got forty thousand florins out of the Privy Purse for her ' friend ' (or what?) . . . For the moment she is staying with her 'friend' (or what?) in Lucerne.

Bülow, from the Triebschen villa, challenged Zander to a duel, and left it at that; but Cosima first importuned Ludwig for an audience, and then wrote him a characteristic letter:

On my knees I humbly beg my King to write the letter for my husband so that we may not be forced to leave the country in disgrace and shame. Only your Royal word can re-establish our insulted honour . . . How would it be possible for my husband to work in a town where the honour of his wife has been doubted. My Royal

Master, I have three children to whom I must transfer the honourable name of their father without any stain.

This was all very well, but rather too histrionic. Ludwig was not her King nor was number three Bülow's child. To the astonishment of Europe, Ludwig took the unprecedented course of writing, and allowing to be published, the letter Cosima demanded with such vehemence. The Bavarians, and the world in general, laughed sardonically and quoted ' the lady doth protest too much, methinks '—or its German equivalent.

Bülow received the Royal letter rehabilitating his wife's honour on the 11th. Next day Wagner wrote to his lifelong friend, Mathilde Mayer :

Really I had meant strongly and energetically to put the alternative before the King. Either I procured justice by breaking my silence, declining all future Royal benefits and separating completely from him, or he himself provided the necessary justification by issuing a highly honouring public Letter. He has now decided to do the latter : in a few days the Royal letter will be published.

It was : on the 19th.

It was of course addressed to Bülow and in it the King said :

As I have been in a position to obtain the most intimate knowledge of the character of your honourable wife, it only remains for me to discover the inexplicable reasons for these criminal insults.

It is not much wonder that amidst all these goings-on Blome reported to Mensdorff that ' some people begin to think the King is going mad '.

July, 1866

During this fate-filled month while Germans were still killing Germans, Italians Austrians, Austrians Italians, Ludwig was at Berg. Paul, now given by the King the name of Friedrich for their sole and private use, was also at Berg in-waiting and had again fallen into disfavour.

He wrote Ludwig the first of another series of extraordinary effusions :

BERG : *July 1, 1866.*
Tristan Day.

Beloved Ludwig !
Tear your faithful Friedrich out of the horrid mood into which the sudden change of yours has put him.

O Heavens, must a word again destroy my beautiful dream ? Must the poor Friedrich once again lose everything ? For God's sake, no ; it cannot be !

No warm hand-shake responds to my pressing ! . . . Oh, I am unhappy ! I could not suffer more from a ' Go for ever '.

For God's sake soothe my pains ; favour your unhappy friend with a conversation about that incident ; only that can give me peace.

In fear and hope,
Your
FRIEDRICH.

Then a reconciliation took place :

July 13th [Berg].
In the night at 11.15.

Most Beloved Angel !
Exalted miracle !
Only a few lines will I send you in order to say what my heart's desire is ! May sweet dreams be with you and may everything that is dear to you on this earth be present !

Sleep well, angel of my heart, and give one more thought to your most faithful,

FRIEDRICH.

July 14th, 1866 [MUNICH].

Most Precious Ludwig !
Just come back from Church I find the enclosed telegram. I send it to you at once in order that you may have some news from the distant friend at once. I shall post the letter to Wagner to-day . . .

July 17th, 1866 [*Wednesday*].
[MUNICH].

Innermost, beloved friend !
Pray forgive me for only now answering your dear letter but the contents of it have upset me so much that

I first of all needed a little rest in order to collect myself.

Most precious and noble angel, you know how much I appreciate your burning and most sincere love, and you know that I reciprocate it in the same degree that I share everything with you—the agreeable things as well as the disagreeable.

I wish I were able to fulfil all the wishes which you express in your letter.

I hope to be in a position to send you and the Friends a telegram to-morrow.

Courage, perseverance, noblest, and the victory is ours !

After a time of trial the reward is bound to come— and it will not fail to come !

How I long to be near you again. I feel well when I am with you.

You know that I only live for you— . . .

A thousand—nay millions of greetings and embraces I keep besides those I am sending you now.

In love I press you to my brotherly heart.

For ever your most faithful

FRIEDRICH.

The telegraph system to Berg was by now in working order and on the 21st Ludwig used it to telegraph to Triebschen, telling Wagner something that he had, apparently, confided to and discussed with Paul : he meant to Abdicate. This upset the applecart completely. Wagner had no use what-ever for a throneless King without a Civil List and, in his heart, never had much use for the moon-sick boy with the intelligence, outlook and sexual proclivities of a perpetual adolescent. Paul in Munich was also informed, presumably by telegraph, of the great decision. He at once sat down at his desk :

July 21st, 1866.
In the evening at 7.30.
[Saturday.]

My Exalted Friend !

You will scarcely believe that I was hardly strong enough to get home.

I am very much disturbed by your resolution and by the ease, yea equanimity, with which you agreed to take that *terribly serious* step by which you may destroy the great plan of yourself and the Friends, and by which

you may destroy us all. A stream of tears for you and
your young life has at last relieved me.

Oh, Ludwig, you are destined to do great things, and
only in your present position can you realize them—
and achieve the great aim.

Unless I receive a counter order to-night I shall go
to-morrow morning at five o'clock to Miesbach ! The
day after to-morrow to the hospitals.

I have just received a note from a young girl saying
that I had better not go out late at night as there is danger.
They say that the Müncheners are very excited about me.
God will help ; I am not frightened.

Once more I entreat you to think twice before you act !
I embrace you with all my heart,

FRIEDRICH.

To do Paul justice he, from beginning to end, tried
to give Ludwig what he considered good advice. But
although like most introspectives Ludwig loved asking for
advice, he hated taking it. Paul—and many others—urged
him to go and inspect his wounded and defeated soldiers,
but that was not his humour. On the 22nd Paul wrote :

July 22nd, 1866.

. . . The main purpose of my little letter to you, only
star of my life, is to indicate how you may show a beautiful
feature of your nature in expressing your sympathy and
interest in the brave wounded soldiers of your Army. I
am sure it would be the greatest success with the Army
and with the whole country.

I will tell you what exactly gives me the courage to
make this proposition. I need not assure you that it is
the most faithful Friedrich who is talking to you, he who
always wants the best for you, and who wants your
people to adore you.

I went last night to the inn to which I often go in the
company of two gentlemen, a captain and a clergyman,
both of them devoted to you in love and faithfulness.
The clergyman backed up by his friend the captain, said
to me : ' Highness, you know how much we admire and
love you, because everybody who knows you must love
and admire you. Couldn't you induce our most gracious
and amiable King to visit the wounded ? You are the
friend of the King, Highness ; the people know that, and

everybody hopes for the best and is glad to know that a young man of such noble character is with the King—as a friend ! '

I answered that one has to be very careful as it is dangerous for a person who is easily affected by sea-sickness to pay that sort of visit, and that, in addition, I could not take the responsibility of exposing you to the risk of infection with consequences which could not be foreseen. Whereupon he continued : ' Oh, I wish the King would appoint you to visit in his name all the hospitals in town and possibly also those outside Munich. Your name, and your relationship to the King, would make an indelible impression on the wounded and on the Army and then they would say : " The King has sent his Adjutant to find out how they all were, and it is Prince Taxis, his friend and favourite, whom he has sent." One would have to publish it in a Bavarian newspaper so that this act of liberality of the King might be known to the people.'

Forgive me if I have said too much and let me again assure you of my faithfulness and devotion,

Embracing you,
Your FRIEDRICH.

While snubbing and opposing Ludwig's responsible Ministers, Wagner was always careful to flatter his favourites. On the 26th Paul wrote :

MUNICH, July 26th, 1866.

. . . I am always prepared to do everything for you. Whatever may be the consequences for me—I am prepared to travel to the distant Friends, if you, angel, order it.

The message from ' the Great Master ' to the ' faithful Friedrich ' touched me very much.

The presents have not yet come.

Expecting your commands re Wagner,

I embrace you with all my heart,
FRIEDRICH.

On the 27th Paul again wrote from Munich :

Dear Exalted Friend !

I hasten to let you know that letters and presents from Triebschen have gone to the post.

To Frau von Bülow I wrote to-day.

In case Quaglio has sent the scenes and decorations which were expected, will you please let me know if there are any further scenes you may want. I would put them together here and then send the whole thing to the Residenz so that nobody could notice anything . . .

If the King would not himself visit his wounded soldiers and personally thank them for risking their lives for Bavaria he, succumbing to pressure from Paul—backed by the Clergyman and the Captain—at last reluctantly permitted his Personal Aide-de-Camp to do so in his name.

Having done as best he could a job the King should obviously have done himself, Paul was summoned back to Berg. Ludwig had a much more urgent and important mission with which to entrust him.

So ended July 1866.

Hohenlohe correctly summarized the political position in his diary when he wrote :

There are positions, like that in which Bavaria found herself in 1805, when one is forced into an un-German alliance without the possibility of escape.

Ludwig was not, however, allowing the scene painter Quaglio—or even Wagner—to have everything their own way. If the Great Master would insist on exercising his talents as a Statesman, Ludwig was going to show in practical fashion his mastery of the technique of the stage. While Bismarck was putting the finishing touch to his cunningly conceived Austro-Bavarian Peace conditions, the King of Bavaria was busy devising scenery and costumes for Schiller's drama *Wilhelm Tell*. Had he not been to the living scenes themselves for inspiration? Had not the Editor of an obscure Swiss journal therefore hailed him as a great King? Some of the costumes designed for the republican hero of the play were made to fit Ludwig himself, and, wearing these, he paraded his room. The Bavarians in general considered that Ludwig had a kingly and imposing carriage. In 1935 Prince Ludwig Ferdinand described his first cousin's carriage and appearance at the age of nearly forty as ' majestic '. But there were a few shrewd observers who thought otherwise of the twenty-year-old Monarch. Young Moy, son of the Grand Master of Ceremonies to the King, acted as page to the Sovereign at a Chapter of the Knights of S. George over which Ludwig presided, and the impression left on his young mind was that the King walked in the procession in an affected and theatrical manner. To be blunt, Ludwig was inclined to strut and, even now, many highly-placed Germans do not always recognize the difference between a strut, a stride and a distinguished walk. Moreover, Ludwig was apt to screw up his courage for the Court dinners, ceremonies and public appearances he hated by consuming beforehand quantities of red wine and champagne—a mixture calculated to make anyone walk and talk oddly !

After he had swallowed Bismarck's Peace pill with distaste and difficulty, but without choking, Ludwig wrote to the King of Prussia offering him ' joint ownership with himself of Hohenzollern, the venerable castle of our ancestors '. King Wilhelm accepted, and an official manifesto was issued in due course, announcing this, and stating that Prussia and Bavaria were now joint guardians of the future of Germany ! As a matter of fact Bavaria had already lost her proud and ancient place in the German Empire—and Ludwig already knew it.

As usual with Ludwig, his personal history was being secretly made behind the scenes. We have seen how both Wagner and Paul were scared to death at the very idea of abdication. However, an alternative scheme after Ludwig's own heart was suddenly evolved and Paul was packed off post-haste to Triebschen in disguise. Really it was much better than dressing Paul up as Lohengrin and setting him off in a boat across the Schwan See, and Paul's description of the incident is unconsciously quite amusing :

TRIEBSCHEN, *August 7th, 1866.*

I have just left the intimate circle of the Dear Friends and have retired to the cosy little room which we shared when we were here together.

Yesterday, directly after arrival in Zürich, I telegraphed to the Dear Friend asking whether I could stay with him, and was received with the kindest hospitality. Hans has kindly left so that I might have the room which you know so well.

Beautiful memory !

Before the Sandman comes to put me to sleep I hasten to give you an exact account of my journey.

On Monday at six o'clock in the morning I left Munich and arrived safely and unrecognized in Zürich. There I decided to stay the night and to take the fast train to Triebschen next morning, because I wished to arrive there by daylight so as not to attract attention.

I am in Hungarian dress, and called myself Friedrich Melloc from Prague when I wrote my name in the book at the Hôtel de l'Epée, and said I was a war refugee. I wear tied black trousers (breeches), a velvet coat and a little Polish cap. I have Hungarian boots up to the knee and the whole suits me very well indeed, so Frau Vorstal tells me.

This morning at 11.15 I arrived at Lucerne and at twelve o'clock I was with the precious ones at Triebschen. All the details I will tell you verbally. Everybody is well. My affairs go well so far and I think I shall be able to leave Triebschen on Thursday morning. Probably I shall make a little detour on my way back—via Friedrichshafen and Ulm—in order not to pass Lindau again. Perhaps I shall again spend Thursday night at Zürich and come home on Friday.

I preferred to write—according to the advice of the Friends—as being safer than telegraphing. The precious one is very excited and needs rest. He and Frau Vorstal send their deepest greetings. May God protect and *keep you on the Throne*. This is their wish and my own, because only then can we achieve our high ideal. The results of my mission are best given to you verbally, and I believe that you will approve them.

We were all very glad to get your telegram of to-day. Our thoughts are very much with you on the Krummkopf.

Although we have all been through a great deal since we last met, our meeting was very cheerful.

Hans was with us for dinner. While I am here he stays in Lucerne. I also met Herr Dräseke, a friend of Bülow and Wagner.

In the evening we had some music and the first half of the second act of *Die Meistersinger* was played. It was heavenly, divine ! Wagner is working, is willing to go on, and only begs to be left in peace so that he may finish the work he has promised. He will leave politics alone.

But now good night, in my thoughts I salute you a thousand times.

Your sincere and faithful

FRIEDRICH.

Meanwhile Duchess Maximilian Josef sat at Possenhofen across the lake from Berg weaving her matrimonial spells. Never forgetting that she was a daughter of Maximilian I, she felt strongly that all her daughters should wear crowns. Ludwig Victor, youngest brother of her son-in-law Franz Josef of Austria, had been to Possenhofen to pay court to Sophie, but he was only a younger son and was not personally very eligible. Gazing from his tower window across Lake Starnberg to the Isle of Roses and romantic Possenhofen, Ludwig did not very much mind what sort of a dream his great-aunt Louise Wilhelmina cherished so long as it remained a dream, but if ever the mother's plans to do the best for her unmarried daughter should include himself, then she would speedily find that she built on quicksand. If ever a moment came when Elsa would demand from Lohengrin his name—his reality—he would vanish. He had been writing to Sophie the sister of his first friend Gackl and whom, because he never possessed him, he always loved. He had allowed Sophie the great privilege of reading some of Wagner's letters.

Ludwig wrote to Sophie :

HOHENSCHWANGAU, October 18th, 1866.

. . . Would you have the kindness to explain to me the sort of rumours with which—as you say—you have been plagued lately ? I take it that Wagner's letters are now with Friedrich ; there is no doubt of his faith and discretion although, lately, he has given me reason to be discontented with him in some respects. Friedrich is now with his parents in Regensburg . . . I intend to stay here until the beginning of December . . .

Why Ludwig was so ' discontented ' with Paul that he sent him on furlough under a cloud can only be inferred. In Ludwig a degree of sensitive perceptivity that was almost pathological entailed his intimates living continuously in a state of high tension ; the slightest incident could bring about a catastrophe : a smile or a caress ill-timed or with-held ; an unduly familiar remark ; a laugh too much, or a sigh or tear too little—and the whole feverishly erected romantic house of cards collapsed in ruins.   Unlike some of his successors, Paul would never have fallen into the vulgar error of mistaking familiarity for intimacy.   Therefore the causes of the break probably lay beyond the borderland of reason.   Ludwig had long secretly felt that he no longer held first place in Paul's heart. .Paul was doing exactly what Wagner had done over Cosima and, as long as he had no one else, Ludwig put up with it and quarrels were always succeeded by reconciliations.   Now Ludwig's own secret longings and hopes were elsewhere ; but what is not unbe-coming in a King can be treason in a subject.

Paul of Taxis had been appointed to a close and confiden-tial post in the first suite given by his father King Max II when his elder son reached the age of eighteen.   Related to both the Bavarian and Austrian Ruling Houses, and having for three years been Ludwig's closest and most confidential friend, he could not be dismissed like a valet caught thieving. Ludwig had to trump up some sort of an explanation that would pass muster with the Royal Family and Society.   He had already prepared the way by telling Sophie that Paul was out of favour.   He now proceeded to close the episode.

Ludwig wrote to Sophie :

MUNICH, *December 27th, 1866.*

. . . Friedrich became too haughty and so I had to remove him ; a better one is now in his place ; Kunsberg is faithful, reliable, true and open . . .

Paul's last letter to Ludwig is undated, but must have been written somewhere about the middle of December, because by the 27th (the date of the letter to Sophie) Friedrich had been secretly discarded :

My Own Beloved Ludwig !
    What in the name of all the Saints has your Friedrich done to you ?   What did he say that no hand, no good-night, no *Auf Wiedersehen* favoured him ?
    How I feel I cannot say ; my trembling hand may show you my inner disquiet.

I did not intend to hurt you. Forgive me ; be good
again with me, I fear the worst—I cannot stand this.
May my notes climb to you reconcilingly. Amen !
Forgive your unhappy,

FRIEDRICH.

Like every human tie he sought to establish, Ludwig's
relationship to Paul was doomed from the beginning. It
could not be otherwise because it was basically unreal and
false. Owing to delayed adolescence, or some other cause,
there may have been, at the outset, spurious elements of
spontaneity and sincerity in Paul's excessively emotional
responses to Ludwig ; if so, they soon evaporated in the
hothouse atmosphere to which they were exposed. Quite
young men occasionally continue to indulge in schoolboy
substitutional emotional satisfactions after they leave school ;
but, given normality, an end to them is bound to come.
It usually does so when the boy begins to experience the
phase known as calf love ; and it can come quite suddenly.
The lad becomes free, and no longer stands shiveringly on the
brink between boyhood and manhood.

Within two months of the beginning of their friendship
gossip had, as we already know, reported to Ludwig that
Paul was leading ' a frivolous life '. Munich was, and is,
a small city ; its Society was restricted, and the young Prince
Paul of Thurn and Taxis could not possibly hope to amuse
himself unobserved and undiscussed. Fundamentally, Ludwig was at once impulsive and suspicious. At first he would
accept all Paul's disclaimers but, soon, doubts would begin
to creep in. Inevitably Paul began to provide corroborative
evidence against himself. Anyone studying closely this
strange correspondence will be driven to the conclusion that
while in its earlier stages Paul was ingenuous and sincere,
very soon he began to play a part—to write and act what
was expected of him rather than what he felt. During 1865,
while Ludwig was obsessed by Wagner, his emotional
demands on Paul would not be excessive. There may
even have been a quarrel—their first. While Wagner was
in Munich Paul had not been necessary to Ludwig ; then
Wagner was banished and the little luxurious palais in the
Barer Strasse empty. Worse still, Ludwig had discovered

that Cosima was Wagner's mistress and that he was the father of at least one of her children ! Soul-sick, he re-called Paul to be with him and the second and more highly pitched phase of their emotional friendship began. Then, attended by Voelk, Ludwig and Paul stole off to Triebschen together, stayed together in Wagner's villa, and returned to Munich sworn fellow conspirators and champions of Wagner.

In the middle of June, Ludwig and Paul, again attended only by Voelk, were staying in the little villa on the Isle of Roses in Lake Starnberg. By July 1st the friends were at Berg and there had been another quarrel—possibly bred by emotional satiety. Then another reconciliation, and Paul was soon on the way back to Triebschen with the abdication proposal.

Reading between the lines, it is quite plain that before Paul became Ludwig's friend and Adjutant he liked an evening out. He had a ' favourite inn ' which he frequented and where he met the convenient clergyman and captain. Moreover, there were feminine influences and he had received ' a note from a young girl ' warning him that he should not stay out late at night as he was in danger ! The mention of ' a young girl ' was a fatal mistake. From a letter not quoted here we know that Paul on another occasion failed to write an expected letter to Ludwig because he had to dine in some far-away Munich suburb to meet another ' young girl '.

Paul found Ludwig's Abdication letter to Wagner so shattering that, instead of sitting down at once and answer-ing it, he had to take ' a little rest '. The little rest lasted at least forty-eight hours—to Ludwig eating his impatient heart out at Berg—an eternity. Were some of those hours spent with the young girl ?

There was a further delay involving another dereliction of duty on the way to Triebschen. Quite unnecessarily, a night was spent incognito at an hotel in Zürich, and another on the way back. All his promises that Ludwig would in future have ' no cause for blaming me or my life ' and ' never to make another *faux pas* ' were broken.

Paul finally disappeared from the life if not from the

heart of Ludwig who, by inference, passed final judgment on his friend when he told Sophie that Paul's successor, Kunsberg, was 'faithful, reliable, true and open'. Of Kunsberg we know nothing—so he too must have been another disappointment.

CHAPTER SEVEN

THE EAGLE AND THE DOVE : 1867

SPEAKING nationally, the moment chosen for the announcement of the King's engagement to Duchess Sophie in Bavaria, his first cousin once removed, was most propitious. In November, beginning at Bayreuth, Ludwig made a progress in great state through war-ravaged Franconia—Bamberg, Würzburg, Aschaffenburg, Nuremberg and the battlefields around Kissingen. He laid wreaths on the graves of soldiers and visited wounded soldiers in Würzburg hospital. In unique Nuremberg, which his grandfather had lately charged him to defend against vandals, he attended a citizens' ball and, according to the local Press,

> . . . danced unceasingly for four hours with partners of all ages and conditions and conversed freely with all the gentlemen who were presented.

Nuremberg so delighted Ludwig that he remained on privately for some time, paying visits to studios, workshops and factories. He was present at a performance of Verdi's *Il Trovatore* (then somewhat of a novelty), and was so delighted that he commanded another performance, and sent for Otto to come from Munich and share his enjoyment. During this progress the Bavarian people vociferously expressed an almost fanatical devotion to the person of Ludwig who seemed to them a Fairy King indeed.

The official announcement of the King's engagement was made on New Year's Day. Ludwig I wrote to his grandson :

ROME, *January 1st, 1867.*

May God's blessing, dear Ludwig, rest upon your marriage ! I have for some time read in the looks of beautiful Sophie that you are deep-rooted in her heart . . . Happiness at home is the greatest blessing on earth. How

116

happy I shall be to carry your first son, my great-grandson, in my arms !

Ludwig telegraphed Wagner :

Walther confirms to the dear Sachs that he has found his faithful Eva—Siegfried his Brünhilde.

To Cosima he wrote :

My love for her is deep and loyal ; but The Friend will never cease to be dear to me beyond all others.

Bavaria was delighted to have a young and lovely native Princess as Queen ; that one of her sisters was Empress of Austria and another, the heroine of Gaeta, had been Queen of Naples and the two Sicilies was nothing to Sophie's disadvantage. Ludwig, like his father, might have gone north for a bride and just then the Bavarians loved the Prussians less than ever—if that were possible.

Ludwig and Sophie showed themselves everywhere together ; they danced the Française at a ball given in their honour by the new Prime Minister of Bavaria, Prince Clodwig of Hohenlohe-Schillingsfürst ; they appeared in state at the Theatre. There was a Court ball at the Residenz. Worst of all, grandfather Ludwig wrote a sonnet in which, with the maximum of unoriginality, he compared them to Venus and Adonis. If he had Shakespeare's second-rate poem in mind the comparison was particularly inept.

For a few months Sophie was almost a queen. Paul had fallen permanently into disgrace ; Wagner was in banishment ; no other favourite had, so far as could be discerned, appeared on the horizon. But Ludwig's incurable habit of turning human beings into romantic poetical phantoms had again triumphed ; he was now ' Heinrich ' and poor Sophie ' Elsa ' ; he was ' the Eagle ' and she ' the Dove '. Had she known of the telegram to Wagner and the letter to Cosima, would it not have frozen her heart ? To Sophie herself Ludwig wrote as early as January 19th :

It is painful for me to send you these lines . . . You know that I have not many more years to live . . .

On the 27th he told Frau von Leonrod that he had ' an awful headache ' and, on the 31st, ' I have a real longing to hear from you ', adding that he ' would like to go to Rome with Gackl ' ; it almost seemed as if he still loved the brother better than the sister !

However, for the moment, everything—on the surface—appeared promising. A handsome new state wedding-coach was ordered. Immediately below his own suite in the Residenz Ludwig had made on the first floor at the west end of the Royal apartments an exquisite little boudoir for Sophie, furnished and decorated with delicate taste. It was reached from Ludwig's study in the top storey wing by one of those uncomfortable, narrow corkscrew staircases inevitable in a palace if you are to pass from one floor to another unseen. Never occupied, it remained for years an empty shrine for tourists to gape at.

The sad story of Ludwig's brief infatuation for Sophie has been so often vamped up from old newspapers and third-hand gossip that it is best told simply in his own words. In forcing himself to imagine that he was in love with his cousin Ludwig was, as in so much else, self-deceived ; but at least there was something pure, perhaps indeed noble and aspiring, in this pathetic self-deception. Practically all repressed conflict is a struggle to escape into, or out of, sex : millions of men had emerged from early sexual conflict by marriage ; why then did Ludwig fail to do so ?

As for Sophie, her memory is for ever consecrated by her blameless life and heroic death. Even before its dawn their love—if love it could be called—was doomed to frustration. The shadow of Wagner—strong, dark, menacing—stood between Ludwig and Sophie, just as, from the outset, the shadow of Cosima, strong, dark and possessive, stood between Ludwig and Wagner. Ludwig, though young, headstrong and a King, staged a losing fight. And who was little Sophie to pit herself against a man whose long and rugged path to success was strewn with broken love affairs and shattered friendships ! Perhaps what follows are the most extraordinary ' love letters ' ever written by a handsome young man of two-and-twenty to a lovely young girl of his own age ; throughout this brief ten months' corre-

spondence every reference to Wagner is urgent and alive ;
every greeting to Sophie perfunctory and conventional ;
they tell in the words of the protagonist the whole—or almost
the whole—story :

Ludwig to Sophie :

February 5th, 1867.

My dear Elsa !
. . . Give me pleasure by writing very soon (perhaps
to-morrow morning) to Wagner ; I know how happy
He will be to get a letter from you.   And now, heartily
good night !

Your loving
faithful HEINRICH.

Ludwig to Sophie :

February 5th, 1867.

My dear Elsa !
I have just left Aunt,[1] repentant, weeping and cough-
ing—the good Aunt must always interfere, either willingly
or unwillingly.   Now I am writing to Wagner.   Sleep
well ; Greetings to Aunt ; refresh yourself with Shakespeare's wonderful poetry.
Heartfelt greetings !

Your faithful HEINRICH.

Ludwig to Sophie :

February 7th, 1867.

My dear Elsa !
Albert has just sent me the enclosed successful photograph of Us Two ; will you please have the kindness to
give it to the Empress in my name.   Perhaps she will
like it.
Heartfelt greetings,

Your faithful HEINRICH.

He wanted to give Elizabeth a more important present
but is not sure if it would be welcome :

Ludwig to Sophie :

February 8th, 1867.

My dear Elsa !
Do you think the Empress will accept anything for
to-morrow or not ?   I appeared in Austrian uniform

[1] Sophie's mother, Duchess Maximilian in Bavaria (1808–1892).

during the third Act in the Theatre—to the astonishment of the audience. How are you? What did you do in the evening? What did the Empress say? Sleep well and sweet dreams.

A thousand inmost greetings from the bottom of my heart.

Your faithful HEINRICH.

Ludwig to Sophie :

February 12th, 1867.

My beloved Elsa !
We should be very happy if you should find yourself able to come to dinner to-day at 4.30 o'clock with Mother, *en petite famille*, as yesterday. Please let me know soon whether it is agreeable to your mother or not. I hope you will also come to *King Lear*. God bless you and give you strength for your painting, singing and modelling . . .

On the 17th he wrote Sophie : ' The God of my life, as you know, is Richard Wagner '—hardly a very comforting or reassuring assertion to a prospective bride !

On the 19th, 20th and 21st Ludwig again invited Sophie to dinner, using a new style of notepaper with the name ' Heinrich ' engraved across the top. As, in his heart of hearts, Ludwig knew that he was not giving—could not give—himself to Sophie, the operatic fiction may have afforded some obscure psychological absolution to his tortured conscience.

The tiresome invocation continued : (as in the one dated February 5th) ' Have you written to Wagner? Have you read his Autobiography? ' In some of his best letters Ludwig reiterates his dislike of his aunt Amalie of Greece :

Ludwig to Sophie :

BERG, *February 25, 1867.*

My Beloved Sophie :
Only two hours and the horrible approaches : the deaf and completely nailed [i.e. cracked] man, and the plump and always interfering fat noodle, his Queen. I really can't help writing these awful things about them. How different Queens can be ! On the one side such a stout, gossipy creature as the fat formless Greek Majesty,

and on the other hand a Queen such as you shall become ;
an angel, a flower, full of spirit and beautiful !—To-
morrow the whole family, probably, will be fed by my
mother ; and then to Meyerbeer's nonsense, to the hot
Africa where someone dies romantically under the
shadows of trees, while a real doodle-di-dum is going on.
Quelle fête ! Dearest sister of my elephant, aunt of the
sparrow's child, so I shall see you only to-morrow (and
not to-day ; my heart is longing for you) amidst the
hurly-burly of the family feeding !—Greetings to the
monster of the sea who teaches you the art of singing ;
think of me and a thousand greetings from,

Your faithful LUDWIG.

Ludwig to Sophie :

(Undated.)

My dear Elsa !
How I would have loved to be with you in the same
box . . . the Greek woman is too awful ! I hope the
pills will give me a good rest ; think sometimes of your
loving

LUDWIG.

Ludwig to Sophie :

(Undated.)

Here gossip is carried so far that it is said in the town
that I do not love you any more. O world ! O men !
How curious that your mother is ours—she is probably
with the old bitch, the Greek woman. Oh, to kill her
like a chicken ! I don't think I will go to the theatre
to-day . . . Heil to you ; but ruin to the wicked,
fat *Malchen.*

After the state ball at the Residenz the most important
function in honour of the Royal engagement was one given
by Clodwig of Hohenlohe. Wagner liked to declare that
it was he who induced the King to give the first political
post in Bavaria to a man who was pro-Prussian ; and, for
once, Wagner was justified in his boasting. Ludwig liked
Hohenlohe personally and appreciated his lofty character,
personal charm and courtly tact ; but the deciding factor
was that, as a man of wide culture, he fully appreciated the
genius of Wagner, and Ludwig and Wagner both hoped

that under such reassuring auspices, the banishment would be ended.

Ludwig to Sophie :

March 3rd, 1867.

Are you going to the Fifth Act after the ball ? To-morrow I shall come to you and bring a portrait of *Maria* [Stuart] on porcelain ; I will also bring the crown and will put it on your head. If it should be too heavy or too large I will get another one made, because I would like to see it on your head at the wedding ; a beautiful head such as yours, which is so dear to me, deserves to wear the highest of all earthly ornaments ; this symbol of earthly Majesty and the ruler's power. Good-bye then. Innermost blessings from, your

ever faithful, HEINRICH.

Ludwig to Sophie :

BERG, *March 3rd, 1867.*

. . . As a compensation I read the history of *Maria* until one o'clock ; there was a terrible gale outside, I was alone in my tower and the winds played round it ; I was in Scotland in my thoughts, with all the dear friends, I really feel as if I had lived with them.

Ludwig to Sophie :

March 5th, 1867.

Beloved Elsa !

Your Heinrich doesn't feel too well to-day and will go to bed early. Do sleep well . . . I send you herewith the interesting and well-written essays by Porges about the creations of Wagner, and his system. Oh, do write to him soon, the dear and distant friend ; you will make him eternally happy by so doing. All my love.

from your faithful,
HEINRICH.

Then, still thinking only of the Queen instead of the woman, he commanded Baron von Lutz, the chief of the Royal Cabinet, to bring the crown from the Royal Treasury in the Residenz so that, with Merk the Munich Court Jeweller in attendance, it might be altered to fit Sophie's small head.   It had been made in Paris in 1806 for Karolina of Baden, the Consort of Maximilian I when, because of his friendship for France, Napoleon I agreed to him changing his Electoral Bonnet for a King's Crown.

Wagner reached Munich on March 9th in order to observe personally how his protégé Hohenlohe was behaving as Prime Minister !   He at once sent a note to the King announcing his arrival, and was granted an audience for the following day.   He found the Royal Family thrust into mourning by the death on the day of his arrival of the first wife of Duke Karl Theodor (Gackl).   In spite of his love for Gackl, Ludwig found great solace in Wagner's arrival and the prospect of an early meeting, and why should not Sophie and her brother—in spite of their grief—do the same ?

Ludwig to Sophie :

March 9th, 1867.

My Beloved Elsa !

Perhaps it will give you some pleasure if I send you to-day a joyous ray of light and glamour into the lonely and sad house of mourning and death.   W. feels a little tired after the long journey.   He sent me the enclosed little note, which please send back soon.   How much I am looking forward to to-morrow !

Ludwig to Sophie :

March 10th, 1867.

. . . How happy I am to have seen Him again and talked to Him after nine long months.   Poor you ; how much you have to suffer these days.   I sympathize deeply with you all.

In his next letter, the words ' good night, my dear ' and ' from yours ' are in inverted commas in English.

MUNICH, *March 10th, 1867.*

My Beloved Elsa !

I enclose ½ fl. Gulden for the damage done to your dress.   I try to think of all sorts of means whereby to get rid of the mother of my brother and the widow of my father before you arrive on Wednesday ; I must succeed. I dare say you will be rather frightened by the smell of

the corpse surrounded by a weeping family. I feel so
cosy in my beautiful apartment and am just writing
in my diary an account of my talk with Him. Many
greetings to good Gackl; try to squeeze out of him
whether he still loves me, and assure him of my faithful
friendship and my deepest sympathy in his heavy loss.
  And now ' good night, my dear ',
  A thousand greetings ' from yours ',

HENRI.

Ludwig to Sophie :

March 11th, 1867.

. . . One of these days He shall be given a suitable apartment on the Starnberger See, into which He will move in
May. In June there will be newly-produced performances of *Lohengrin* and *Tannhäuser*. What raptures that
will give me ! On the 14th of this month Bülow will
come here ; and also Semper will be called upon by us.
  And now farewell,
      Think lovingly
          Of your happy HEINRICH
who finds it so difficult now to weep and mourn.

On the 13th, Ludwig told Sophie that '. . . Mozart's
famous *Requiem*—which I had specially ordered—was
magnificent '. Either he was echoing something Wagner
or somebody else had said to him, or he had a real glim-
mering of what music means. On the same day he indited
a second epistle to Sophie—an emotional screed in which
he contradicted the assurance of happiness with which the
foregoing note closed. His fundamental dislike of the idea
of marriage was forcing its way to the surface :
  Ludwig to Sophie :

March 13th, 1867.

My Dear Elsa !
  Please forgive me for bothering you at this late hour.
To nobody but you will I tell what I suffer. I am so truly
happy about our engagement, and because the Precious
Friend is here—and at the same time I am so utterly
unhappy and miserable. Oh, God, my dear Elsa, in
spite of all my happiness my heart aches. Gackl, who is
so close to my heart that I would gladly go through fire

for him without trembling for my own life, is wounded.
Oh, should I come near him in danger ; I would bear
every pain on earth with pleasure for him. How it
hurts my heart. There is nobody in the world whom I
acknowledge to be above me ; nobody can order me ;
but if he would reign I would leave the Throne, yes, even
transfer the Crown to him. I would serve him, gladly be
obedient to him whatever he might want—to him, but
to no one else on the whole earth. I entreat you, do make
it possible for me to talk to him quietly and cosily as soon
as he comes back ; he shall see how faithfully this friend's
heart beats for him unto the end ; once he has seen that,
well and good ; let him go to Rome in God's name. I
will forget my grief as much as I can, but I would like
to have the consolation of knowing that he is, and always
will be, my friend. O God, to nobody on earth could he
possibly be more precious than to me—not even to his
own mother. To think of the possibility of his death is
unbearable—I would go mad. And now, good night,
sweet life. This evening I received a dear letter from the
Friend.

Your faithful HEINRICH.

The man's emotional temperature was so erratic as to be
incalculable. The foregoing was obviously written late at
night and would seem to be real : yet, next morning, he was
overjoyed when the draft of the ' terrible ' ceremonial for
their wedding was submitted to him—and terrible it was—
lasting from ten-thirty in the morning until ten o'clock in
the evening with a brief respite from three o'clock to six.
Ludwig to Sophie :

March 14th, 1867.

Good morning, my dear Elsa ! How are you ? I am
happy and full of joy. The Ceremonial for Our Wedding
has been put before me. It is magnificent but terrible.
How much more beautiful it would be if we could have
it all in a little church on the Starnberger See.

Ludwig then planned an unprecedented, an almost
inexcusable, action. Sophie's mother, Duchess Maximilian
(Ludovica), was not exactly a tactful woman, yet, when
Ludwig, as he liked to do, came courting at night to Possenhofen, or to their mountain home at Bad Kreuth, she had

lights placed all over the house and all the servants had
to be on duty in state liveries. This exasperated, indeed
horrified, the hermit lurking in Ludwig's secret soul. Did
the Duchess know that Ludwig had arranged for his fiancée,
a young girl, to go alone and secretly to visit Wagner in
Munich ? The Ducal family were mostly anti-Wagner ;
nevertheless, the interview between Sophie and Wagner
took place as planned in Munich at the town address of
Sophie's eldest brother Duke Ludwig. The servants were
sent out of the way and Duke Ludwig's wife herself opened
the door ! This odd procedure was probably made easier
by the fact that the marriage, being a morganatic one, the
lady had not Royal rank and was known as Baroness Waller-
see. Wagner duly reported that : ' he had looked into
eyes out of which shone anxious love for the King '.

Ludwig's reaction to the episode is hardly that of a
lover.

Ludwig to Sophie :

March 17th, 1867.

To-day I shall enjoy the happiness which you enjoyed
yesterday. W. comes to me to-day at 1 o'clock and we
shall have a couple of beautiful hours of cosy talk together ; think of Us !

Ludwig to Sophie :

(Undated.)

. . . In about half an hour I will come to you and
show you a letter from the dear Friend, who is perfectly
enchanted with your charming and sublime nature.

Sophie had beauty, grace and charm but, although
Wagner was no great courtier, he knew better than not to
be ' enchanted ' had she been as ugly as Margaret Maltusch.

Ludwig to Sophie :

March 21st, 1867.

. . . Not till half-past one did I go to bed as I had lost
myself in a very interesting book about Louis XIV.
Frau von Bülow wrote me a letter which made my heart
rejoice. I enclose it because it contains news about the
beloved distant Friend.

Ludwig to Sophie :

March 25th, 1867.

. . . This morning I received another letter from Frau von Bülow who recommends that man Putlitz, whom the Precious Friend insists on having as Intendant of the Theatre. I do not agree at all with Him, because by continually bringing foreigners here He has done much harm to Himself and to Our cause . . . My trust in Hohenlohe is diminishing, and it is difficult, during these perplexing days, to find an able Minister. Frau von Bülow writes that the autobiography has been taken up again. I am glad of that because it really is written in masterly style. It is wonderful how Wagner remembers so clearly the details of His life, so rich in deeds and in sorrows.

The Ducal family were in residence at their imposing Munich house, the Prinz Luitpold Palais in the Ludwig Strasse ; it was upon the landing halfway up the handsome staircase that the ' brother and sister ' busts of Sisi and Ludwig stood alone. In one of the smaller rooms the body of the Heroine of Gaeta was embalmed before being placed in the crypt of the Private Chapel in Schloss Tegernsee. These stately rooms were degraded when Hitler turned the palais into a picture gallery of horrifying examples of ' National Socialist Art '.

Ludwig to Sophie :

BERG, *March 30th, 1867.*

. . . Oh, I do wish you were here, beloved Elsa, I would come over so often . . . Now, I think I will write to the precious distant one. Oh, what wonderful days the month of May, the month of delight (Wonnemonat), will bring to Us. Then, at last, He will return ; and that will be the beginning of a new era, a time of glorious creations after the sad times of separation . . .

Ludwig to Sophie :

April 2nd, 1867.

My Beloved Elsa !

I send you herewith letters from the Precious Friend. If only he would give up the idea of Putlitz !

A thousand heartfelt greetings from the loving soul of,

Your faithful HEINRICH.

Ludwig to Sophie :

April 3rd, 1867.

. . . Probably I shall start on my journey on Saturday—not for Rome, but to the country where our Saviour suffered and died for Us—for Jerusalem.

Ludwig to Sophie :

April 3rd, 1867.

. . . Either on Saturday or on Monday I shall start with Mother for Jerusalem . . . I feel like Gottfried von Bouillon, I am full of enthusiasm, am enchanted . . . I hope to see you to-morrow.

Then Wagner arrived suddenly to spend a few days in Munich. The Queen Mother, Jerusalem and Godfrey de Bouillon, were immediately abandoned.

Ludwig to Sophie :

MUNICH, *April 7th, 1867.*

A great deal has happened since we saw each other last. When I came back to my room on Thursday after the Opera I found a letter from Our Precious Friend which told me that he had arrived . . .

Fresh political and dangerous news made me decide *not* to undertake my journey.

Ludwig to Sophie :

MUNICH, *April 14th, 1867.*

. . . To-day I received the enclosed telegram from the Precious Friend. On the 15th of this month the Bülows will arrive here and then everything will go quickly, as I most certainly hope, towards the great and longed-for aim ; I wish you would soon get to know Frau von Bülow : she is a great woman and as intelligent as she is charming. I am sure that my Elsa will like her. Otto is now in Naples ; he climbed Vesuvius . . . Oh, if you could only hear this wonderful work but, although you can't just now, you will be able to do so in the happier times which are coming to Us. That I know for certain ; yes, we shall be very happy together and God will give Us His blessing. Bülow is a very able musician, but personally unbearable.

Ludwig to Sophie :

MUNICH, *April 28th, 1867.*

. . . Yesterday I received a letter from W. who is looking
forward very much to coming here in May. He also
writes a lot about politics ; amongst other things, he tells
me that Aunt Sophie is said to have uttered the most
detestable things against me last summer. That is so
like her, the Ultramontane, blind woman that she is.

Ludwig to Sophie :

BERG, *May 6th, 1867.*

. . . To-morrow, after the Audience, I hope to come and
see you . . . On the 4th I had a dear telegram from
Wagner—it was exactly three years since we first met
each other ; oh, do write him soon.

Ultra-sensitives, when their feelings have been exacer-
bated, are unforgiving. An inner voice warning them that
they are vulnerable to a pathological extent, their obvious
compensation is to refuse to enter into competition. All his
life Ludwig when faced with difficult situations fled to the
mountains. Should anything wound his sensitive soul or
offend his kingly dignity he immediately reacted unfavour-
ably ; not even the Beloved Friend was immune. In
March, as we have seen, Wagner was in Munich, and was
received in audience by Ludwig with customary warmth.

By the 22nd he was back at Triebschen and Ludwig telegraphed him in extraordinary terms. Sophie may not
have been intellectually brilliant, but she was high-spirited,
young, sensitive and, if not exactly in love with Ludwig,
was in love with the whole romantic idea, with a vision of
herself as the beautiful bride of a remarkably handsome
young man, and the adored Queen of the Bavarians. In
Royal circles, even more than elsewhere, the office of King
and Queen have religious, indeed, quite rightly mystical
significance. Even so, her heart must have felt chilled with
apprehension as it gradually dawned on her that she was
being treated, not as Ludwig's best beloved and future bride
and Consort, but as the embodiment of a musician's dream.

While Wagner was in Munich in April Ludwig insisted
that he should come again in May for the purpose of cele-
brating the third anniversary of their meeting. For this

purpose he had some time before, with great exactitude, ordered from Bechstein the famous combined piano and writing-desk that was to make easier Wagner's laborious work as a composer. Ludwig's plan was to hire the Villa Prestele near Starnberg, install the piano as a surprise, and Wagner was to settle down there for the summer and divide his time between writing inspired operatic masterpieces and inspiring the King.

But like so many of Ludwig's dreams it didn't work out quite like that.

Ludwig to Sophie :

BERG, *May 14th, 1867.*
Wagner does not come before the 20th ; i.e., after the completion of the Second Act of *Die Meistersinger.*

The unbridgeable chasm between the Kingly Friend and the Great Friend was the composer's inviolable artistic conscience and sublime artistic egotism. Wagner could not accept the tentacles of Ludwig's obsessive love and retain his creative genius. The fire of great genius destroys as stubble all that comes between it and its own fulfilment.

Wagner, dedicated at the time to the formidable and exhausting task of scoring the *Meistersinger,* was chained by creative imperatives to his desk and had no mind for Maytime make-believes on the banks of Lake Starnberg. Ludwig, who never did a day's solid hard work in his whole life, was slow in learning that a man or woman doing the task they were uniquely born to do is sacred. It is greatly to his credit that, eventually, Ludwig did learn this truth, and that Wagner was the one human being from whom he accepted lies, evasions, snubs, deceit, greed, and a hundred other humiliations. He was, for once, expressing stark reality when he wrote to Sophie : ' The god of my idolatry is Richard Wagner. ' But before accepting his god without any reservations (as man always must) there were a few more battles with himself to be fought and won.

Wagner now began to hedge about the prolonged visit to Starnberg, and Cosima, who in some ways knew Ludwig better than Wagner ever did, wired from Munich to Triebschen warning the Master that if he did not keep his promise at Whitsuntide there would be a complete break between him and the King. Perturbed, she wrote to Ludwig broaching the disappointing news ; he replied that 'a refusal now' would grievously wound him, but 'Siegfried the hero would bow to the will of Wotan the God'. But that was not quite the same as saying that Ludwig von Wittelsbach could, as yet, bow to the will of Richard Wagner—or Richard Geyer, whichever was his real name.[1]

Ludwig to Sophie :

BERG, *May 21st, 1867.*

. . . Your singing yesterday enchanted me so much I cannot suppress the wish to hear you again to-day ; just to-day it would be beautiful, because to-morrow I must give myself up to Wagner who comes here in order to celebrate his birthday with me.

If Ludwig found his god in Wagner the composer found his protecting goddess in Cosima. Her power lay in the fact that she ever fought to enlarge and foster Wagner's creative freedom ; Ludwig's impotence in that, unwittingly, he sought to fetter and smother it. Under Cosima's tactful pressure Wagner duly arrived in Munich and was at once commanded to luncheon at Berg. Ludwig, always courteous to women, also invited Cosima, but tactfully she excused herself.

Asserting that the Villa was not quite in order, Wagner went temporarily to Munich, only moving out to Starnberg a week later. The day after the luncheon, without seeing Wagner, the King of Bavaria and his brother Prince Otto with Captain von Sauer in attendance set off on a visit to Eisenach to see the Wartburg, ostensibly to get some ideas for the scenery for *Tannhäuser.* But what an odd moment to choose—the day after Wagner's long-awaited visit had at last begun !

Wagner was by now almost as worried as Cosima.

Ludwig returned to Berg for a night and immediately left again for a visit to the Zillerthal and Achensee where he could easily have gone at any time.

Ludwig's uncanny intuition may well have told him that

[1] Mr. Ernest Newman has treated his perplexing question very exhaustively in his great biography of Wagner.

Wagner dallied in Munich (which they both hated) not because the Villa Prestele was not ready—Cosima herself had been out to see to all the preparations before the Master's arrival—but because he so obviously preferred the society of Cosima to that of the King.   That was intolerable. Then Ludwig, who was by no means a fool, and who was kept extremely well-informed by his police and those who feared Wagner's return to Bavaria, may about this time have become definitely convinced that Cosima and Wagner were lovers ; that they had from the beginning lied to and deceived him, and that by extorting from him a certificate of their honour they had smirched the honour of the King of Bavaria before the world.

Only five weeks earlier Ludwig had written to Sophie, a young unmarried girl affianced to the King of Bavaria, and besought her to ' get to know Frau von Bülow '.   This he would never have done were he already convinced that Wagner and Cosima were lovers.

Whatever the occasion of the break in the friendship between Ludwig and Wagner, here lay the cause.   Even Hohenlohe, had he wished, could not have made it possible for Wagner to return permanently to Munich, although the house in the Barer Strasse was still waiting for him. And Hohenlohe may no longer have approved of a possible return ; on May 25th Ludwig, as we have seen, told Sophie that his ' trust in Hohenlohe was diminishing ' and, four-teen days later, ' fresh political and dangerous news ' caused him to abandon his longed-for pilgrimage to the Holy Land.

In June, before finally shaking the dust of Munich off his feet, Wagner sent to the *Suddeutsche Presse* the valedictory letter containing the famous injunction : ' Seek, Germans, Roman strength and Greek beauty.   You shall discover both ; but you will never attain Gallic spontaneity.'   The *Suddeutsche Presse*, a Liberal paper, was supposed to be a Government organ, although this was officially denied by Clodwig Hohenlohe.   It was even said that it was financed by Ludwig himself—which was nonsense.

The letters with their Wagner themes continued and Ludwig wrote :

BERG, *June 25th, 1867.*

My Beloved Sophie !
    Good night, my sweet (Wesen), read in Tristan
        With heartfelt greetings,
                    Your faithful LUDWIG.
Very soon we shan't be any longer Sophie and Ludwig
but Lohengrin and Elsa.

In June, Elizabeth of Austria was at Possenhofen and
from there travelled direct to Ischl, where there was an
Imperial villa surrounded by an extensive park and magnificent mountain scenery, and where she received the following letter from Ludwig :

BERG, *July 3rd, 1867.*

You can have no idea, dear Cousin, how happy you made
me.   The hours recently passed with you in the railway
carriage I consider among the happiest in my life ; never
will their memory fade.   You gave me permission to
visit you at Ischl ; if the time comes for this ardent
hope to be fulfilled, I shall be of all men upon earth
the most blest.   The feelings of the sincere love and
reverence and faithful attachment to you which I cherished
in my heart even as a boy makes me imagine heaven
upon earth, and will be extinguished by death alone.   I
beg you with all my heart to forgive the contents of this
letter—but I could not help myself . . .

The letter remained unanswered by Elizabeth, probably
because at Possenhofen she had been told by her mother
and others a great deal about Ludwig's strange behaviour
to his fiancée Sophie.   The unusual warmth of the letter
suggested the anticipation of criticism, and an attempt to
discount it in advance ; Elizabeth got Franz Josef to answer
without ever mentioning the idea of Ludwig visiting them
at Ischl.   He swallowed the obvious hint and the proposed
visit never took place.
    Ludwig to Sophie :

HOHENSCHWANGAU, *August 25th, 1867.*

. . . Oh, how wonderful it will be when We Two shall
be here alone in the rapturous Hohenschwangau.   I am
sure that you will love it just as much as I have loved the

dear castle and the surrounding country since the earliest days of my childhood. You will grow fond of it very quickly, because here is the source of strengthening and refreshing quietness, and of the consecrated poesy ; unfortunately my present stay is completely spoiled by Mother who tortures me with her endless love ; she has no idea of rest and every sparkle of Poetry vanishes in her company. Wagner promises the *Meistersinger* score for our wedding. I don't think there is anybody on this earth who has such absurd ideas as Mother . . . but I will not bore my dear Elschen with all my complaints, because you won't be having too rosy a time with Aunt Sophie in the house ; but pain is short and joy eternal. From the bottom of my heart I greet you, my dear Senta, Elizabeth, Elsa, Isolde, Eva, Brünhilde—and accept my warmest thanks from the depths of my heart which beats faithfully for you.

Sophie had received Frau von Leonrod, who wrote to Ludwig :

FREISING, *August 24th, 1867.*

Her Royal Highness was so gracious and charming that I am completely enchanted ; especially when Her Royal Highness spoke of Your Majesty her beautiful deep eyes radiated divinely. The voice of Her Royal Highness is so beautiful that it really sounds like music.

What his best, dearest, and earliest woman friend must have felt and thought when, only two days later, she got the following letter can only be imagined.

Ludwig to Frau Baroness von Leonrod :

HOHENSCHWANGAU, *August 26th, 1867.*

The happy feeling which inspires me now that I have shaken off the burdensome bonds—which I knew would turn out unfortunate for me—can only be compared with the rapturous sensations of a convalescent who at last breathes again the fresh air after a dangerous illness. Sophie was always dear and precious to me as a friend and darling sister, but she would not have done for my wife ; the nearer the date of the wedding came the more I dreaded my intended step. I felt very, very unhappy and so I resolved to free myself from the self-imposed bonds and chains ; for Sophie also it was not too difficult to give back her word because she saw for herself that we do not suit each other ; so we avoided misfortune, and now we both have the possibility of making an engagement which promises to make us happy ; I am sure that she will pick a happy *parti* in the near future and, so far as I am concerned, I am not in any hurry ; I am still young and marriage would have been too premature anyhow.

The twenty-second anniversary of Ludwig's birth was celebrated as usual on August 25th. His wedding to Sophie, which was to have taken place on that day, was by an official announcement unexpectedly postponed until October 12th. In September, Elizabeth, on her way home to Vienna from Zürich, heard further curious stories about the relationships of the King and Sophie, and disliked them more than ever. On October 4th Duke Maximilian Josef intervened. A curt undated note from Ludwig to Sophie says :

Your parents want to break off our engagement and I accept the proposal.

On October 7th, less than a week before the postponed date, the wedding was again officially put off, and Ludwig gave Sophie the blow for which she must have long sub-consciously been prepared. He no longer used their special private Heinrich notepaper :

Adjutancy of
His Majesty
The King of Bavaria.
            HOHENSCHWANGAU, *October 7th, 1867.*
My Beloved Elsa !
    As the wedding day was forced upon me like a hot-house plant, just as the day of the engagement was, I consider it my sacred duty to tell you something now when it is not too late. Always you have been precious and dear to me, I love you with true and sincere affection, I love you like a dear sister ; and this feeling, which is deeply rooted in my heart, shall never leave me, and so I would like to beg for the continuance of your precious and amiable affection ; should you remember me with sorrow and bitterness it would cause me deep grief.

When we wrote to each other a great deal the summer before last, and when I gave you proofs of my friendship and trust, your mother pressed me to make a decision ; she thought I had infatuated you, because she did not believe in the existence of a friendship without ' real ' love. You will remember the answer which I gave to you and to your mother through Gackl. When I then heard how unhappy it had made you, and that you would have to go away, and that we should never see each other again, it gave me great sorrow ; I was deeply touched by the proofs of true love which you gave me ; my affection for you grew deeper so that I was carried away into asking for your hand. The reason I ordered all the preparations for the wedding, talked and wrote to you about it, put it off and, at the same time, did not want to give it up, was not in order to cheat you or, as you may think, to go back slowly and step by step ; oh, no, I certainly did not want to deceive you. That was quite beside the question. I acted in the firm belief that everything would lead to a satisfactory conclusion. Now I have had time to test myself, and think the whole matter over, and I see that my true and faithful brotherly love is now, and always will be, deeply rooted in my soul ; but I also see that there is not the love which is necessary for a matrimonial union.

I owe you this, dear Elsa, and I beg for the continuance of your friendship when you give me back my word ; and, when we part from each other, please let us do so without ill-will and bitterness and please—I ask you heartily for this—do keep all the souvenirs which I gave you, and allow me to keep yours. They will always remind me of a time which will never cease to be precious to me and of a dear friend and relation for the happiness of whom—who is so close to my heart—I will pray to God daily. Should you within a year's time not have found somebody with whom you think you could be happy, and should it be the same with me (which I think is not altogether impossible), then we could join ourselves together for ever—that is to say, of course, if you still felt like it ; but now it is better to part and not tie ourselves for the future. I must say again that the interference of your mother in our affairs as they were last winter was very unfortunate. Should there be ill-will and bitterness

—which are the fiancés of hatred—in your soul may a good God give you mercy so that you may recognize in this, my sincere confession, the proof of the most pure and faithful friendship. May the Father—and that is my deepest wish—who is above Us all guide you to the way of true happiness, my faithful beloved Elsa ; you do deserve it. And now farewell, do not forget,

Your heartily affectionate and

faithful, HEINRICH.

PS. Will you please be so very good as to let your parents know the main points of this letter.

The next day Ludwig confided to his diary :

Sophie got rid of (abgeschrieben). The gloomy picture fades. I longed for, am athirst for, freedom. Now I live again after this torturing nightmare.

Sophie's brother Karl Theodor (Gackl) wrote to Ludwig :

After the information which I gave my mother she considers all further communications are superfluous. She thought, however, that your behaviour justified different expectations ; but now, knowing your opinion, she considers the matter as definitely settled. A continuation of the correspondence is, of course, out of the question.

Naturally Elizabeth was incensed ; writing to her mother she said :

SCHÖNBRUNN, *October 19th, 1867.*

How much both I and the Emperor are shocked about the King you can imagine. There is no expression for such behaviour. I cannot imagine how he can ever dare to show himself in Munich after all that has happened. I am glad that Sophie takes it all so quietly ; she never would have been happy with such a man ; I only wish twice as much now that she may at last find a good one. Who will it be ?

On November 28th, the day on which the marriage was to have taken place, Ludwig wrote in his diary :

Thanks be to God, the fearful thing was not realized.

To this day the beautiful wedding-coach rests unused

in the Marstall Museum, housed in the old Royal Riding School where Ludwig and Otto had their first horseback lessons. Beautifully painted, several of the panels depict episodes in the life of Louis XIV whereas only one deals with Wagner and represents the interior of a crowded theatre 'during a performance of a Wagner opera. Nearby is a fine example of the coach-builder's art made for Ludwig himself in Paris in 1870–1871 and seldom used. The rococo sleighs are there, also state harness, coaches, sleighs, saddles belonging to the Electors and Kings of Bavaria. On the walls hang pictures of nearly every one of Ludwig's favourite horses. Once, when speaking of the defection of a friend, he said : ' Only animals are honest and faithful.'

Now we must go back six months in search of a possible explanation of the cause of the unforgivable humiliation inflicted upon Sophie by Ludwig before the whole world.

On Saturday, May 11th, when Ludwig was twenty-one years and nine months old, just three years after his first meeting with Richard Wagner the Great Friend, and while daily writing pseudo love-letters to Sophie, Ludwig met another Richard who, out-rivalling the ' Great Friend ', became ' Richard, Beloved of my Heart ' ! The King was at Berg, and when his hack came across the courtyard from the stables to the front door that morning it was in charge of someone he had never seen before. The cavalcade consisted of the led horse, a young groom, two Royal footmen in blue and silver cut-away coats, silk hats with wide silver-braided rims and hat-bands, tight white buckskin riding-breeches, white gloves, and black calf-length riding-boots. The young groom in charge who led the King's horse, and who was directly responsible to the Chief Stable Master, his own father, instead of a lackey's embroidered coat, wore a close-fitting Eton jacket of bright Bavarian blue cloth admirably calculated to show to advantage the rider's graceful, sinewy figure. He was between twenty-six and twenty-seven years of age, and had some time before completed his Army service. His name was Richard Hornig. His family was not Bavarian but Prussian and originally hailed from near Breslau in Silesia.

As from the hour of their first meeting Richard Hornig

was to play a part in Ludwig's life second only in importance
to that filled by Wagner, an account of his family background and personal characteristics is essential. He was
born at Basedow in Mecklenburg on September 10th, 1841,
five years and thirty-two days before Ludwig. Richard's
father, Ehrenfried Hornig, who was brought up amongst
horses, became Chief Horsemaster (Stallmeister) to King
Maximilian II and, with his young family, went to live at
Rohenfeld-on-Donau, the headquarters of the Royal Stud
Farm and Training Establishment which had branches at
Bergstetten and Neuhof. Ehrenfried's photograph in old
age shows a handsome strong face with good eyes, bushy
eyebrows, grey hair thinning somewhat in front, and a
heavy grey moustache. He looks a prosperous yeoman or
a retired senior non-commissioned officer, efficient, experienced, and accustomed to responsibility and obedience.
His wife, well and carefully dressed in the German bourgeois fashion of the times, had plenty of dark hair smoothed
back over the ears, well-kept hands and blue eyes. Richard,
in appearance, took after his father. Not tall, or big, he
had the horseman's perfect figure, lean and wiry with ' a leg
for a boot '. He had a beautiful seat and, like all born
horsemen, looked his very best when mounted. His hair
was blond and, in earlier years, somewhat inclined to be
wavy. His fine, wide-set eyes were blue, his complexion
very fresh with a good deal of colour. Deriving from a
family of gamekeepers and huntsmen, shooting, riding and
country pursuits were his passion. Nevertheless he was
fond of music, especially that of Wagner, but his greatest
passion was what Bavarians call ' hunting ', but which the
English call Field Sports.

Reaching the age of eighteen he had to do his compulsory
service in the Army and naturally chose the Artillery. Like
most young soldiers, he was proud of his uniform and rushed
off to have his photograph taken. That of the rather
frightened-looking youth who has not yet learned how to
wear his uniform, much less to feel and look at home in it,
does not do Richard justice, but is the best available. It
would obviously be a mistake to think of the position
Hornig soon came to occupy in the King's entourage as

anything faintly like that of an English peer occupying the high ceremonial part at Court of the Master of the Horse. It would be equally incorrect to think of him as merely a groom as Clodwig of Hohenlohe, who ought to have known better, described him. The correct translation of König-lischer Stallmeister is equerry. The nearest approach in England to the office Hornig occupied in Bavaria is that of Crown Equerry, an office from which in England, as in Germany, much of the glory has departed with the coming of the motor-car. As the active deputy of the ornamental Master of the Horse it was, and in a reduced measure still is, the business of the Crown Equerry to provide riding and driving horses, and all horse transport, for the Sovereign, the members of the Royal Family, and the entire Royal House-hold. This in itself, especially when no other means of transport were available, was an onerous and exacting task. In addition, this Official was sometimes, as in Bavaria, responsible for the breeding, purchase and training, of all the Royal horses ; he controlled all stabling, coaches and carriages ; harness, state and ordinary, relays for long journeys, and so on. A forage-master, generally a retired senior non-commissioned officer, was in charge of the forage. No reception of a foreign Royalty, no Royal marriages, funerals, coronations, progresses, or other public ceremonial, no private visit of a Prince to his tailor or a Princess to her dressmaker, could take place without the intervention and assistance of the Crown Equerry.

The Bavarian Court was comparatively simple. Munich is, it is true, a small city and the capital of a small country ; nevertheless, Richard Hornig's post was no sinecure. The geographical position of the capital in the centre of Europe made inevitable frequent official and semi-official visits from foreign Royalties. Moreover, during the reign of Ludwig II visits to remote castles, chalets and mountain huts not only made it necessary for Ministers and officials to wait on him, but entailed the provision of an elaborate mounted messenger service. In all there were about five hundred horses in the Royal stables ; some of the hunters cost as much as ten or twelve thousand marks. Ludwig's endless mountain journeys were made in a four-horse car-

riage with outriders, or in one of his fairy-like golden
illuminated sleighs, and relays had always to be provided.
It is clear that none but an expert could successfully cope
with such onerous duties. It is true that, in the best sense,
Hornig had risen from the ranks inasmuch as, having learned
to ride when a child, he began his service in the Royal
stables under his father as an apprentice at the age of
twenty-one. He was a real lover of horses, a brilliant horseman and, of course, a skilled whip. His pleasing personality, resource, and intimate knowledge of every phase of
his business made him an invaluable servant. More than
once his personal courage and skill saved his Royal Master's
life. As everyone with any acquaintance of the subject
knows, a mutual love of horses is a strong bond. Until the
advent of the motor, the head groom was never in any
English county home looked upon as a mere servant ; so
far as horses and equine knowledge were concerned he was
the teacher and friend of each member of the family ; he
was passed on from one generation to another, enjoyed
privileges often amounting to intimacy, and was invariably
looked upon and treated by everyone in the family as a
friend. In the families of the nobility and gentry the office
of head groom was often hereditary.

The rapidity with which the lifelong intimacy between
Ludwig and Hornig developed is evidenced by the fact
that, in the beginning of July, some eight weeks after they
met, Ludwig, with Hornig as his chosen companion, set out
on a journey which was, to him, something not unlike a
pious Moslem's pilgrimage to the holy places. He tore
himself away from Richard Wagner at Berg to go off on a
jaunt with Richard Hornig.

The first halt was at Eisenach to do homage at the Wartburg. Like all Germans, Ludwig was immensely impressed
by this magnificently situated castle with its watch-tower
commanding far-flung views of the Thuringian forest and
plains. But it was its historic and romantic associations
and remains which, gripping Ludwig, never once let him go,
and which inspired his last architectural folly, the castle
of Neuschwanstein. Rightly, Ludwig bowed before a fine
example of one of the few Romanesque palaces in existence,

and was deeply moved by its associations with Walter von der Vogelweide, Wolfram von Eschenbach, and the hordes of minstrels, singers and pilgrims that infested the Court of the Landgrafs in the twelfth and thirteenth centuries. Even more captivating to Ludwig was the magnificent, ancient Sängersaal in which Wagner had placed the vocal context in the Hall of Song in *Tannhäuser*. There and then Ludwig vowed to create in Bavaria his own Wartburg, with its Romanesque frescoes, Sängersaal dedicated to Wagner's music. Neuschwanstein is massive, unconvincing, dull ; the only quality in which it proved a peer of its prototype is its incomparable site.

By July 10th, travelling incognito as the Count von Berg, Ludwig reached Paris and, with Hornig, put up at the Hôtel du Rhin in the Place Vendôme. The Empress Eugénie, for whom he had a romantic predilection, was absent but, while fully respecting his incognito, Napoleon III received him and took him to Pierrefonds where he found Viollet-le-Duc's absurd restoration of a mediaeval feudal stronghold entirely to his taste, and no doubt thanked Napoleon and the Empress for having ordered and paid for its creation.

The Emperor gave him lunch at Compiègne, where he felt ' wrapped in the spirit of Jeanne d'Arc '. Greatly as Ludwig was impressed by the Louvre and Tuileries, he found his true French spiritual home at Versailles—and the Paris Exposition where he spent whole days.

On July the 26th King Otto, who since his abdication of the Greek Throne had lived in the Royal Castle at Bamberg, died very inconveniently. Ludwig had to tear himself away from Paris—but not before he had bought a huge ' Moorish Kiosk ' and other monstrosities at the Exposition —and, as etiquette demanded, hastened to Bamberg to offer his condolences in person to ' the Greek bitch '.

There can be little doubt but that the advent of Richard Hornig in May led to the break with poor Sophie in August if indeed it did not cause it by finally proving to Ludwig that, for him, normal happy love for any woman was impossible. But Richard, Beloved of my Heart did not permanently oust the Great Friend by any means.

At the beginning of September Ludwig sent Düefflipp, his Court Secretary, on a confidential mission to Wagner at Triebschen. Whether the results were reported verbally or in writing is not known, but on December 13th Ludwig wrote to Düefflipp :

> I am astounded that you find the affair between Wagner, Frau von Bülow and Frau von Schnorr may not be quite kosher [*sic*]. Should that sad rumour be true, which I cannot make up my mind to believe—should there be adultery in the play—love . . .

Wagner again arrived in Munich during the last week in December, and the wizard was, somehow, able to convince Ludwig that no matter how often he chose to commit adultery, it was always quite kosher !

CHAPTER EIGHT

FLIGHT FROM REALITY : 1868–1869

1868

IN February 1868 Prince Ludwig, the King's eldest first cousin and seven months his senior, was married in Vienna to the Archduchess Maria Theresa of Austria-Este. It was an important occasion because, should Ludwig and Otto die without children, Prince Ludwig would succeed to the Throne.[1] The Archduchess, as the direct senior successor of Charles I through his eldest daughter Minette Duchess of Orleans, was considered by strict Legitimists as the rightful Queen of England and, in their view, Prince Ludwig's son by her, the present Crown Prince Rupprecht of Bavaria, is the rightful King of England ! The Crown Prince, a fine soldier, a great patriot and a great gentleman, is content to confine his pretensions to allowing his children to sport the Royal Stuart tartan when they appear in the kilt.

Ludwig was unable to be present at the state entry of the bride and bridegroom into Munich. It was, quite truthfully, announced that he was in bed, but few people believed it, and Lipowsky, the King's Cabinet Secretary, went so far as to see Hohenlohe about ' the reports concerning the King ' and to complain of ' the people of Munich and their evil tongues '.

Ludwig I asserted that he would never die ; but, like ordinary folk, he did so at his residence in Nice, the Villa Diesbach, on February 29th in the presence of his two sons, the Princes Luitpold and Adalbert. Probably the twenty years that had elapsed since he abdicated because of Lola Montez were amongst the happiest of his life ; she, thirty-two years his junior, had already been eight years in her lonely and obscure grave in Greenwood Cemetery, New

---

[1] Which he in fact did as Regent ; assuming the style and title of King Ludwig III on November 8th, 1913, because of the incurability of King Otto.

York. He was taken home to the beloved Munich he had done so much to create and buried with imposing ceremonial in the Basilica of S. Boniface which he had caused Ziebland to build for him, not knowing it would house his own sarcophagus and that of his Consort, Queen Thérèse, who behaved with much dignity over the Montez turmoil.

The verses which Ludwig I wrote as captions to Karl Roffmann's classical landscapes that decorate the Hof-Garten arcades are fading, which is perhaps just as well. But the magnificent Ludwig Strasse remains, as do the Ludwig's Kirche, the Sieges Tor, the Propylaea and, above all, the Glyptothek with the Greek and Roman original sculptures of the first rank which he collected. Then, there is the Widmann's equestrian statue of himself, unveiled in his presence and that of his grandson Ludwig whom he made Crown Prince too soon. Ludwig loved and admired his grandfather and was as sorry as any young man of twenty-three can be about the death of an old man of sixty-eight ; but he was suffering from toothache, the miserable aftermath of the Sophie episode and, as he had lately told Clodwig Hohenlohe, was ' much concerned about the independence of my Crown and the autonomy of my Country '. In June he also told Hohenlohe during an audience at Berg that he distrusted, and was indignant with, the Ultramontane Party.

On June 21st the first performance of *Die Meistersinger* took place in Munich. Wagner, assisted by Cosima, supervised the production and Bülow conducted. Ludwig insisted that Wagner should sit beside him : ' So ought the poet to accompany the King.' At the conclusion of the performance Wagner bowed his acknowledgments to the plaudits of the audience from the Royal Box. Frau Eliza Wille, who was present, said ' the want of form in such a proceeding as this shocked and hurt me ! ' But she was a Republican and, like Socialists and Communists, they are very easily scandalized by breaches of Royal etiquette. However, Wagner and the King were, as usual, enraptured with themselves and, in a lesser degree, with each other ; Wagner meant the part of Pogner in the opera to be considered as a monument to his friend Otto von Wesendonck.

Doubtless he considered this more than ample compensation for the large and frequent gifts of money he had received from Otto, and for robbing him of his wife. Otto's feelings about the transactions are not on record.

The first ten days of August were spent by Ludwig at Kissingen where, accompanied by brother Otto, he went to receive the Tsar and Tsaritza. Ludwig thus described the occasion to Frau von Leonrod :

BERG, *August 29th, 1868.*

. . . I spent a week at Kissingen with Their Russian Majesties ; the place itself, the surroundings and the monotonous life, are altogether against the grain . . . Nothing is more strengthening for body and soul than to move about in God's free nature ; and on the tops of mountains the soul is nearest its creator—it is more beautiful there than in the fumes of towns where the real seat of joy certainly is not. At Hohenschwangau everything is ready for the building of the new castle. It will be in the romanesque style and the pictures and statues therein will represent the poetical and consecrated spirit of the best period of the Middle Ages . . .

On September 28th Sophie was married to the Duc d'Alençon, grandson of Louis Philippe King of the French. For the occasion the hall at Possenhofen was transformed into a chapel ; the bridegroom and his father wore the insignia of the Bavarian Order of S. Hubert, and during the banquet (probably as a conciliatory gesture to Ludwig) the Wedding Chorus from *Lohengrin* was played. Ludwig was not of course present but, on the wedding eve, paid Sophie a private visit. Hohenlohe, who was a guest in the Castle for the marriage, recorded that his room had ' a villainous bad smell ! '

That Ludwig was far from broken-hearted finds additional proof from the fact that when, in due course, the bride and bridegroom paid him the usual formal visit of courtesy he described himself as ' bored to death '.

1869

Wagner visited Munich in November (1868) and was granted an audience ; nevertheless when, just before Christmas, he sent Ludwig a present of the score of *Lohengrin* bound in four volumes, it was not acknowledged. On January 11th (1869), speaking of the King, Wagner wrote to Nohl :

> I must tell you quite honestly that I may as well face the fact that one day I shall see myself deprived of any protection and without any benefits from there.

To Ludwig's ancestors Bavaria owes so much architecturally that there was little left for Ludwig II to do, especially in Munich. He therefore turned his thoughts towards domestic architecture. Indeed, his dislike of Munich and the whole bias of his temperament made this outcome inevitable.

Ludwig to Frau von Leonrod :

MUNICH, *January 7th, 1869.*

> . . . Unfortunately I cannot yet move into the upper apartment because my study and the red salon won't be ready before March. The small Winter Garden, which you know, is going to be enlarged during the summer and it will be made magnificent by the Moorish Kiosk, the grotto, and the picture background representing an Oriental garden with a pond, kiosk, swan, boat and peacock, so that one can imagine oneself to be in Oberon's fairy garden. Near the Linderhof, not far from Ettal, I am going to build a little palace with a formal garden in the Renaissance style ; the whole will breathe the magnificence and imposing grandeur of the Royal Palace at Versailles. Oh, how necessary it is to create for oneself such poetic places of refuge where one can forget for a little while the dreadful times in which we live.

Maximilian II had a small hunting lodge in the woods near Linderhof ; having had it put in order, Ludwig went there to stay in May and within a week the plans for the new castle were put in hand. There, in nature's wildest and most magnificent surroundings hitherto echoing only the sounds of the hunter, the woodman and ski-runners, where in winter the weather is so severe that the deer had to be handfed daily by the foresters, Georg von Dollman planned at Ludwig's command a florid French palace surrounded by exotic gardens, terraces, fountains, statuary, a temple, an artificial waterfall and, most incongruously,

had erected nearby a Moorish kiosk. An artificial cave
copied from the famous blue grotto at Sorrento was, however,
with its brilliant light and artificially coloured water, the
supreme attraction. Ludwig's incomparable eye for a
beautiful site never failed and, like Chiemsee, Neuschwanstein, and the projected Falenstein, Linderhof is magnificently placed. From his father's modest hunting-lodge
Ludwig, as he loved to do, watched Linderhof being built
stone by stone. It was an architectural projection of his
necrological passion for Louis XVI and Marie Antoinette
and was conceived as a memorial to them, and to Louis XIV
and XV. The first castle Ludwig built, it is, on the whole,
perhaps the least satisfactory. People write and talk as if
he had dotted the land with castles whereas he only built
three—Linderhof, Neuschwanstein, and Chiemsee—which
was never finished.

Once Linderhof was begun Ludwig had what he needed
most ; an absorbing occupation that would keep him away
from his capital. His creativeness was of course entirely
derivative ; nor need he be reproached with that, for it is
all most people can hope for. True, he employed no great
architects ; there were none to employ. His caperings in
stone were characteristic of his period and no worse than
a respectable London iron bridge bedizened in a kilt of
Scottish granite and called a tower. Those were the days
of towers. Look at Balmoral. Look at the sham ruins
and sham castles and gingerbread gazebos that besprinkled
so many of the gardens and parks of England.

Whether accidentally because he was obsessed by the
beginning of Linderhof, or deliberately because he was
nursing a grievance, Ludwig for the first time failed to
congratulate Wagner on the anniversary of his birth in May.
Worse still, in August, Ludwig's birthday month, Wagner
spent two days alone in the pleasant little town of Starnberg
gazing across the lake at the Schloss, but had to return to
Triebschen without being summoned. This must greatly
have pleased Duchess Maximilian Josef, who would no
longer allow the name of Wagner to be mentioned in her
presence, and who had ostentatiously adopted the views
of those who regarded ' the whole Wagner business ' as a

dangerous craze of the King's. She could afford to 'become haughty' as there was now no possibility of her youngest daughter becoming Queen of Bavaria.

Here it will be reasonably convenient to deal with an odd episode in Ludwig's life that cannot be fitted into any strict chronological order. Although spread over some period of time it was merely an episode, but an illuminating episode, unexpected as, superficially, it appears to be uncharacteristic. Probably one reason why Ludwig instinctively avoided women was because he was in a curious, weak way as wax in their hands, especially when, as with Elizabeth of Austria and Cosima von Bülow, they had strong characters and strong wills. Moreover, he may have had a guilty feeling that he owed them any reparation that it might be in his power to bestow.

Elizabeth Ney, the only sculptress he ever knew, came into Ludwig's life about this time. She was a remarkable woman in her own right and is important to us because her artist's bi-sexuality seems to have enabled her to have understood Ludwig better than any other woman he ever met. Moreover, we are not only fortunate in having a very full and vivid account of their relationship, but most of her letters to Ludwig have been preserved.

Elizabeth has in history a secure little niche as a sculptress. A Westphalian by birth, she was a grand-niece of Napoleon's Marshal Ney and, where her own passions, interests and prepossessions were unconcerned, she was not unworthy of the 'Bravest of the Brave'; completely a product of the Romantic movement she went everywhere, met everyone and did everything that, by the conventional standards of the day, she ought not to have done. Always, as such women must, she was in the heights or in the depths, her prototypes being of course the Récamier, George Sand and de Staël. Baptized Francesca Bernadine Wilhelmina Elizabeth, she managed to survive even that handicap. She was of course anxious socially and professionally to hitch her modest wagon to a glittering star—like thousands of others of both sexes all over the world. Sometime about 1868 she made up her mind that she was going to fascinate the young King of Bavaria and inspire him to walk in the

paths of what she considered artistic and political righteous-
ness.   Fortunately for Wagner she was a sculptress and not
a composer or theatrical impressario.   Her bust of herself,
and her full-length portrait by Kaubach, show her to have
been tall, graceful, passionate, determined and, although
predominantly feminine in temperament, looking like a
self-willed boy.   Elizabeth had already tried and failed to
conquer the Bavarian capital when, copying the tactics of
Lola Montez and Cosima von Bülow, she decided upon her
second invasion of Munich.   It has never been made quite
clear how—after a prolonged siege—the undefeatable
Elizabeth ultimately gained Ludwig's interest—most probably by appealing to his passion for building ; indeed, she
was quite equal to becoming (temporarily) a stonemason
if that would aid her ambition.

For a time she had great influence over Ludwig, her
romantic French family background being an immense
help.   Long before they met he commissioned Degan, who
afterwards became his building-adviser-in-chief, to design
a studio residence for Elizabeth.   It was, by her desire,
Tuscan and pretentious, and until about 1910 one of the
sights ' of Schwabing, the Chelsea of Munich, where it
stood prominently in the Maria-Josefa Strasse.   Ney named
it the ' Steinheil Schlösschen ', and another little bit of
imitation Italy was added to the Bavarian capital.   As
fond of dressing-up as Ludwig himself, Elizabeth wore
Oriental robes when she received all artistic and Bohemian
Munich.

In spite of this well publicized and surely not incon-
siderable success Ludwig persistently refused to receive the
sculptress in person.   All down history kings have built
costly seraglios for lovely courtesans ; Ludwig is probably
the only monarch—the only man—who built one for a
woman he had never seen.

For one reason or another Ney took it into her head that
Cosima von Bülow was her real stumbling-block and, in
public and private, began denouncing the lady at the top
of her voice.   Like Lola, and Wagner himself, Ney just
could not hold her tongue.   When Wagner's first child by
Cosima arrived very opportunely on the morning when its

putative father von Bülow was conducting the first rehearsal of *Tristan*, it was, as we already know, promptly christened Isolde. Without any avoidable delay on Wagner's part a second followed and was christened Eva Maria; whereupon Ney demanded loudly all over Munich: 'Why not Tristana?'

Upon Cosima pontifically, but unwisely, announcing that it was borne in upon her that she had been selected by destiny to preserve and inspire Wagner, Ney, who had herself experienced many such urges, cried out : ' He has been preserved and inspired by half the female population of Germany; it's disgraceful leaving babies on one doorstep after another in the name of the new music-drama.'   Then, spitefully returning to the hated Cosima as the more vulnerable of the two : ' She might get the King to grant her a coat-of-arms with a cradle rampant.'   This from a young woman who was the gossip of half Europe for her amorous indiscretions and who, having at that moment two men living in the Steinheil Schlösschen, was not unnaturally believed to be ' living in sin ', was piquant and delightful. Ney was a very useful scourge for Cosima and Wagner, and the many enemies they had such a gift for amassing, did not scruple to use her.

When the King's engagement to Sophie was announced Ney decided that he ought to present his fiancée with a bust of himself. She was wrong. She pestered Liebig, Bismarck, and many others to help her to achieve access to the King and again failed woefully.   Had she been tactful enough to approach him through Wagner at a moment when the composer was in high favour she might easily have succeeded.   She made a great artistic sensation during the Paris Exposition with busts of Bismarck and Garibaldi and was received by Napoleon III as ' the grandniece of the Prince of Moskowa '—the incognito in which the ' Bravest of the Brave ' was disguised by Napoleon I. Ludwig during the many hours that he spent at the Exposition must have seen Ney's *Sleeping Faun* and heard it extolled by Hosmer, Hüeffer and by Liebig, who was constantly at the Residenz organizing chemical experiments for the King. When Ney demanded :

'Is he truly as hard to know as people say?'

Liebig neatly countered with :

'No one who lives in a palace is easy to know.'

Elizabeth now took matters into her own undefeatable, masterful hands. She started bombarding the King with long letters. Laying aside the sculptor's chisel she used with such skill, she seized a pen as clumsy as a white-wash brush, dipped it in a vat of flattery, and bespattered Ludwig. An artist herself, she asserted that she, and she only, understood and appreciated one of the few artists ever to occupy a throne. A woman who was never, if she could avoid it, alone, she declared that like his 'Most Enlightened, Almightiest King, Most Gracious King and Lord, Thou King of the Realm of Ideas', she craved for solitude ; like him, she lived for art, poesy, idealism, and was quite ready to come and make a statue of him at the Residenz, Hohenschwangau, Berg, a mountain hut, or any other place whatsoever.

No reply.

By some means she was careful never to avow, Ney got her busts of Baron von Werther and Liebig so placed in the Residenz that Ludwig had to fall over them and break his neck—or else stop and look at them.

However achieved, Ney's two years' siege at last breached Ludwig's castle of isolation. Orders were given that the Odysseus-Sal was to be fitted up as a temporary sculptor's studio and Ney, like many another, envisaged herself as installed for life in the Residenz and the King's chaste (but not too .chaste) Egeria. With the utmost difficulty sittings were arranged. The great day at last arrived. The sculptress was objective and business-like ; the sitter bored. A true artist always puts into a picture or bust more than they actually see ; often more than they realize. A work of art should not be a description but a revelation. The resultant bust bore a striking resemblance to Otto and showed Ludwig as an immature, handsome boy—which is all he ever was. In a stupid plan to awake his sleeping desire the hefty Balyowski once threw herself into the miniature lake in the Winter Garden and cried aloud to the King to save her from drowning. Ludwig rang a bell, told a footman to drag her out, and retired to his study. Ney, much more subtle (remembering the Empress Elizabeth rumours), dressed herself as Iphigenia ; remaining, however, the objective artist throughout, she suddenly recited a passage *at* him from Goethe's *Iphigénie*, and Ludwig was enchanted. Here was reality—as he understood and loved it. The two became friends. Following the bust, a life-sized statue of Ludwig as Grand Master of the Order of S. Hubert prospered. They discussed Ludwig's hopes of redeeming the people through Art as high-falutin as ever Ruskin and Morris were at that moment doing in England. Ney had once crushingly told Schopenhauer himself that sordid political reforms would be superfluous once 'the people' (whoever they may be) were 'filled with the glory of a high creative soul '—a pronunciamento Wagner at his most histrionic could scarcely have bettered.

But none of the few women to whom Ludwig accorded his friendship could let well alone. Over a long period Cosima continuously exposed him to a bombardment of letters which he withstood for the sake of the Great Friend ; the Balyowski, Marie Dahn-Hausmann, Josephine Scheffsky and Ney all, sooner or later, abused their privileges. They interfered in his private life ; worst of all, they aspired to interfere politically. Ney, on hearing that the King was to open the Diet, sent him a long, impassioned letter telling him exactly what to say and what not to say : ' Why should only the few who have the privilege of serious conversation with Your Majesty hear all the wonderful things you say ? ' Most of Ney's letters are preserved in the secret Archives. They are intolerably long, rhetorical, turgid, impertinent and, on the whole, stupid.

Even as a boy Ludwig, as we know, loved bestowing gifts. Ney said he offered her the choice of the Crown Jewels which, proudly, she declined saying she much preferred flowers. Thereafter her Schwabing home was like the Royal Crypt in S. Michael's Church on All Souls' Day.

From time to time the King succeeded in escaping to the mountains. Letters from Ney pursued him. Two letters, the last she wrote him, are worth quoting. Apparently, the night before the first one was written she had spent

a long time unburdening herself to the King—but not
sufficiently.

Next day she held forth on paper. Something of what
Ney wrote is pertinent and revealing :

> I hear Your Majesty asking : ' How can I, after so
> many disillusionments, still have faith in humanity ? '
> With inexpressible sadness I see that contact with reality,
> with life as it is, draws ever farther away from Your
> Majesty. Already it has, for you, almost escaped into
> formless distance. Our earnest conversation last evening
> revealed to me that Your Majesty, *and not without horror*,
> perceives this . . . must overcome by a supreme effort
> of the will every thought, however noble, every emotion,
> however tender, which isolates Your Majesty from life.
> Choose now . . . before Your Majesty has surrendered
> to the self-destroying torture of solitude. Last evening
> Your Majesty asked : ' Is there any man in whose generos-
> ity and high-mindedness I dare to believe ? ' . . . Oh,
> lest the dark demons of utter distrust come at last to pre-
> dominate in your mind, grasp a hand warm with life . . .

In a later (undated) letter she wrote :

> I thought of your words all night long. ' God made
> you as you are. You did not create yourself. There-
> fore you may admit freely what you are.'

Had these words another meaning than that of making
clear that a man may, without vanity, take the measure of
himself ? ' Therefore you may admit freely what you are.'
That, indeed, was Ludwig's inextinguishable desire, eating
his heart-strings, parching the spring of his soul. It was
the explanation of the secret Diary, of his incongruous choice
of intimates—this quenchless ache, never more than momen-
tarily assuaged, to find the perfect friend who would understand his quintessential need to worship, to adore, to enter
with humility and veneration the sacrarium of humanity
where men, by kneeling side by side in fellowship, might
indeed discern God. This, because he chose—perhaps had
no option but to choose—broken road and treacherous by-
paths was Ludwig's shipwrecked quest—fully perceived by
him ' not without horror '.

When Ney bade Ludwig ' grasp a hand warm with life '
she knew that was just what he had always failed to do.
Surprisingly for a woman, she does not mean her own ;
intuitively, or perhaps concretely, she knew that here such
advice would prove useless. She meant the hand of the
noble Justus von Liebig whom first Ludwig's grandfather,
and finally his father, pressed to leave his famous post at
Siessen to occupy the Chair of Chemistry at the University
of Munich, and later ennobled. This man, enlightened
thinker, pioneer scientist, true humanitarian, Ludwig also
loved, even as he loved the illustrious Döllinger.

CHAPTER NINE

THE SECRET DIARY : 1870–1872

1870

'BLOWN into the present which I hate, and where I shall always feel a stranger ' ; feeling forsaken, alone, and spiritually almost an outlaw, Ludwig fled for comfort to the romantic past ; fled to the building of Linderhof in which to enshrine his peculiar vision of the glories of French history ; fled to his friendship for the man disdainfully (and incorrectly) referred to by Clodwig Hohenlohe as ' the horse-breaker Hornig ' ; most fatal retreat of all, he fled for shelter to the pages of a secret Diary.

The inevitable thing about all abnormal relationships, whether between individual and individual, or between the individual and the State, is that they are foredoomed to degeneration. Corruption can only beget, and reproduce, corruption.

Ludwig began his secret Diary early in December 1869 when he was just over twenty-four years of age. It is one of the most fantastic and extraordinary documents of its kind in existence. When a Catholic introvert, by persistence in what he knows to be evil, cuts himself off from his Church, his Priest and his Confessional, he is almost bound to turn elsewhere for relief. Hence such documents as the secret diaries of Ludwig II and Roger Casement.

Ludwig's, like that of Casement, has only incidental historic importance and no literary value or significance whatever. Yet it is not merely a pathological study ; it has intense psychological interest and, meagre though it be, it is the secret record of a mind in torment. It is as far as is known a unique human document. In this pitiable, halting confession a man uncovers his soul. True, he does so for his own escape and release, never, perhaps, really intending the account for any except specially privileged eyes. Nevertheless he had the virgin pages handsomely

156

and ornately bound in two volumes and, inset on the covers as medallions, the porcelain plaques he had made to illustrate the story of *Lohengrin*, using photographs of the young woodcutter of the Valley of the Ramsau as his model for Wagner's hero—with whom he was inclined to identify himself even as the Great Friend identified him (at first) with Parsifal. Accident, malice, cupidity, or mere stupidity having given us this strange sign-post to little known and treacherous human territory we are entitled to scrutinize it for any addition to knowledge that it may afford. After all, the Diarist is over sixty years in his tomb, left no descendants, and everyone directly or indirectly concerned with the tragedy is now subject to the verdict of history.

The extreme introvert is slave to himself and, as such, has no choice but to repress his emotions. Inverted, he or she, apparently contradictorily, ever longs for, and ever seeks for, extrovert relations, outward contacts. The dream-life is filled with wonderful beings richly dowered with magic gifts of love or friendship, impossibly perfect, satisfying, complete. Either all attempts at forming such ideal contacts are made difficult by circumstances, or they are ventured and failure and disappointment inevitably result. Whichever happens, the introvert is mercilessly driven further within, and consequently tends to become more brooding, more secretive, more sensitive and, very often, develops towards human nature suspicion, cynicism or even hatred. Faced with life's healthy, inescapable difficulties and realities the victim is torn by indecisions and internal conflicts. If, sometimes, the prisoner meets, or imagines having met, the perfect friend, the perfect lover, they pour themselves out excessively and—unless equally abnormal—the new friend is at first alarmed, and then withdraws.

If it has not already been adopted as an alleviation, the last, lonely, perilous refuge is a secret Diary. Into such documents the introverted, the disappointed, the disillusioned, yes, even the sanctified (but unsatisfied), pour out their souls. This impulse, this method of escape, has given the world some of its greatest literature ; probably to it we owe in some measure all poetry, art, music and literature.

Ludwig's Diary entries were made very spasmodically ; a few are dated, in some instances the date can be inferred, while others are dateless. Some are long, some short. Owing to confusion, amounting at times to incoherence, it is often impossible to tell exactly where one entry begins and another ends. Therefore an analysis of a few of the more significant and revealing pages is indispensable.

The first entry, which is undated, displays certain characteristics which repeatedly occur. The most notable is the fixation of the King's obsession by Louis XIV and all that concerned that monarch. The motto of Louis, ' Nec pluribus impar ', and the French Royal lilies, seem to have given Ludwig courage and hope only second to that inspired in him by the sign of the Cross. The reference to Oberon, King of the Elves and the guardians of the Treasure of the Nibelungen in the *Nibelungen Lied*, is equally characteristic. Ludwig was very fond of Wieland's epic *Oberon* ; and the first time that he appeared at the Theatre in Munich after his Accession early in the winter of 1864 Weber's *Oberon* was performed by his command. On that occasion he was received by the packed house with the utmost enthusiasm, and the Opera was therefore in his mind associated with romantic, happy, and inspiring hopes and memories. The introvert hugs to his heart his few moments of freedom and happiness almost as slavishly as he chews the cud of his humiliations and disappointments.

Psychologically, and biographically, the most important admissions made in this first Diary entry are that the writer has, in the past, indulged in sensual love, that he has repeatedly ' fallen ', thus betraying his ideals ; that, sick of such love, and longing to achieve its psychic counterpart, he is continuously failing, and ever crying out for help and strength to overcome the evil within. This indeed is the burden of the Diary throughout which opens, as it is to end, with an account of one of many ' falls '.

Page two contains the first example of a joint oath to which Ludwig and someone else put their initials. W. cannot be identified ; he may be the W. whom the King first met on December the third. Apparently, he gave the diarist good advice, and generously tried to help him because we have here Ludwig's own admission that he was already habitually given to violent physical movements ; and, we know from the Empress Elizabeth and others, that his unaccountable fits of restlessness and instability were known and discussed in the family circle. The reference to water may be connected with the habit of cold bathing in the hope of reducing this pathological excitability. It is also noteworthy that Doctors of that period recommended cold baths and washings for the sleeplessness and headaches from which the King suffered agonizingly and increasingly all his life. The efficacy of the cold-water cure Ludwig had already begun to doubt. The R. who drove the King to Pfunden (Pfronten) was most certainly Richard Hornig. Linderhof, Pfronten, Tannheimer, Kofel, Gacht, Weissenbach, Reutte, Plansee, and Ettal, with its famous fourteenth-century Benedictine monastery which Ludwig particularly loved, were all within driving distance of Hohenschwangau. These sleigh or carriage drives were much commented on in Bavaria at the time, more particularly because they mostly took place at night and, preferably, by moonlight. Night secured for Ludwig such intervals of privacy as all kings, and he in particular, naturally required. The artificial moon and—in spite of real water—the fountain in his bedroom at Hohenschwangau were not altogether satisfying. Reality had sometimes to be called in to redress the disequilibrium inherent in make-believe. Indeed, the desolate moon appealed to Ludwig's aesthetic sensibilities almost as much as it did to those of Keats ; but to Keats it was feminine, to Ludwig masculine. The specialists who inquired into Ludwig's mental condition in 1886 thought this driving by moonlight in his fantastically curved and gilded rococo sleigh with its magnificent ermine rug, especially sinister, crediting the poor dead moon with the oddest power over mentally unstable people, as the ignorant do to this day.

Apart from his personal enjoyment of the lovely Bavarian scenery by moonlight, Ludwig did not desire in that mountainous country of primitive roads to find himself, his outriders, his grooms—and his favourite of the moment—all suddenly mixed up together in a ravine or ditch. As a matter of fact he was in many ways much more practical

than some of his Ministers. When making riding expeditions the King invariably did so by day when he could see
where he was going. Moreover, he had bad eyesight and
it is possible that like some short-sighted people he saw
better at night. Vanity prevented him wearing glasses ;
consequently, as he grew older the decorations of all his
castles became gaudier and gaudier ; the embroideries and
gilding brighter and bolder ; the lighting more excessive ;
the colours more brilliant : otherwise he could hardly have
seen them. His cousin Elizabeth of Austria, her brother
Karl Theodor, and all her sisters, suffered from sensitive
eyelids. Strong sun gave them severe pains in the head.
This was why Elizabeth had the practical habit of carrying
a sunshade or fan, although credited with vanity, and with
all sorts of mysterious reasons for doing so.

Linderhof and its surroundings were from the first a place
of overwhelming magic for Ludwig and he would frequently
drive the twenty-odd miles from Hohenschwangau to see
its progress. It was inspired by the Grand Trianon which
the King first saw in company with Richard Hornig in
July 1867 ; but it has none of the Trianon's fine propor-
tions and aesthetic austerity. His secret name for Linderhof was Jmeicos-Ettal, a forced and childish anagram for
L'état c'est moi ! It was his way of saying that here he
was absolute. As self-control dwindled self-assertion in-
flated.

Page three of the Diary contains the first reference to the
Royal bed, which was to Ludwig something almost sacro-
sanct. This feeling was intensified by his admiration for
Louis XIV, although it must be remembered that in all
Royal and high aristocratic circles the State bed was always
something of a fetish, more particularly perhaps in France.

In Ludwig fetishism was strong and, like so much in his
character, remained static. He always seemed to realize
acutely that the Royal bed and the Royal bedchamber
were, in some peculiarly sinister way, indelibly affected
by his behaviour.

On the other hand, he seems to have had the feeling that
in the Winter Garden, in a hut in the woods, in a sleigh or
elsewhere, such acts were somehow less blameworthy.

'The soft cushions of an oriental dreamland' also seemed to him to bring some measure of excuse for this and that. Moreover, anything suggestive of the East fascinated Ludwig.

The frequent use of seals, associated in Ludwig's mind with Royal State and high aristocratic ceremonial, was designed to give broken vows newly undertaken a special sanctity, to emphasize the illusion that the latest repetition of his oath of chastity was even more binding than earlier ones. He adored anniversaries, and the final four lines of the entry refer to the forthcoming anniversary of his first meeting with Richard Hornig.

Page four contains little that is new. The references to useless cold washings, and to the continued need for 'forbearance' (Schonung) are significant : Otto, it should be remembered, was also constitutionally subject to fits of violence and, in both of them, the seizures inevitably grew stronger and more frequent as they got older. It is interesting that outbreaks of violence seem to have caused Ludwig almost as much remorse as did his various 'falls'. The signature is the initials of the German Ich der König instead of the French Louis or De par Le Roy ; it is, as usual in the Diary almost unreadable and rather like that of a drunken man or a lunatic.

Page five is full of the mysticism of numbers by which the King was also obsessed ; occultism and later on some indulgence, it is said, in active Spiritism appealed strongly to his visionary and superstitious nature. The Pagodenburg is another small pleasure house north of the Schloss in the Park at Nymphenburg ; Ludwig was fond of it and sometimes went there with Richard instead of to the Amalienburg. The cypher R.L. on the left bottom of the page is that of Hornig and the King intertwined ; those on the right the same in reverse order ; the middle L.R., joining them into a sort of tailpiece, was made by Ludwig.

The fleurs-de-lis at the head and foot of page six of the Diary are well drawn in a rather schoolboyish manner and are, therefore, probably not by the King who, in spite of his lifelong interest in architectural plans, drawings and elevations, and the elaborate draughtsman's desk and stool in his room at Berg, was but a poor performer.   The smaller lily, at the foot of the page, is surrounded by rays, a favourite idea of Ludwig's.   Here we have for the first time in the Diary the ancient Spanish kingly superscription Yo El Rey (I the King).   This is frequently used afterwards.   Spain, like ancient France and the East, was a country conveniently far away where his turbulent imagination could wander at will without ever having to face, as in his lovely but native Bavaria, the nauseating limitations of reality.

From Clodwig Hohenlohe, an exact and painstaking observer, we have several descriptions of audiences with the King.   At a stated hour a Royal carriage would arrive at the Minister's house in Munich and the journey via Fürstenried to Berg would take two hours—not bad going considering that the distance is some twenty-two miles. Hohenlohe described an audience on July 7th (1870) :

> He gave me his hand, which he seldom does, and was very amiable . . .   The King is always distrustful, which is due to his extremely sceptical nature . . .   It is the King's nature to set people against each other . . .   The King was as usual very acute in his questions and answers. It is a pity that his talents are lying fallow, and that he confines himself more and more to the bad company of the horse-breaker, Hornig.   Yesterday evening he intended driving to the Riss, probably to escape the arrival of the Emperor of Austria.

Oddly enough Ministers—even Hohenlohe—were never formally invited to dine with the King.   In Munich it was unnecessary, but at Berg they had to be given something to eat and a belated luncheon would be served about five o'clock in the still existing pavilion [1] situated on a slight rise in the garden quite close to the house and the road. Ministers were seldom invited to Hohenschwangau because, as it was seventy or eighty miles from Munich, it meant putting them up, and this Ludwig hated doing.

[1] The Schloss was abused during the Hitler régime, and has far from benefited by being occupied by U.S.A. troops during and after the Second World War.   Repaired, and a good deal altered, it is now the residence of Prince Albrecht (b. 1905, e.s. and heir of the Crown Prince Rupprecht).

On September 16th Ludwig wrote to Frau von Leonrod from the Saierhütte, one of his many mountain eries :

> These last few days I have been reading a lot about the history of France to which I feel very much attracted . . . I returned quite pleased with my excursions to Landshut and Schweinfurt . . . The generation of strong-willed men with courage, energy and strong convictions, such as I want and am in need of, has died out ; one only meets with vagueness and indifference, and that is why I feel so forsaken and lonely on this earth, like a left-over from better times, blown into the present which I hate, and where I shall always feel a stranger.

The far-reaching events of 1870–1871 belong to the main stream of history—and we are only immediately concerned with the manner in which they affected Ludwig. Just before Sedan he wrote to Frau von Leonrod ; his letter shows how, at first, Bismarck's chicanery deceived even the well-informed :

BERG, *August 28th, 1870.*

. . . How I long for the mountains. On the mountains there is freedom, and there men never bring their pain. Woe to those who began this awful war in that irresponsible way ! The terrible judgment already begins ; his faithful friends all leave him ; even the Empress and his people ; all the means which he uses in his last efforts to save the situation fail, and have a contrary effect. There is no close understanding between Sovereign and people, no bond of love which binds Ruler and subjects together as in other countries where they have shared all their joys and sorrows for centuries in mutual faith. Now becomes clear the outrage of Napoleon's usurpation in the theft of the bloody crown, and in the resurrection of the Throne which was achieved with lies and fraud. How the criminal deed is shown up now in its horrid nakedness. But I am sincerely sorry for the poor Empress for she is a noble and charming woman and is only responsible for a very small part of the crime of her infamous husband.

You can imagine how pleased I am at the brilliant victories of my brave troops ; who could have dreamt of such extraordinarily rapid results. Those quick and

decisive victories of the Germans over the famous undefeatable French Army ! . . . All the same, with all my
strength I am longing for an early Peace which shall be
lasting and blessed for the whole of Germany, but especially for my beloved Bavaria.

As Bismarck well knew, the establishment of a German
Empire without the active and sympathetic support of
Bavaria was unobtainable. Following the tactics he had
so successfully employed after the Seven Weeks War he
sought to beguile Ludwig by carefully keeping on his iron
hand a conspicuous, reassuring velvet glove. It never
deceived Ludwig or, for that matter, the Bavarian working
classes with whom the Franco-Prussian War, while being
fought, was far from popular, [1] although once successfully
over they of course joined in the cheering.

Bismarck coaxed Ludwig to be present at Versailles, as
the spectacle of the Head of the House of Wittelsbach
beseeching his Hohenzollern cousin to assume the Imperial
Crown would have served to emphasize Prussian aggrandisement before a watching world. Dressing the hook with a
gaudy fly, Delbruck said : ' let us give him one of the famous
historic suites—possibly the bedroom of Louis XIV—and he
will be so enraptured that he won't notice the absence of all
normal conveniences '. Ludwig hesitated. On October
18th he wrote to Lorenz von Düefflipp, his Court Secretary,
from Linderhof :

> His Majesty is more and more convinced that it will be
> impossible for him to undertake the planned journey to
> France. His Majesty therefore thinks that it is necessary
> to pretend an illness such as extension of the sinews ;
> will Herr Düefflipp please let this be known to the general
> public and the Army.

Two days later the Bavarian Cabinet arrived at Versailles
where the Envoys from Würtemberg and the smaller
German States were already assembled. Then Holnstein
who, it was said, coveted the office of Prime Minister, somehow got himself appointed Ludwig's special Envoy and set

[1] The Bavarian Landtag rejected neutrality by sixty votes to fifty-
eight.

off secretly for Versailles. Holnstein was after all a soldier and Sigmund von Pranck, the Minister of War, was indignant about this unofficial journey, as were the Ministers who knew nothing about it or its objects. He openly boasted to the Grand Duke of Baden that it was he who induced Ludwig to entertain the Kaiser idea. He got into touch with Bismarck, who did not trust him but, quite prepared to use him, drafted the Kaiserbrief and Holnstein hurried off with it to Berg and—the story is threadbare and inaccurate —tricked Ludwig into signing it. Bismarck recorded that on November 23rd about ten o'clock in the evening ' the Bavarian Treaty is made and signed. Germany's German unity is secure, and the German Emperor too.'

Ruggenbach, the Baden Envoy, said :

There was not likely to be another King in Bavaria who would offer the Imperial Crown to someone because he had the toothache.

In an expansive moment the Versailles conspirators permitted themselves a little unbuttoned levity. Bohlen said :

It was really funny what Holnstein told us about his interview with the King of Bavaria while he had toothache.
' And the way I wrote to him to bring him round,' boasted Bismarck . . . ' It was Holnstein who did most in this matter. He played his part very cleverly . . . What order can we give him ? [1]

Bismarck's official view of Ludwig, dressed up for history, was somewhat different :

. . . from his Accession soon after (March 10, 1864) I remained in friendly relations with him, and in a comparatively brisk correspondence, that lasted until his death, he always impressed me as a businesslike, clearheaded Ruler, full of the German national spirit, but caring greatly for the preservation of the Federal principle of the Constitution of the Empire, and of the Constitutional privileges of his country. I remember, as something outside the domain of practical politics, his uppermost thought in the Versailles negotiations, was that the German Empire, with the Federal Presidency,

[1] *Reflections and Reminiscences* (London, 1898).

should alternate between the Prussian and Bavarian Royal Houses. The doubts as to how that unpractical idea was to be made practical were put an end to by the negotiations with the Bavarian Representatives at Versailles, and by the result of them, according to which the rights which he exercises to-day were conceded in principle to the President of the Federation, and thus to the King of Prussia, before the title of Emperor was discussed.

While what is called history is being made human beings are inevitably beset by private anxieties and preoccupations.

In August Wagner married Cosima von Bülow ; his mission to Versailles was Otto's last public official act, and in November he retired from the Army ; about the same time Ludwig met with a serious horseback accident and never rode again. A good walker, a fair climber, and an excellent horseman he was thereafter deprived of healthy exercises that he loved, and this was the cause of him putting on weight in his later years. The Crown Princess Friedrich of Germany suggested to Clodwig von Hohenlohe that Princess Elizabeth daughter of Prince Friedrich Karl of Prussia would make Ludwig a suitable wife. Hohenlohe thought that probably the ' pretty, gentle-looking girl lacked the necessary energy to influence the King '. As she was not yet fourteen this was more than likely.

Prince Ludwig, in the Bavarian Upper House declared that :

A firmly established German Empire will be able to open those permanent friendly relations with the neighbouring Empire of Austria-Hungary which are the sole guarantee for the peace of Europe.

1871

On January 6th Ludwig wrote from Hohenschwangau to Frau von Leonrod :

. . . It is really painful to see Otto in such a suffering state which seems to become worse and worse daily. In some respects he is more excitable and nervous than Aunt Alexandra—and that is saying a great deal. He often does not go to bed for forty-eight hours ; he did not take

off his boots for eight weeks, behaves like a madman,
makes terrible faces, barks like a dog, and, at times, says
the most indecorous things ; and then again he is quite
normal for a while.   Gietl and Solbrig examined him and
if he does not follow their advice *soon* it will be for ever
too late !

On January 18th Wilhelm I was proclaimed German
Emperor in the Hall of Mirrors at Versailles, and it was
everywhere recognized—and, in order to mollify Bavaria,
publicly admitted by Bismarck—that without the concur-
rence of King Ludwig II this could never have happened.
Bismarck's Machiavellian dealings with Holnstein—a quisling before Quisling was born—were of a piece with the
forged Ems telegram by which he had precipitated the war
in the previous August.   Nevertheless, it was known by
some, and felt by many, not only in Bavaria but throughout
Germany, that Ludwig's support of the brand-new Empire
was anything but cordial.

There is very little authoritative evidence in existence as
to what Ludwig really thought and felt about the events
of the beginning of 1871.   Werther, one of Bismarck's many
spies in Bavaria, and a most unreliable one at that, reported
to his employer at the end of February that, owing to disgust
at the whole political situation, Ludwig desired to abdicate
in favour of Otto.   The foregoing letter to Frau von Leonrod proves that he had known for months, perhaps years,
that any such project was impossible, and Ludwig was at
all times very far from being disposed to transfer his Crown
to the head of his uncle Luitpold.   In a letter from Munich,
dated March 24th, he gave Frau von Leonrod the real
reasons for his action ; in politics, especially where Prussia
was concerned, he was very much of a realist :

   . . . It was in Bavaria's own interest that I acted as I
   did ; if I had not sacrificed for the crown and the country
   what I did we should have been forced before long to
   sacrifice much bigger and more important things.   Moreover, it is clearly foreseeable that by then we could not
   have even pretended that we did it voluntarily—and
   that would injure our whole political future, and our
   position in the new Reich.   Oh, we have had to go

through terrible times. In my short reign we have already had two wars ! That is very hard on a peace-loving Sovereign. Soldiering, if indulged in, makes the manners and customs of the people rough and wild, and makes them unable to conceive big and supreme ideas. It blunts them for spiritual enjoyments, and these, and these alone, are, in the long run, able to captivate ; these alone give real pleasure and inner satisfaction . . . I should like to show you (before long I hope) my new Winter Garden which is just finished. It represents an Indian landscape with the Himalaya Mountains in the background . . . It is two o'clock now . . . I must go to bed.

On March 29th Gietl wrote to Ludwig concerning Otto :

The four doctors unanimously consider it necessary that the seriousness of the situation, as well as the serious consequences of his behaviour, should be explained to His Royal Highness. Unless Your Majesty gives other orders, I think I shall myself have to undertake that task because I have known His Royal Highness since he was born, and because I have observed him longer than anyone else.

It is impossible to understand Ludwig II without giving some attention to the case of Otto. Hitherto this has been impracticable because no one was allowed to see the forty-odd bound volumes of the daily Medical Reports stored in the Secret Archives. On June 16th Ludwig wrote to his mother :

. . . I did not want to accept your kind offer of a sum of money because last year I had the impression that you said in rather a regretful tone that you wouldn't be able to go to the mountains for financial reasons ; that is why I then made a certain sum available for you . . . I am very upset about Otto's health ; it is such a pity that Gietl's warnings did not help at all. If Otto does not do something now it will soon be for ever too late ; then nothing can be done and he will go towards his own ruin.

On June 29th a characteristic entry appeared in the Diary :

Drive to Schlux . . . Sworn in memory of the oath in

the Pagodenburg on 21st of April . . .   Soon I will be a
spirit ; heavenly airs are around me . . .   I repeat it,
and as truly as I am the King, I will keep it, not again until
the 21st September.   Then to try it otherwise ; at the
third time it succeeds.   Remember the 9th of May 3
times 3 !—Febr.—April—June—Septemb.   Fragrance of
the lilies !   The King's delight . . .   This oath has its
binding power, as well as its potency by

De Par le Roy

LR

D   P   L   R

Solemn oath before the picture of the Great King.
' Refrain for 3 months from all excitement.'   ' It is not
permitted to approach nearer than one and a half paces.'

Louis

Given at Hohenschwangau in the year
of our Salvation 29 June 1871,
Of our Reign the eighth.

Next comes what is practically the sole reference to
contemporary history in the Diary :

On July 15th and 16th 1871, the victorious German
Armies entered Munich.

They were led by the Crown Prince Friedrich of Prussia,
Queen Victoria's son-in-law and afterwards for some ninety
days second German Emperor.   Wearing a victor's laurels
and his brand-new dignity of Imperial Highness and Crown
Prince of the German Reich, many Bavarians welcomed him
tumultuously ;   many with a dislike for all things Prussian
that is endemic.

Hating war, Ludwig welcomed Peace, and poetically
hailed its advent in his Diary.   The adored friend whom
he greeted on July 17th with rapture after long absence cannot be identified.   The reference to the nameday of the
Empress Elizabeth is noteworthy inasmuch as she is the
only woman mentioned in the Diary, and even she only
once :

Feasts, Theatre, drive, the presence of the Crown Prince
of Pr. *very* disturbing and disagreeable !

On the 17, at half-past ten o'clock at last saw again the

adored friend after a long separation ! Blessed embrace.
—Happy hours, garden, sat in Grotto, faithful until
death.—Oath in thought projected before the balustrade
of the Royal Bed of Lilies. 18 July—*take it well to heart.*
(Madame de Montespan by Capfigure (?) read. On the
24. July to the Kreuz berg, fragrance of Lilies, 2 days
there, read Montespan, Marie de' Medici. Walked in
the dear world of the mountains—and Alpine bells
sounded rapturously and blessedly as if announcing peace.
Peace come ! . . . Began Don Carlos by Pongne some
days Berg (became acquainted with Dr. Wechser, author
of ' Mazarin ' . . . Inquisition scene feast in the tent.
29 July have been at the beloved place [unreadable]
. . . 1 and 2 Aug. . . . (Alhambra) Diane de Poitiers.
Saw Ship of the Dutchman on the Schöttel [unreadable].
Meal, trip on the Lake by moonlight on the 3 the Name
day of the Empress down, swift drive . . . Later on to
the Schachen, saw preparation for the great Oriental room.
Redeemed Sept. or Oct. ! ! ! Strong is the magic spell
of the desirer ; stronger that of the renouncer . . .

The words ' feast in the tent ' seem to indicate that it
was about then Ludwig started getting groups of foresters,
peasants and grooms together in a tent at night for feasting,
drinking and crazy horseplay of one sort or another. These
gatherings naturally caused unending gossip and were of
course a final development of his miserable *nostalgie de la
boue.* Elizabeth of Austria had a similar predilection for
visiting peasants in their huts and sharing their rustic (but
not amorous) amusements.

On July 23rd Ludwig, from Berg, repeated in a letter to
his aunt Queen Amalie of Greece the opening words of this
Diary entry :

Very disturbing was the presence of the Crown Prince
of Prussia who rather pushed himself into the limelight.
Of course I had to invite him *bon gré, mal gré* . . .

On September 2nd Ludwig from Berg wrote to Frau
von Leonrod :

. . . That this last war, which in many respects ended
so gloriously for Bavaria, should have forced myself and
my country into the iron clutches of that damned German

Reich with its Prussian colouring—that just this unhappy war which is enthusiastically loved by so many of my people should have done it—is a most deplorable dispensation of Providence. The popularity which, thanks to the quickness of my resolutions and my political sacrifices, I enjoy especially in Northern Germany does not at all make up for what I have lost.

A fortnight later he wrote his mother :

BERG, *September 17th, 1871.*

I told Gietl to go and see Otto at Hohenschwangau, because it is absolutely essential that he should begin to lead another life, and that he should follow the advice of the doctors ; already it is almost too late, because he simply won't listen to the doctors.

In October Herr Robert von Mohl, the new Baden Diplomatic Envoy, was granted an audience by the King at Berg and described the occasion as follows. It gives a vivid picture of Ludwig's way of life when at his favourite Berg :

I expected wonders in the Schloss and garden and was much disappointed. The garden really consists only of a wood, at the bottom of which runs a small footpath along the shores of the lake, and some flower beds ; the Schloss is small, narrow and extremely simple, especially the rooms of the King himself, though his rooms in the Residenz are overladen. The domestics were very queer. I knew that the King lived quite alone at Berg, except for a few servants, and with no high Court officials, only an Adjutant who lives in a separate building, and whom he often did not see for weeks, and the Cabinet Secretary who also lived in a separate building. But I was surprised to find the Schloss itself completely unguarded and without any order. There was a policeman at the entrance of the Schloss, but nowhere a porter or a servant. Nobody knew anything about my audience, and I did not know how to get to the King. I searched for the Adjutant and when I at last found him he said he had no orders and refused to announce me. Finally he agreed to take me to the Schloss. To the intense astonishment of the Adjutant we found there two Ministers waiting in an awfully cold antechamber for an audience. As it was so very cold we gladly accepted the Adjutant's suggestion to go for a walk in the Park and there wait for the King's commands . . . The King was in black and very elegantly dressed, wearing the Baden House Order and looking very well . . .

While I was waiting I looked at the rooms. On the first floor I found them very simple ; no—or rather only a few—unimportant and medium works of art and old furniture. In the passages and halls were all sorts of servants, footmen, kitchen boys, housemaids and so on, in not very distinguished liveries ; the whole house smelt very disagreeably of photographic salts. In short, the mixture of Royal Household, monasterial seclusion, and disorderly bachelor establishment, was very queer. In these conditions the young Lord lived for at least three-quarters of the year, completely alone, hardly seeing anyone except his Cabinet Secretary, occupied in reading books about the century of Louis XIV, and usually riding out late in the evening in the company of some grooms until long after midnight, or voyaging alone in his little steamboat on the lake.

On October 23rd, from Partenkirchen, Ludwig again wrote to Queen Amalie of Greece :

Otto's state is deplorable. He is in the best way of becoming just like Aunt Alexandra ; he suffers from a morbid over-excitement of the whole nervous system which is quite terrible.

Next comes page eight of the Diary. It is mostly made up of notes of expeditions. There are the usual pledges to abstain from passionate embraces, the usual invocations to the Lilies, and to the ' Great King '. The page is interesting because it gives the fullest account available of the relationships of Ludwig and Hornig. Their friendship, apart from its basis, seems to have been sincere and lasting. Certainly once they met they never parted and although in the end—like everyone else—Hornig testified against and abandoned his King, he was, all things considered, extraordinarily faithful and loyal. The oddest thing about the relationships of these two was that Ludwig, obsessed though he was with ideas of absolutism and delusions of grandeur, was—as with Wagner—always human and humble with Hornig, treating him in the pages of the Diary as in all ways a friend and equal. It was quite extraordinary of Ludwig to write ' Vivat Rex et Ricardus in aeternum ' as if the King and his equerry were equals. If he any longer believed in a theological heaven Ludwig certainly held that the royal circle (where he expected to be seated beside Louis XIV) would of a certainty be divided by a handsome *ruelle* from the space allocated to common angels. Ludwig and Hornig have had a row and a reconciliation, and Ludwig loved both. He has somehow convinced himself that their relationships were not only beautiful but meritorious and even pure, yet chronicles the fact that in one month they met in the Amalienburg three times. He means of course met privately because, in the ordinary performance of his duties, Hornig saw the King intimately and constantly. Whether Ludwig's penchant for the Amalienburg arose from artistic, or less avowable, reasons it is impossible to say, but it inspired him to have a replica, which he named the Hubertus hut, erected at Linderhof which he also used as a rendezvous for himself and Hornig ; another hut similarly used was built into the cleft of a great tree called by Ludwig ' Richard's linden '.

The reference to the magic ring of the Nibelungen which conferred ' the strength of a giant and the power of renunciation ' on its wearer, and the further reference to the third act of *Lohengrin*, seems to indicate that in January Richard had given the King a ring which was to strengthen and protect his Master : on the other hand, it may mean that the King, obsessed by the idea that he was indeed Lohengrin, bestowed a protecting ring on Richard, even as Lohengrin bestowed his upon Elsa of Brabant. In Lohengrin's pure idealism Ludwig always saw a pledge that, eventually, his own ideal aspirations would triumph over his sexual temptations.

Page nine is a mere amplification of the foregoing. The L.R. on the left bottom of the page and the Ludwig in the middle were written by the King ; the Richard and L.R. on the right by Hornig. The ' Indian Hut ' was of course the one in the Winter Garden on the roof of the Residenz.

The reference to Racine's *Esther* which he describes as a ' magnificent drama ' on page ten of the Diary is a further indication of the King's often deplorable taste. He was delighted with this confection and had it frequently performed ; he attended the rehearsals and, after the first production, sent for Ernst von Possart, the Director of the National Theatre, and pointed out that the producer was wrong in certain respects ; it was subsequently proved that the King was correct. He had formed a large and valuable library concerning the Louis XIV period and had amassed a fine collection of prints and illustrations. He possessed a prodigious memory, and his knowledge of his chosen period made him a formidable, if not a very inspired, critic. This entry also shows his intense interest in historic Memoirs. He liked exhibiting his remarkable memory and, if he were assured of a sympathetic hearer, would reel off long spasms of bad prose and worse poetry. Moreover, he liked listening to fustian, and encouraged Wagner in his incurable habit of spouting aloud his own writings on the very slightest provocation—or even without any provocation at all. Many a long evening at Triebschen, and later at Wahnfried, was spent in this way.

1872

The first secret Diary entry of this year, somewhat curtailed, is as follows :

. . . Reconciliation with Richard beloved of my soul . . . On the 21st, the anniversary of the death of the pure and exalted King Louis XVI. Symbolically and allegorically the last sin. Sanctified through this expiatory death, and that catastrophe of the 15th of this month, washed of all mire, a pure vessel for Richard's love and friendship.—The ring, consecrated and sanctified in the water, gives the wearer the strength of a giant, and the power of renunciation.—Kiss holy and pure . . . only one. I the King. The 21 Jan. 1872—*Vivat Rex et Ricardus in aeternum—Pereat malum in aeternum.*

The next entry reads :

3 Febr.—Hands not once more down on penalty of severe

punishment. In Jan. Richard was with me here three times . . . ! On the 31 Court Ball Ride with R. in Nymphenburg, (Amalienburg). *D e P a r L e R o y.* It is sworn by our friendship, on no account again before 3rd June . . .

R.   Ludwig Richard   R.

Like an old man Ludwig was at the age of twenty-seven already living largely in the past. Again recalling the first meeting with Hornig he wrote :

On the 6th March 1872. In just 2 months it will be 5 years since that blessed 6th day of May 1867 when we learned to know each other, never more to separate, and never to leave each other until death. Written in the Indian Hut.

In an entry under March 22nd :

About this time sent frequently for the singer Nachbauer. Heard heavenly songs. Serene mood. Easter.[1] Enlightenment, Heavenly light . . . On the 10 April rode with Richard in Nymphenburg (Pagodenburg) . . .

A letter to Nachbauer throws an interesting light on Ludwig's simple and charming Wittelsbach attitude towards such artists as pleased him and whom he liked :

April 21, 1872.

My dear Nachbauer,[2]

I was very glad to receive your happy news from Riga to-day. I always enjoy hearing you sing ; but I would be particularly glad if the three performances of *Tannhäuser,* and so on, could take place on the three specified days in May. Without certain conditions your Director in Riga does not want to agree to that ? I am very curious to know the conditions.

Let me assure you, my dear Nachbauer, that I shall always remember you with the most sincere and faithful feelings of friendship—even when I have left the town,

---

[1] In 1872 Easter Sunday fell on March 31.

[2] Nachbauer, Franz (1830–1902), tenor singer, member of Hoftheatre 1866–90, created part of Walter Stolzing in *Die Meistersinger* in Munich on June 21, 1868, when Ludwig infuriated the Müncheners by insisting on Wagner sitting in the Royal box.

which I shall often do, now and in the future. You may
be sure of this, much beloved friend !   I close in order to
resume reading a highly interesting book which I have
begun and which I cannot leave.   I hope that you enjoy
reading the books which I have sent you lately about
Haly.

Hoping to see you soon !   With heartfelt greeting from
your loving friend and gracious King,

LUDWIG.

One month after writing this letter Ludwig received
from Dr. von Solbrig a long report concerning poor Otto
which is important because it throws light on Ludwig's
own case, and reveals, especially in the last paragraph, a
naïve self-satisfaction that seems to have been characteristic
of those psychiatrists who afterwards attended Ludwig
himself.

On the fifty-ninth anniversary of his birth (May 26th)
the foundation-stone of the New Theatre on the hillside
outside Bayreuth was laid by Wagner and, in the evening,
he conducted the Ninth Symphony in the charming Old
Opera House in the town.   Ludwig refused to be present,
contenting himself with sending a telegram.   Important
as was the anniversary of the birth of the Great Friend,
and momentous as was the occasion, neither were mentioned
in the secret Diary and therefore were, presumably, not in
Ludwig's secret thoughts as was ' le 6 Mai cette Journé si
importante pour tout ma vie ' associated with Hornig.

The composer delivered a eulogy on Ludwig, as well he
might, and, amongst a crowd of notabilities garnered by
Wagner, Nietzsche added intellectual distinction, if not
aesthetic grace to the proceedings.

In spite of Ludwig's dislike of the widowed Queen of
Greece, she was, naturally, one of the very few people with
whom he could freely discuss Otto.   On June 20th he wrote
to her from Hohenschwangau :

My inmost thanks for your kind thoughts : poor Otto's
state of health is really deplorable.   Unfortunately he is
not better yet ; he is much worse than Aunt Alexandra.
His nerves are in a state of irritability which is difficult to
imagine.   He very seldom dresses, hardly ever goes out

into the open air, often looks like a wild animal, and
suffers from the most horrible hallucinations ; it is really
a terrible fate.

A Diary entry gives glimpses of how Ludwig passed the
summer :

> (On the 21. July H. for absolutely the last
>   time . . . meal Y el R.)

Under Richard's linden, drive, 18. Excursion to the Plansee, Kocherbrunnen . . . Read
extracts from Dollinger's Lecture (Louis XVI and
beginning of the so. Rev.) R. rowed, back, then Berg,
carriage.
Berg up to the great Ahorn [1]—Left on the 19. July.
Moon, rest Ammerland,—Berg, a few days
there, ovation, steamer, dinner, Tirolean singers
Beuerberg on the 24 night in tent, Moonlight
out [unreadable] back towards
morning, Sedlmayr [a lacquey] drove with me, left next
day in the afternoon for Kramatsberg.

D e   p a r   l e   R o y

LR.

By the lily gained the power to resist all temptations
      throughout the whole year.
LR.

Kramatsberg the 26th July, 1872.
Vivat Rex in aeternum!

On August 27th Ludwig is at the Halbammerhütte, a
mountain retreat which he had furnished with curtains,
rugs and so on, all of which had been birthday or other
gifts from Frau von Leonrod. There he could escape into
his own past :

> . . . All these dear things remind me of you whom
> from my earliest childhood I have to thank for so much.
> I shall *never never* forget that . . . You understand me
> so well, and only a very few people do. By most of them
> I am misunderstood so that, naturally, I felt rebuked by
> the world and retire more and more ; it does me so much

[1] Ahornopf, some fifty miles south-east of Innsbruck, 9,750 feet.

good to talk to you to whom my heart clings in faithful and innermost love since the happy and blessed days of my childhood. I spent my birthday with Otto at Berg and found him, thank god, a little better. He would only consent to come to Hohenschwangau on condition that he need not go back to Nymphenburg. That, of course, the doctors could not permit.

Next day from Berg he wrote his mother :

Fortunately I found Otto less excitable than I expected. He still does not like to go out, and still pretends to have boils on his feet. As we drove along he continually buried his head in his hands—did not look at me, and always saluted much too late when the people had already passed by . . . After half-past one at night he drove back to Nymphenburg.

In her House Chronicle the poor Queen Mother made this sad entry at the end of the year :

Otto ill during the winter. Upon the advice of the doctors, and of Dr. Solbrig, he was removed to Nymphenburg on February 26th where we may see him only very rarely. Unfortunately Dr. Solbrig died on the 31st of May of this year. Dr. Gudden took over the medical attendance Nov.–Dec. 1872.

This is the first time Gudden's sinister name is mentioned by any member of the Royal family.

The one gleam of light in this tragic darkness was Ludwig's unfailing love for Otto, and the selfless devotion of the Queen Mother to the grown son whose mind was steadily deteriorating before her eyes. She went regularly to Nymphenburg, where in the earlier stages he was confined, to see Otto and, when his habits became so erratic that there was no relying on his ever keeping an appointment, she would wait patiently for hours in an anteroom in the hope that eventually he would come and speak to her. Often the poor mother had to go away disappointed.

Ludwig's year ends as fatefully as it had begun in the pages of the Diary.

1872
Juré

                                        Louis

Au nom du Roy Louis XIV
An oath, holy, and never to be broken New
Year's eve
1873 !—
I swear and solemnly vow by the
pure and holy sign of the Royal Lilies
Inside the impassable, invulnerable
balustrade enclosing the Royal Bed.
During the year just begun as much as
ever possible bravely to resist every temptation ;
and never to yield if at all possible
either in acts, words, or even in thoughts.   In this
way to purify myself more and more from the dross,
which unfortunately clings
to human nature, and so to make myself more worthy
                              of the Crown which
God has given to me.
Bonne dans la chambre du Roy, dans la balustre,
sacre et infranchissable agnouille sur l'estrade la tete
protege par la dai du lit Royale
Neo cessabo neo errabo.   Dieu m'aidera . . .

CHAPTER TEN

VARICOURT : ANOTHER ROMANTIC FRIENDSHIP :
1873

LUDWIG, as a fox-hunter would say, always rushed his fences. Most normal young people think of life as ever-lasting ; from early manhood Ludwig was haunted by the conviction that his would be short. Thus he was inwardly driven to demand spring and harvest in one, the flower and the fruit must be there to clutch—simultaneously.

On a Friday in March of 1873 Ludwig spoke to Baron von Varicourt for the first time and another of his exotic hothouse friendships burst and prematurely blossomed. Rapturously he exclaimed : ' Hail to the bearer of such a name ! '

He demanded his new friend's genealogy and—a tactful move from a singularly tactless man—got it in French. Varicourt, aged twenty-nine, was a seasoned soldier, having fought in the Bavarian Army against Prussia in 1866 and against France in 1870–1871. He had served successively in the Chevaux-Léger, a cavalry regiment of which La Rosee had been Colonel and for which Ludwig had a pre-dilection ; later on he was posted to the Cuirassiers. Ludwig immediately appointed Varicourt his personal aide-de-camp and, for a time, another abortive friendship flourished.

The most trivial letter has a validity that no paraphrase can convey. Varicourt's letters to Ludwig are, like him-self, so narrow and wooden—so utterly without charm—that only a few need be quoted, and those solely because they establish facts or evoke an aspect of Ludwig ; their value to us is that they inspired him to be more objectively outspoken about himself than do any of the fulsome screeds exchanged between him and Wagner, or indeed between him and anyone else. Amongst much else they bring out with frightening clarity the unique capacity that human beings have for self-delusion when swayed by their emotions.

In that simple fact abides all the immeasurable danger of
shipwrecked souls and shattered civilizations. In spite of
Ludwig's assertions to the contrary, Varicourt's family was
not outstandingly distinguished, and none of its members
rendered unforgettable service to France or the French
monarchy, and in his honest, clumsy way Varicourt tried,
and failed, to make Ludwig see this. Ludwig's insistence
on the absolute privacy of his letters is evidence of their
outspoken sincerity.

On April 3rd, twelve days after their first meeting, Ludwig wrote :

My Dear Freiherr von Varicourt !
     I am, as you know, specially interested in the history
of France and in the history of French Royalty during the
past centuries and, as I read a great many books on the
subject, it gives me pleasure to see now and then plays
about those periods, performances of which are given for
me alone. Such plays are to be given in the Residenz
Theatre to-day ; one is about Louis XIV, and the other
about Louis XV. Perhaps you would like to see these
plays ? Amongst all the people I know you are the only
person who, I think, deserves to attend these performances in my box. Will you therefore be in the ante-
chamber at 7 o'clock so that we may go into the Residenz
Theatre together. First of all, I do not want to increase
the number of those who envy you, and secondly I
always wish to avoid unnecessary talk about these performances ; I therefore trust that you will *not* say *the
least* thing about it. I feel urged to say that I am truly
proud at having a Freiherr von Varicourt as my aide-de-
camp ; I have been for years interested in your ancestors
whose history is so closely connected with that of the
Royal House. Auf Wiedersehen until to-night. I send
my kindest regards and remain, with the sentiments of
special grace and confidence,
                              Your King,
                                        LUDWIG.

This letter reached Varicourt by hand and, very adroitly,
he rushed back to the Residenz to answer it in person ;
he had already realized Ludwig's impetuosity and im-
patience, but had not yet quite grasped the fact that, not

only his letter, but every aspect of their relationships, must be fulsome, heated, florid and histrionic ; his verbal thanks were therefore a trifle lacking in warmth. Next day he wrote to Ludwig :

MUNICH, *April 4th, 1873.*

The profound impression which the infinite favours of Your Majesty awoke in my soul is so vivid that Your Majesty's most obedient servant cannot keep it to himself but feels obliged to offer to his most gracious King and Master his deepest thanks.   How will it ever be possible for Your Majesty's most faithful servant to repay by active proofs of his faithful devotion the smallest part of Your Majesty's most gracious favours.   Full of repentance that, by badly chosen words, I should have caused—if only for a few moments—in Your Majesty's mind the slightest doubts of my feelings of happiness and satisfaction, I most humbly beg Your Majesty's pardon.   I am full of happiness about my new appointment.

Ludwig is, for the moment, content.   He is the central figure of a play and returns frantically to his blue desk in his blue study :

April 4th, 1873.

. . . My most heartfelt thanks for your letter which made me very happy . . .   Let me assure you that I also think with inmost joy of the hours which I had the pleasure of spending with you in the Theatre and in the Winter Garden ; I am also glad to hear that you did not mean those words as they sounded to me.   The feeling of being able to trust you like a rock inspires a sentiment of most faithful attachment in me for you, and the true and sincere friendship which I entertain for you I will keep until death.   I swear that you shall remain your own master just as much as if you had left the Army.   If you want to travel just let me know quite frankly ; do or leave undone whatever pleases you ; it is my only wish that you may live *many many* years without troubles and griefs and that you may be happy and content.   I send you my heartfelt greetings, and remain
              Your King, LUDWIG, who esteems you
     greatly and who is convinced of the purity of
                              your character.

If Varicourt imagines that his new post is a sinecure he is soon undeceived. Next day, April 5th, the King again burst forth :

> . . . You know that you owe the appointment as aide-de-camp to my interest in the history of France in the past centuries, and to my unlimited confidence in you and my true and sincere friendship . . . The majority of my people—as regards their political opinions—are miles away from my own, and hate to be reminded of Royal history and of the times of absolute Monarchy. I wish, my dear Freiherr von Varicourt, that you should promise me on your sacred word this very day in writing that you will not show my letters to you to anybody, nor talk to anybody about them ; secondly, that you will not let out a word, especially about my political opinions, nor about anything else I may discuss with you. I firmly believe you because the word of a Varicourt is as sacred to me as the Bible . . . Do write to me as often, and in as much detail, as you like. You have no idea what joy a letter from you can bring me.

Two days later, sending Varicourt his photograph, Ludwig wrote :

> *April 7th, 1873.*
> . . . I enclose a pair of fleur-de-lis links with diamonds which I had originally ordered for myself. I give them to you because you are much worthier to wear them inasmuch as two of your ancestors suffered heroically for this high emblem of Royal France. The photograph is in remembrance of our meeting on Thursday last. The memory of those hours is dear to me as an unforgettable dream ; only now has the Winter Garden received its true consecration because a Varicourt honoured it with his company. But from now onwards I shall force myself to write less enthusiastically, and not too often, to you because you might become haughty. You might show this wantonness, and thereby enlarge the number of your enemies and enviers. That I will not have. And I should like to add that whoever dares to speak maliciously about you will have to reckon with me. Your enemies I consider as my personal enemies . . . I will never doubt you ; rather will I doubt God and the whole

world. The nimbus that radiates around your name is indestructible in my eyes.

Ludwig and Varicourt must have spent the entire day and part of the night of the 9th April at their desks. Ludwig leads off :

April 9th, 1873.

. . . The other day, after supper in the Grotto, you said you would tell me the story of your life, saying that you did not want me to doubt you. You told me some things of your youth, about tricks which you used to play in the Institutes, and so on. I had the impression that, at the beginning, you had intended to tell me more but that, while talking, you changed your mind and thought it better to curtail your story. This must have been the case as you could not possibly have thought that the little which you had already told me could make me feel disappointed in you ; this matter has bothered me ever since, and I beg of you to write me *quite sincerely* whether I am wrong or right in thinking that . . .   That you are also in the spiritual sense the descendant of your magnanimous and heroic ancestor I firmly believe—this I can tell by my inner infallible voice. ' High above all the power of doubt shall stand my friendship ! ' God be with you ! Let me enjoy a letter from you to-day, and greeting you a thousand times most heartily, I remain,
Yours friend and gracious King,

LUDWIG.

A few hours later Ludwig ' enjoyed a letter ' sure enough. He is told that although for eight years Varicourt did his duty as a soldier he did not find satisfaction in mere routine work and in riding a horse. He had no interest in Munich Society and only kept in touch with a few friends. He saw no chances of promotion and therefore decided to leave the Army after the war of 1870–1871. He wrote all this down at great length and in his reply Ludwig discloses more about himself.

Post-haste came Ludwig's by no means unwise answer :

April 9th, 1873.

. . . The steadiness and purity of your character appeals to me very much . . .   I only complain that in the

times in which I am compelled to live there are so few
characters of that kind. I do not in the least doubt that
your brain will make it easy for you to make up for
missed opportunities. Be that as it may, your ancestors
live in you, and because of the deeds of your ancestors
and those of your father—you shall for ever remain dear
to me. You are embittered and discontented—as I must
conclude from your verbal and written utterances—by
impressions which you received during the years of your
education. I am also disconcerted by sad experiences
connected with politics which I had to go through very
soon after I ascended the Throne. That is why I am cold
to most people and keep them at a distance. I now live
more in my beloved books than in the hateful present. I
understand your need for independence so well—it is a
good and noble impulse. It is true there are a lot of
boring and tiring things in the life of an aide-de-camp,
especially being on duty in the ante-chamber, and the
desire for compensations in the form of excursions and
short journeys is only natural. I should like it so much if
you would always let me know your wishes quite frankly ;
you will never make me angry by doing so—that would
be quite impossible with a Varicourt. I repeat, you shall
do everything that you may want. Although you have
sworn to my flag as a soldier I do not consider myself as
your real King—because your real master is, strictly
speaking, Henri V [1] the legitimate King of France and of
Navarre. Oh, how I wish you could also find in reading and studying the greatest of joys. This wonderful
absorption in captivating books is such a compensation
for the evils of life. I now finish my sixth letter to you,
and think about the horrid sixth of October about the
terrifying details of which I read last night in the books
which your father sent me : on the sixth of October of
this year you shall receive the marble bust of my Queen
Marie Antoinette, whom I adore as if she were still alive.
She was pure and exalted like an angel of God. God
bless you !

Varicourt came to supper and, because Ludwig hated
going to bed on account of his nightmares and sleep-broken

[1] The Comte de Chambord, grandson of Charles X, called by
legitimists Henry V of France.

nights, they talked and talked, and talked. Then, obeying the introvert's urge to introspection, next day Ludwig lived the cherished hours over again in writing ; the extravagant idealism of his devotion to Varicourt is the measure of the loneliness of an empty heart :

> I am happy in the remembrance of the hours which I spent with you yesterday, but this feeling is mixed with sorrow because I had the impression that last night you were quite different from what you were the other day. I found that at the last moment you were very serious and disconcerted. I shall have no rest until you let me know the reason of this—or whether I was mistaken. I take it that you will give me your word never again to give way to a feeling of bitterness or grief; the thought that you will always remember me in friendship would be a blessed consolation to me ; the contrary would make me ill.
>
> Just as with you the feeling of friendship for me has its deep and sacred roots in Royalism, so my friendship for you arose through reading Royalist historic books—you cannot reproach me because of that. Of course this feeling was strengthened by getting to know you personally, and by the verbal exchange of true feelings, but still more so by our correspondence. Each of your letters is something very precious to me. And now, God bless you ; may He take care of you and pour His richest blessings over you and keep you now and evermore. With this prayer in my heart I finish and shall remain until death your faithful friend, and gracious King,
>
> LUDWIG.
>
> PS. Your character is noble and exalted all through ; every word you said to me yesterday proved that afresh. The most beautiful and the most longed-for death for me would be to die for you. Oh, could that happen soon, soon ! That death would be more desirable for me than anything else the world can offer.

Varicourt was indeed gauche in the rôle of passionate correspondent for which Ludwig had cast him as relentlessly as he cast all his intimates for parts which suited his fantasies, but so often outraged the facts. Nor was Varicourt a brilliant, or even a sympathetic, correspondent ;

yet the foregoing letter inspired him to something a little more high-falutin than usual. Except Wagner at his worst, nobody could ever be sufficiently magniloquent to collaborate with Ludwig in his more sublimated moods. Such moments, as he confesses, ' dominate the whole man '.

Ludwig to Varicourt :

April 16th, 1873.

. . . To have had the pleasure of getting to know you, the noblest of men, makes me happier than I can say. The hours we spent together seem to me more of a dream than a reality. I will close with the words which Schiller, in one of his finest dramas, *Don Caesar and Don Manuel*, lets the reconciled brother say : ' So I will seize this brotherly hand which is the closest to my heart on earth and nothing shall separate us but death.'

Ludwig to Varicourt :

April 17th, 1873.

. . . With inmost joy I think of Our last meeting which made me so happy. Believe me, should you again fly into a temper—which I am sure will happen again because your moods change so quickly—I shall always remember that it is your temperament and not your intention which is to blame ; I shall always know how to differentiate between the two.

Certain incompatibilities cannot be reconciled, and it is Ludwig's basic tragedy that he was always trying to establish intimacies for which there were no foundations. Between April the 18th and 23rd there happened between Ludwig and Varicourt something which each of them, for his own reasons, desired to gloss over. Varicourt was quick-tempered and crude and something he found unacceptable, some morbid suggestion, verbal or otherwise, antagonized him, and he reacted immediately and violently. Feeling guilty, Ludwig climbed down. A letter from Varicourt to him written between the 18th and the 25th of April is unfortunately missing. Probably Ludwig, as he had a way of doing when a letter annoyed or hurt him, immediately destroyed it ; but we can infer its contents from Ludwig's letter of April the 25th to Varicourt.

The missing letter was, in fact—although neither recognized it at the time—the beginning of the end.

Ludwig to Varicourt:

April 25th, 1873.

There is something in your letter I keep wondering about. You write that you appreciate most highly—as you express yourself—my favours of a purely spiritual nature. Please explain to me why you emphasize that particularly, as it is a matter of course that they were of a purely spiritual nature. But you emphasize it specially; please write me the reason why? It is an enigma to me which I absolutely cannot understand; that is why I ask for an explanation of this curious and *completely incomprehensible* phrase. It would hurt me deeply if only the shadow of a doubt were to come between us.

Then he summoned Varicourt and they had another of Ludwig's interminable talks:

April 26th, 1873.

My Dear Freiherr von Varicourt!

I am so restless that I must write to you at once. I am still full of all you told me to-day. The four hours we spent together disappeared like lightning. I am so utterly happy that words cannot describe it. Yes, my God, not only your name, but also your person, is surrounded with an earthly nimbus in my eyes. May you be blessed in that you succeeded in retaining the gold of your pure and noble feelings amidst the whirlpool of life which deteriorates so many people. To-day it is five weeks since I first knew you and I thank Heaven for sending me Our friendship: in my heart you reign as absolute King. To you it shall belong until my latest breath. I feel as if in a rapturous dream since I knew you. During these last weeks I have lived in the highest heights of ether . . . Your letters are much more precious to me than all my possessions, castles and pictures, and the memories in my soul connected with you and the hours I have spent with you are the most wonderful of my present life. May God protect you and take care of you and keep away all sorrows.

Faithfully loving you now and evermore in most sacred fervour, firmly and faithfully standing by you in all need, and only to be separated from you by death.

I am, and remain until my last breath, your sincere and true friend—*not your* King because in reality you are mine,

LUDWIG.

They go to Berg together for a week, after which Varicourt returned to Munich—and Ludwig to the mountains and to his neglected Diary in order to try and there recapture in retrospect something of the inexplicable rapture aroused in him by Varicourt's mere presence :

1873.   Page eighteen of the Diary.

On the 21 March spoke to Freiherr von Varicourt for the
    first time.
On the 23 appointed him A.D.C.—
Hail to the bearer of such a name.
About this time (3rd April) with Freiherr von Varicourt
    in the Residenz Theatre. *The Fan of the Pompadour*
    and the *Secret Audience.* Then
    supped with him in the Winter Garden (grotto)
    (7–1 o'clock)
Wrote much to each other—
High over all power of doubt my friend-
    ship shall remain. After
    the Feast of the Resurrection supped again with him
    until 2 o'clock on the 27 April.
Leonhard the Periwig-Maker in the Residenz
    Theatre.
Eight days in Berg on the 15th supped with Freiherr von
    Varicourt in the Kiosk, then drive
    in moonshine along the lake from 10 o'clock till $\frac{1}{4}$ to
    4 in the morning together.
    The thought of the friend, destined by Providence, the
    looking-up to the exalted magic name which he bears.
    Varicourt will always strengthen me.

Telegram from Ludwig to Varicourt :

KOCHEL, *May 23rd 1873 at 6.20.*

To-day, on the 22nd of May, I remember with inmost joy the same day in March, and hope to do so for much longer than 22 years. Heartfelt greetings.

LUDWIG.

Ludwig to Varicourt :

May 26th, 1873.

I must firmly oppose a passage in your last letter. You write that you are quite an ordinary man—that you really are not. I cannot possibly allow my best friend to be belittled and attacked—not even by himself.

The other day I had a very realistic dream when I was spending the night on the Hochkopf, a mountain hut not very far from Walchensee. You had to fight a duel ; on the last evening I said goodbye to you full of pre-monitions, thinking it was for the last time in this life. Oh, I earnestly hope that this moment will never arrive !

Ludwig to Varicourt :

June 11th, 1873.

. . . You see that I haven't changed my feelings in the least. Once the feeling of friendship for you made me call you by your Christian name, and Thou (*Du*). I should be very glad, and it would make me extremely happy, if you, in one of your next letters which I expect soon, would do the same and call me by my Christian name, and Thou. Oh, please do fulfil this wish. I am so hoping for it. I wish your moods would not change so quickly . . . I believe that in your melancholic moods you are quite capable of doubting my friendship for you.

LUDWIG.

Varicourt to Ludwig :

MUNICH, *June 11/12, 1873.*

I was bad-tempered towards the end of my visit to Berg because I was prevented from keeping an appoint-ment by the delay in taking my leave. That was the only reason. That I do not in the least doubt the con-fidence and the friendship of my King I think I can best prove by saying :

Ludwig ! Friend ! Believe me, always believe me !
Your Majesty's faithful and obedient servant,
and in devoted friendship,

VARICOURT.

However, Ludwig once again overlooking Varicourt's moodiness invited him to drink tea on Sunday, June 15th at nine o'clock in the evening.

Ludwig to Varicourt :

June 16th, 1873.

. . . I firmly believe in thee as in the spirit of good, the power of the pure and exalted. Quite lately you said to me, and also to Count Holnstein, that there are moments when you think of ending your life. I expressly beg you *never again* to listen to such inner voices ; the thought alone that you might really do so causes me the pains of hell.

In life and death,
Your faithful and sincere friend,

LUDWIG.

This letter makes it clear that Varicourt was confiding in Holnstein more than, in the circumstances, he had any right to do.

Varicourt's next letter was more or less a repetition of all the others. It was his final screed to Ludwig who, for the first time, kept him waiting eight days for a reply. Whether Varicourt realized it at once or not, by showing that something else was more important than Ludwig's whim, he—like Paul—had committed the unforgivable sin ; nor can it be denied that Ludwig was indulgent to a friend who is out of his own mouth proved guilty of frequent brusqueness almost amounting to deliberate rudeness.

BERG, *June 25th, 1873.*

My Dear Freiherr von Varicourt !
I take up my pen in order to thank you heartily for your last letter and to send you inmost farewell greetings as I am going into the mountains soon for some time ; it is not necessary for me to assure you that I shall often think of you because you know my feelings of friendship for you.

I am glad that I can think of Our last meeting on the 15th inst. with unclouded joy for there was not the slightest discord. During my last excursion I read the third volume of Walsh which I return herewith with my very best thanks to your father.

Whether I am near to you or far away, I shall always continue to cherish my feelings of friendship for you which you know, dearest friend ; and I believe I know you so well that I can rely on your faithfulness.

I send you my inmost greetings and best wishes for your welfare and remain,

Your faithful friend,

LUDWIG.

Five or six photographs of Varicourt preserved in the secret Archives of the Royal House show him to have had a pleasant enough looking face, a soldierly figure, repressed, dissatisfied mouth, and a general air of self-restraint that it might be exaggeration to describe as sulkiness. Of marked mentality, unusual charm, grace, or spirituality there is not a trace. It is difficult to believe such a man could reciprocate any great warmth of friendship, much less the peculiar form of exotic ardour demanded by such an equivocal relationship as Ludwig thrust upon him.

As the laws of attraction and repulsion between human beings are inexplicable it is impossible to do more than infer what attracted Ludwig to Varicourt. Loneliness; the isolation of his peculiar temperament reinforced by the isolation of kingship had, doubtless, much to do with it; and these were undoubtedly reinforced by his abiding sense of his own inadequacy. Then there was the need all Royalties feel to escape from the restrictions of convention and etiquette and establish a rich and fructifying human relationship: 'Call me Thou.' That is understandable. Less so was the morbid strain of Chinese ancestor worship, but what is quite inexplicable is the hunger for self-abasement, so overpowering that Ludwig, who revered kingship and the crown, could, for a time, bring himself to believe that in a stolid, middle-aged, surly and discontented soldier he had found a reincarnation of the ancient chivalry of France. One even worthy to wear the lilies of 'the Great King'; and—memories of Paul and Wagner—one whose presence as a guest 'consecrated' the Winter Garden.

Their friendship was hailed by Ludwig as that of David and Jonathan, and, like Jonathan the king's son, Ludwig was anxious to give even his shirt to David. Varicourt must use 'du' to him as if he were also a king or a close Royal relative; most inexplicable of all—Varicourt was to be Ludwig's king. Then, no more earthly comparison being sufficiently superlative, Ludwig declared that he was possessed by Varicourt as S. Paul was possessed by Christ !

If there is something distasteful, something distressingly abnormal about Ludwig's abasement before Wagner, there is also something fine and noble in the humility of a man who merely inherited a crown before a man dowered in his own person by genius. But to explain the excesses of abasement wallowed in by Ludwig before the utterly commonplace Varicourt is a task that must be left to the specialist in morbid psychology.

The second half of the year 1873 was the most miserable period, so far, that Ludwig ever spent. Although nothing to that effect has been recorded, it can hardly be doubted that the intensity of his brief friendship for Varicourt— it lasted only thirteen weeks—entailed a corresponding reaction ; his overwhelming loneliness drove him again to the mountains.

Moreover, Otto's mental health was so steadily and rapidly deteriorating that to keep up even the pretence that one day he might recover was no longer possible.

In August the Royal Family, following the custom sanctified from childhood, met at beloved Hohenschwangau to celebrate the twenty-eighth anniversary of Ludwig's birth. The Queen Mother was there and Otto joined them. Because she was a silent woman Queen Marie has always been dismissed as negligible. But she was first and last a devoted and unselfish wife and mother, and what must have been her hidden thoughts when she recalled the first August she, their father, Ludwig and Otto had spent together in this exquisitely situated house that they all adored. She must have had forced upon her that awful realization that one son was hopelessly insane, and the other distinctly abnormal.

Dr. von Gudden, with a tactlessness that was on a later and even more tragic occasion to prove incredible, so timed his routine report on the state of Otto's health that it reached the Queen Mother on the morning of Ludwig's birthday feast : with the food and wine with which they in ancient fashion celebrated the occasion the long-suffering mother and her elder son had to swallow medical details about her younger son and his beloved only brother so repellent that they have been banished from this volume.

The Queen Mother's retrospective entry in the House Chronicle is poignant in the eloquence of its bald simplicity :

> On Sunday August the twenty-fourth at eleven o'clock in the evening Otto came again to Hohenschwangau with Ludwig (the first time for two years) !
> For the first time celebrated Holy Christmas with Ludwig and Otto at Hohenschwangau.
> Then Otto away to Fürstenried.

Fürstenried where, on that happy day in young summer time, Otto and Ludwig fed the fishes in the pond and gazed at their faces reflected side by side in the laughing water.

With Otto incarcerated in Schloss Fürstenried, it was not only the first, but the last, time that the doomed little family spent Christmas together at Hohenschwangau.

After the entry about Varicourt, Ludwig closed the secret Diary and did not open it again for four years and four months. Therefore, for that period, we know with certainty very little about his inner life. Deprived of the companionship of a man who for a few months he almost deified ; cut off for ever from Otto whom he adored—because he never dared to visit Fürstenried—Ludwig rapidly deteriorated in every way.

As he had long feared, Ludwig now knew for a certainty that he, no more than Otto, could possibly escape madness and, transfixed with horror, he beheld his symptoms growing more like those of Otto day by day. They say that, having crossed the borderland, those who are mad are happy, but waiting for the moment when they must cross is the hell of all hells.

As, with inquisitional probing, Ludwig, gripped by fiendish torture, saw hope relentlessly recede, he, like many another before and since, snatched greedily at such assuagements as were demanded by his diseased brain—and what fellow-wayfarer could have the callous temerity to judge him harshly !

CHAPTER ELEVEN

RETROGRESSION : 1874–1879

1874

IN January Wagner, the building of whose new Festival Theatre at Bayreuth was being held up for lack of funds, appealed to Ludwig, who replied : ' I must come to your rescue.' This he immediately did to the extent of three hundred thousand marks. Gulden (florins) had recently been converted into marks, and at the rate of exchange of twenty marks to the pound this donation represented fifteen thousand pounds. Never quite reconciling himself to Munich being abandoned as the Wagnerian music capital of Europe, Ludwig had disapproved of the Nibelungen cycle being given in Bayreuth in the spring of 1871 ; nevertheless, he had given Wagner seventy-five thousand marks towards the expenses of the festival in the old opera house.

On January 25th, the day he sent off the money to Wagner, Ludwig had the ill-omened duty of for the first time personally receiving from von Gudden his official report on Otto, of whom he was now in charge. Saddening though the document inevitably was, Gudden, whose judgment was poor, felt justified in holding out some hope that the patient's condition might improve. If he really believed that, he was the only person in Bavaria acquainted with the facts who did so. These two, King and Alienist, were destined to meet again.

Like Otto, Ludwig, as we know from his early letters to Anna of Hesse, was subject to dreams, and on February 23rd wrote to Queen Amalie of Greece a letter which indicates either that he did not (as was probable) believe Gudden, or that he had more reliable sources of information.

> When I awoke the other day, after having dreamt very vividly of you and Uncle Otto, I received your dear letter . . . Mother is, thank God, well ; but unfortunately Otto is worse. The doctors say that probably he will not recover at all from his nervous illness . . .

On April 29th Ludwig's first friend Gackl married for the second time and chose as his bride the lovely Infanta Maria Josepha of Portugal who, only sixteen and a half years old at the time, was Gackl's junior by eighteen years. Many years later Duchess Karl Theodor described the occasion. Ludwig, breaking his custom of years, received her warmly. She was taken to a gala performance of *Lohengrin* and seated at the King's right hand. As she had never been to a theatre before the girlish bride sat entranced, quite forgetting to be civil to her host. Far from being offended, Ludwig watched closely her interest in the opera and afterwards told her he was delighted to see her so carried away. Next day he sent her flowers and a set of scenes from the opera as an expression of his thanks to her for *listening* the evening before.

Perhaps no custom of Ludwig's aroused more critical comment than his practice of having operas and plays performed for himself alone, yet—his buildings apart—this practice, and the money he gave to Wagner, were his wisest extravagances. Far from being a whim, seeing an opera or play alone was to him a necessity. No sensitive person who has ever listened to opera or any other form of real music in public but has longed for Ludwig's power to banish the audience. Why many people go to opera, play or concert is a mystery ; certainly it is not to listen ; often it would seem that they do so merely to whisper and cough. Then, when he wanted to hear a singer with a lovely voice, but an ugly face or ungainly presence, Ludwig hid their airs and capers, their inane posturings and gestures behind banks of lovely flowers, and most of them didn't like it, although they welcomed the handsome fees and costly gifts that followed. As a matter of fact, few aesthetic experiences in life can have equalled a performance of a Mozart opera in the lovely, empty, Residenz Theatre given by a good cast and a fine orchestra before the lonely king sitting almost invisible behind the curtains of the Royal box. A king who, like a great artist, entered and left silently and in darkness a temple without fanfare and without retreat. Music is a spiritual experience, and perhaps the one advantage of the radio is that it enables it to be experienced, as it should be, in semi-darkness and alone. In those days, as is still the barbaric practice in some concert halls, the auditorium lights were never turned down and Ludwig had to sit with a battery of opera glasses and greedy eyes riveted upon him instead of on the stage. For a man who hated being stared at it was torture.

On July 12th Wilhelm I of Germany passed through Munich on his way to Kissingen and, to Ludwig's chagrin, he was unable to make up an excuse for not going to the railway station to be civil to his Uncle whom he would not refer to as Emperor ; as usual, he confided his troubles to the receptive Frau von Leonrod :

HOHENSCHWANGAU, *July 16, 1874.*

You can imagine what it cost me to see again the King of Prussia—to whom I have had to give up so many rights, and to whom Bavaria has given such essential services, and helped to gain many a victory. Instead of being grateful Prussia treats Us as if We, and not poor France, had been its enemy during the last war . . . In dear poetic Hohenschwangau, in precious Berg, on the shores of the wonderful lakes, in the lonely huts of mountain tops, or in the Rococo magnificence of my rooms at Linderhof—in these places it is my greatest and never-ending pleasure to study historically interesting books because in them I find consolation and balsam for all the bitter and painful experiences of the sad presence of the hateful nineteenth century . . . Probably Otto will never recover from his deep-rooted nervous disease . . . I foster a kind of religious cult for the memory of that beautiful and profoundly unhappy Princess (Marie Antoinette) who came through all her heavy destiny purified, who had real greatness of soul, and was as exalted, sublime and Royal in the darkest jail as on the first Throne of Christendom. I can never read her history without being deeply moved.

Ludwig's extravagant emotional outpourings to his friends obscure the fact that, when writing as a Sovereign, he could be clear and, for a German, concise, and no one knew better how to decline an unwelcome visit with ease and courtesy. A letter of his, one of the many he addressed to Bismarck, not only illustrates these points but is another example of how, throughout their correspondence, as the bullying destroyer of Europe admits, Ludwig held tenaciously to the rights of Bavaria, and never lost an opportunity of restating and re-asserting them. If he referred to the first German Emperor as King of Prussia in a private letter, he would use no such discourtesy when writing officially :

HOHENSCHWANGAU, *July 1874.*

My dear Prince—It would not only be of the greatest interest to me, but it would also afford me the liveliest pleasure to speak with you and give verbal expression to the very high esteem I feel for you. To my sincere grief I learn that the horrifying attempt at assassination,[1] for the failure of which I shall ever be thankful to God, has had a bad effect on your health, so precious to me, and upon the course of your cure.

It would therefore be presumptuous on my part, were I to ask you at once to take the trouble to come to me, now that I am staying in the mountains. I thank you from the bottom of my heart for your last letter, which filled me with sincere pleasure. I place my firm trust in you, and believe, as you expressed yourself to my Minister von Pfretzschner, that you will stake your political influence on making the Federal principle form the basis of the new order of things in Germany. May Heaven preserve your precious life to us for many years ! Your death, or that of my honoured Emperor, would be a real misfortune for Germany and for Bavaria. With my most heartfelt salutations, with particular esteem, and deep-seated confidence, I remain always,

Your sincere friend,

LUDWIG.

That these protestations of grief and horror at the attempted assassination of Bismarck were sincere is proved by a note written to Queen Amalie of Greece on August 6th from the Tegelberghütte near Hohenschwangau : ' I was also much upset by the horrible attempt on Bismarck's life, and am glad that it was not made by a Bavarian. The Emperor Wilhelm is really very chivalrous.' Bismarck replied to Ludwig reiterating his favourite lie that ' under

[1] Kullman's attempt on July 13th, 1874.

the Federal Constitution of the Empire, the independent position of Bavaria was inviolable '.

In August, with Holnstein and General Schamberger in attendance, Ludwig started suddenly for Paris, where he stayed with Hohenlohe-Schillingsfürst at the German Imperial Embassy which astonished him by its magnificence. Peremptorily refusing to waste his precious time on boring official or semi-official engagements, he spent his days sight-seeing and his evenings at the Théâtre français. He visited Versailles with its art treasures, its gardens and fountains and, for him, its sacred memories were given first place.

For some unknown reason he had a serious row with Holnstein, who went to bed in a sulk and left his master to visit Fontainebleau on his own. Few things in Ludwig's life are more inexplicable than the way he clung to this brusque, coarse-voiced traitor. Holnstein of course shared most, if not all, of Ludwig's curious secrets and, knowing the man, it would not be out of character if it were proved that he retained the highest Court office in the Realm by the least scrupulous of means. Ludwig never really liked him, nor he Ludwig—yet they clung together, each nursing a cherished hatred.

Ludwig had invited to stay with him at Hohenschwangau a new-found friend. They made excursions together, particularly to Linderhof, by then well on the way to completion. The new favourite was Alfred Karl Nikolaus Alexander, Count von Dürckheim-Montmartin. He was then just over twenty-four years of age and a loyal, chivalrous, somewhat stupid person, and Ludwig, with his usual impetuosity, had, almost at first sight, promoted him and appointed him his personal aide-de-camp, a hasty exercise of his Royal prerogative of which the Minister of War disapproved. On their third day together at Hohenschwangau, September 9th, the King sent a note and a present across to Dürckheim, who immediately wrote :

> I have just received Your Majesty's most gracious letter and the wonderful album of Linderhof which will be a precious souvenir for all time of those days which live in my soul like a fairy dream . . . Every pulsation of my heart belongs to the Monarchical principle which for me is

embodied in the Person of Your Majesty. I am always prepared to shed the last drop of my blood for the triumph of Kingship and the Person of the Sovereign.

In spite of the fulsomeness of this baroque rigmarole Ludwig's confidence in Dürckheim was justified and, when the hour of trial came, he was certainly one of the few apart from the peasants who was prepared to shed the last drop of his blood for his King.

It was a sign of Ludwig's trust and confidence that within a few weeks of their meeting he sent Dürckheim to Nymphenburg to report personally on the condition of Otto:

> There are some favourable changes in the health of H.R.H. Prince Otto . . . Two days ago he gave up the strict fasting . . . He is now much happier, less self-centred, and less absorbed by horrid dreams and, although he still sees only Baron Branca, H.R.H. more often took part in the general conversation at dinner . . . To-day started with the warm baths . . . The strongly religious atmosphere seems to continue . . . but whether this improvement will last, or whether it is only the stillness before the storm, it is difficult to say.

On October 12th, very quietly, in the little Church of Waltenhoven near Hohenschwangau, Marie, the Queen Mother, was received into the Roman Catholic Faith and every human being who knows of her existence must hope that in its wide and hospitable arms she found not only assuagement of her past and present griefs, but new strength for the greater sorrows that were yet to come.

1875

On May 18th Sir Robert Morier, Her Britannic Majesty's Chargé d'Affaires in Munich, writing about the death of Princess Alexandra the King's insane aunt, to Sir Henry Ponsonby, Private Secretary to Queen Victoria, said that, although the theatres were ordered to be shut, the King shocked public opinion by having his favourite Louis XIV play acted for himself alone while his Aunt Alexandra lay dead, and by leaving Munich the day before the funeral.

This poor lady, who always insisted on being dressed in white and who was always so much in Ludwig's mind, was buried in the Theatiner Church beside her brother Maximilian II within a hundred yards of Ludwig's east windows in the Residenz.

In his report to the Foreign Office in London Morier went on to say that a contemplated visit to England by Otto would never take place, and gave his reasons :

MUNICH, *May 30th, 1875.*

. . . his state has much worsened during the last month and the whole town is talking of an esclandre which happened on the occasion of the Corpus Christi Festival three days ago. The King, who is cross with the Church, would not attend, or allow the Princes to take part in it. This seems to have worked on Prince Otto's mind (whose hallucinations have of late taken a religious turn) and, just as the procession was entering the Cathedral, he burst through the cordon of soldiers lining the streets, rushed in (dressed in a shooting jacket and wideawake) and threw himself on the steps of the altar before the officiating Archbishop and began in a loud voice a general confession of his sins. It was with the greatest difficulty that he was conveyed into the vestry and got into a quieter state of mind.[1]

What Morier refrained from saying was that the merry Otto accused himself of having committed the unforgivable sin against the Holy Ghost.

A few days later Ludwig wrote to Queen Amalie of Greece what turned out to be his last letter to her, because she herself died soon after :

BERG, *May 19, [1875].*

Although it is always painful for the survivors when a member leaves the family circle for ever, it really was a very good thing in the case of dear Aunt Alexandra. Her continuous sufferings from her nervous disease were seldom interrupted by moments of happiness.

[1] Morier, Sir Robert Burnett David, 1826–1893 : quoted in *Henry Ponsonby, His Life from his Letters,* by Arthur Ponsonby (London, 1942, Macmillan), p. 340.

Ludwig to his Mother :

HALBAMMER, *June 14, 1875.*

Otto suffers more than ever from tormenting hallucinations and religious scruples.

A special performance of *Götterdämmerung* was announced for August 6th in Munich at which Ludwig and Wagner met for the first time after an interval of seven years.

Before leaving home for another visit to France, as an extraordinary concession to public opinion, Ludwig, amidst popular enthusiasm, reviewed some fourteen thousand Bavarian troops in Munich. He was intent on spending the thirtieth anniversary of his birth at Rheims where the French kings were crowned, once more saturating himself in memories of Royalist France. Again he was accompanied by Holnstein.

Ludwig to Frau von Leonrod :

BERG, *August 28th, 1875.*

Yesterday back from Rheims. I visited all the places which have any association with Royalism . . . My hotel was close to the house where Saint Joan once lived. Opposite I had the wonderful cathedral which I could not stop looking at . . .

Ludwig to the Crown Prince Rudolf of Austria :

Fortunate and enviable one, to whom it is granted to spend so much time with the august Empress, pray lay me at her feet and beseech her in my name graciously to remember her faithful slave, who always honoured her from of old, and will do so for ever. It was great comfort to me when Louis sent me an assurance from Godollo last October that the Empress would curb her impetuosity in riding. Never in my life should I recover from my grief if any accident were to befall her. God forbid such a thing ! And may he preserve you and me from such an appalling experience.

I will have your portrait framed, so that I may always have it before my eyes, together with that of the Empress. For nobody on earth is so dear to me as you and she are. Please remember me most cordially to the Emperor. I am spending these winter days most gloriously among the mountains, absorbed in fascinating books, which are my dearest pleasure.

The Crown Prince Rupprecht of Bavaria has a collection of over a hundred portraits, sketches and photographs of Ludwig.   Scrutinizing them for the purposes of this biography was a sad, haunting, indeed a humiliating experience, exemplifying as they do, how sanity can tragically decline, self-control vanish, youth and beauty prematurely decay. There is amongst those of Ludwig a photograph of Rudolf in cavalry uniform taken not long before his mysterious death in 1889 and, if ever ultimate despair looked out of a pair of haunted eyes, it looks out of his.   Fated alike to failure, frustration and finally self-murder, Rudolf and Ludwig were twin souls.   These two men seem to disprove the popular theory that environment and economic status govern the destiny of the individual and not atavism. Those two men were King Ludwig II of Bavaria and Rudolf Crown Prince of Austria-Hungary.   Both men were brilliant and the collection as a whole bears witness to the truth of Dryden's couplet :

> Great wits are sure to madness near allied,
> And their partitions do their bounds divide.

1876

In the spring of the year Ludwig resided for a period in Munich as a King.   He held all the customary Court Ceremonies and entertainments, received the members of the Royal Family and foreign Royalties, the Cardinal Archbishop, the great Officers of State, and the members of the Cabinet, in the magnificent suite of state rooms overlooking the Hofgarten.   Reached by the Emperor's staircase, a triumph of German Renaissance art, they stretched from the white hall through the throne room, the Barbarossa hall and the great ballroom to terminate fittingly in the Gallery of Bavarian Beauties from which Stieler's portrait of Lola Montez had long since disappeared.   Wearing the full dress of a Bavarian General and the riband collar and Grand Cross of S. Hubertus and the Collar and Grand Crosses of S. George and the Austrian Golden Fleece,

Ludwig was an imposingly kingly figure, his great height carrying off a measure of portliness that would have dwarfed a shorter man.

There can be few who remember that Royal reception ; possibly the only person now alive who was present is the Crown Prince Rupprecht, then a lad in his first uniform. It was the first of the only two occasions on which he came into personal contact with Ludwig, who spoke to him with a kindliness and charm that are vivid memories after the passage of three-quarters of a century.

For those few weeks of that spring Ludwig seemed to have escaped from his cage ; to have resumed his rightful place and regal duties with all the ardour that he displayed when he ascended the throne. But, like Otto's visit to southern Italy and brief return to normality, it was only one of those ambiguous sunsets that so often presage a night of storm.

Those to whom a royal command to attend a state ceremonial is, quite rightly, the accolade of success have small notion of the fatigue and boredom engendered by a ceremonial existence. From childhood to their very death-bed Royal personages must practise the ready smile, the appreciative look, the tactful greetings, the unfailing memory, the cordial hand-shake, whatever their inner griefs.

To Ludwig, whose spiritual home was the Bavarian highlands, whose refuge solitude and books, who in thirty years had failed to find one faithful friend amongst glittering throngs and state cavalcades, the whole pageant of Sovereignty which, at first, he had loved soon became anathema.

For some time Dürckheim, at the King's command, had been spying out for nice, amenable candidates for Ministerial office, and for pliant personalities for the King's secretarial staff. At the end of March he was appointed a Royal Chamberlain and his cup of happiness just boiled over :

March 30th, 1876.

As I stood before Your Majesty I felt a magic power over me, and all the excitement of the last two days, all the worries and troubles which had made my loyal soul restless—all vanished in the magic moment when I saw Your Majesty . . . The search for a suitable Chef de Cabinet

continues unsuccessfully.   The Chef whom Your Majesty
needs must be not only devoted and faithful as a rock—
which, thank God, thousands are—but he must be absolutely trustworthy, must have more than usual acuteness
and ripeness of judgment, great skill, great energy, and
must be of an iron constitution.   I must confess that, at
the present moment, I do not know of anyone who could
guarantee all that.   I have often wondered whether
amongst the present members of the Coalition such a
man could be found.

On April the 9th he reported that ' such a man as the
post calls for he is not yet in a position to name and that
he would not dare to propose anyone whom he could not
guarantee '.

On June 15 Ludwig had to approve of Otto being
gazetted out of the Army, thereby publicly admitting that,
as far as life in public was concerned, his only brother and
heir was finished.   His military career was honourable.
In 1866, like his uncle Prince Leopold, he served with the
Bavarians against the Prussians ; in 1871 he took part in
the battle of Paris and in the siege ; in 1873 he had been
promoted Major-General.   Now, at the age of twenty-
eight, all was over and Ludwig companionless.

As his letters prove, Dürckheim's loquaciousness was so
inherent that not even his faultless loyalty could curb it.
His was not the temperament of a Grey Eminence secretly
shaping the whisper of a throne.   Unmaking, and trying
to make, Ministers of State, dismissing and replacing the
King's immediate entourage, scanning Europe for secret
loans, being the only senior officer close to the King—all
went to his devoted but woolly head and he talked and
boasted.   Friedrich von Zeigler, who had been Ludwig's
devoted and monumentally patient Cabinet Secretary for
years, became a pliant tool and thus unwittingly helped to
bring about his Master's downfall.   Yet, however unwise
some of the advice given to Ludwig by Dürckheim and
Zeigler, and however stupid some of their actions, they had
a proper standing at Court and in the country and were
immeasurably superior to the subservient menials who
were so soon to supplant them.   As for Hornig, the position

he had by now come to occupy in the Royal entourage is
shown by the following letter from him to Zeigler to whom
he writes as an equal :

HOHENSCHWANGAU, *July 15th, 1876.*

My dear Friend :
   . . . On the first night at the Schlux His Majesty
talked himself into a rage which will probably last for some
time . . .   Although it was already very late yesterday
—two o'clock—His Majesty sent a long letter to Prince
Bismarck.   I only know that he said how angry he was
about the Emperor, and that he felt very much offended.
That the Emperor ought to be grateful was of course not
forgotten.   We shall see what the Prince replies ; if only
I could dictate it ! . . .   Since the King left Berg he has
never gone to bed before four a.m.   You have seen for
yourself when he gets up.   Just like Prince Otto.   Please
give my respects to your wife ; with heartfelt greetings,
Sincerely yours

HORNIG.

On the evening of the 5th–6th of August Ludwig was in
Bayreuth for the opening of Wagner's new theatre when
the great occasion was signalized by the first complete performance of *Der Ring des Nibelungen*.   To Ludwig's chagrin
the Emperor Wilhelm I was also there and, as he was not
known as a lover of music and had never done overmuch
to encourage or help Wagner, Ludwig saw in his presence
another covert attempt by Berlin to overawe Munich.
Compelled to sit in the *Fürstenloge* between the Emperor
and Wagner, Ludwig's tumultuous feelings can be imagined.
Hans Richter, who had copied the Ring Cycle for Wagner
at Triebschen, came from Vienna to direct and conduct
the first performances.   Soon he was to awaken musical
England to the delights of the new music by conducting
the Wagner Festival at the Albert Hall ; later the Richter
Concerts were a revelation to Londoners ; created by
Oxford a Doctor of Music, he conducted the first performances in England of *Die Meistersinger* and *Tristan and
Isolde* at Drury Lane, ending up in 1900 as the conductor
of the magnificent Hallé Orchestra in Manchester.
   On that unique occasion on an August evening in little

Bayreuth, Ludwig, whether he realized it or not—and the probabilities are that he did not—was listening to a great modern conductor who established the Wagner tradition and whose interpretations, derived directly from the tuition of the Master himself, were incomparable.

Ludwig, who received a tumultuous reception, far out-vying that given to the Emperor, was astonished that the people were not ' Prussianized '. He stayed at the Ere-mitage where, surrounded by gardens, fountains, artificial ruins and memorials of Frederick the Great's sister, the notable Margravine Wilhelmine, he could forget Prussia and the existing state of things.

Ludwig to his Mother :

> BAYREUTH, EREMITAGE, *August 28th, 1876.*
> The festival performances are very beautiful and interesting ; also I do enjoy staying in the Eremitage which I used to like even as a child. Otto, curiously enough, never wrote or telegraphed for my birthday.

Some two weeks later he returned to Bayreuth, strictly incognito, to pay a visit to the Great Friend.

The subterranean activities of Zeigler and Dürckheim could not of course remain long a secret and very soon rumours were flying about to the effect that because of the good Bavarian money he had squandered on Wagner and his music, and on building castles in such inaccessible places that few of his faithful subjects could even see them, the King was up to his neck in debt and scouring around for a loan in the most unlikely and undignified quarters.

In September Clodwig Hohenlohe, at the German Imperial Embassy in Paris, noted in his Diary that Erlanger the banker ' who has just left me, says that the rumour of the King of Bavaria's money difficulties is a fabrication. If the King were in need of money he would apply to his [Erlanger's] father, who would never refuse him five hundred thousand florins. He described as equally senseless the assertion that a syndicate had been formed here to raise money for the King.' However, Erlanger was wrong and, for once in a way, rumour was correct.

Ludwig to Frau von Leonrod :

BERG, *September 12, 1876.*

. . . Poor Otto ! For a long long time I had no news from him personally about his health ; he seems to suffer more than we all imagined ; he very urgently needs a better doctor. Brattler—as I learnt from Branca—is rather careless . . .

1877

On January 7th of this year Ludwig wrote to his Mother saying that he ' is furious about the articles in the *Augsburger Schmetterer* belittling Wagner's fame.' On the 21st he resumed that, to him, most insidious of drugs, the secret Diary. The whole entry is in French :

In the King's name I swear to-day—the 21st of January of terrible memory, the anniversary of the assassination of the King of France and of Navarre, Louis XVI by name—that what took place yesterday night was the last time for ever ; atoned for by the Royal Blood !—(The Holy Grail). Absolutely the last time under penalty of ceasing to be King ! Sworn the 21st January 1877 at Hohenschwangau (ten years after the year so costly to so many rights). [1]

It is worth recalling that on May 17th of this year the magical strains of parts of *Parsifal* were first heard in London by a small group of cognoscenti assembled in the house of Edward George Dannreuther, an Alsatian residing in a charming little house at number twelve Orme Square, Hyde Park. It was not until five years later that the full score was heard at Bayreuth.

Acting as Zeigler's agent behind the scenes, Hornig sent him the following note :

KENZEN, *July 13th, 1877.*

If he sticks to his intention, the King will write to-morrow to the Empress at Feldafing in order to ask her to permit him to see her once more on the 23rd or 24th, and then go for a walk alone with her on the island, and make a round trip on the lake by steamer. The King is

[1] The reference is of course to the results of the Austro-Prussian War of 1866.

longing for the Empress : what do you say to this ? It
is to be hoped that the Empress will not allow him to
come ; anyhow the letter is not written yet and his longing may cease.

On the 28th Ludwig made a long entry in his Diary.
Partly retrospective, it referred to incidents that took place
on the 7th at Berg and at Hohenschwangau on the 22nd.
Fernstein, where the inevitable oath was signed and sealed,
was a modest hunting-box on the lovely little Fernsee near
the Austrian frontier :

> On the 7 July night in Berg, at Hohenschwangau night
> of the 22nd July 1846 (symbolic—allegorical significance
> (1866)) 1877 year of Redemption !—The Royal Lily
> triumphs and makes any relapse quite impossible !—
> July 30 days still, then never, never, never more. (Sym-
> bolic, allegorical significance) 1877 year of Redemption !
> (30 to 31 years) 1866 time of Lilies (year of the *Nibelungen*
> R W and L.R. Once more a risk of that fall and the
> right to the Crown and the Royal Throne has to be for-
> feited. I, the King. (the 30 July to the 31 during the
> night *des present impossible*).—Saturday the 28 July 1877
> Fernstein. Rain 6 hours there, 3 years (except August)
> Lilies-number, since the first sight of ' Versailles ' 10 years
> since the first visit to the soil of France also in July 10
> since I saw Richard and learnt to know him.—Definitely
> the *last* risk of falling ! *Jour de St. Louis 77* purified by
> Versailles ! Rheims ! *Le souvenir de Louis XIV et de la
> Royaute absolue—Not one* kiss more, no more excitement,
> not in *speaking*, not in *writing*, not *acts*. Magic of the
> Lilies.—Purity, Kinship ! ! ! I bind myself to remember
> without fail to open no more, or get excited. Given
> today, during the year 1877 in remembrance of the
> beautiful days in 1867, that is 10 years ago.
> Fernstein 28th July 1877.
>   RICHARD.   LUDWIG.

On August 28th Ludwig wrote from Berg to his Mother
saying that he doubts very much if she will be able to see
Otto ' who is said to be very excitable ' ; on September 7th
he was at Linderhof and confided to the Diary :

> . . . Birthday on the Schachen . . . Read much in

Wolfram von Eschenbach's *Parsifal* . . . Impressed anew by these immortal sagas and poems because they inspired R. Wagner's wonderful *Parsifal*, the libretto of which the Master sent me in manuscript during the course of this summer. How I long to see this work completed and composed.

Megalomania increased. His first tutor Klass had as usual written to him for his birthday and Ludwig announced that the passage in which the old man said that ' he would like to speak as a father to his son ' was pronounced ' eminently unsuitable '. Klass is to be told this ' either verbally or in writing '.

There is one more Diary entry for this year. It is undated, but appears to have been written subsequent to September 13th :

Au Roy

In this letter is given the *order* and with it also the necessity and possibility of fully abstaining from kisses, *anathema* in *aeternum* ! Therefore conquered at the age of 32 and not quite 3 weeks, the last misfortune. Terribly near the brink of a complete fall, night of the 12–13 Sept. 77. *Damned* be the *blinding apparition* which oppresses our *senses*.—Sworn *never* and *never never* again, in the year of the completion of Linderhof and in the yr. before the beginning of the *Building of Chiemsee* (Versailles).

1878

Like so many others, Ludwig began the New Year with good resolutions which, as usual, he confided to the Diary :

The House of Loretto and the blessed power of Heaven and the Holy Sepulchre which purifies the whole world. Powerful is also the prayer of the religious—they have rich stores or merit. *Espérance d'être racheté par le Sang Royal, innocent et répandu.*—The benediction and kiss of the [unreadable] . . . Emperor and King diminishes the pernicious effects of that fall, it is health-giving, strengthening and it contains the germs of victory and peace.— Valid for 1878. Before number XII of the year of my reign was completed, and therefore the miserable fatal number 13 was still in the ascendant, the 'last' fall occurred !—Shortly before I became 33 years of age (33 (: 3 × 3 :) 9 the number of the steps of the *throne* power of self-command achieved when I have reached this number,) all very near to 31 (13, last number of fall,) now gone [unreadable] penitence is absolutely necessary !

On January 5th he wrote Frau von Leonrod from Hohenschwangau :

I have returned to my mountains after I had the great pleasure of seeing the beautiful and charming Empres of Austria and her son, the highly-talented Crown Prince who is a great friend of mine.

There now comes into the picture a valet or lackey, Alfonso Welcker, whose devotion to his master seems to have been sincere and constant. As, during the last eight or ten years of Ludwig's life, he exercised considerable influence behind the scenes and, towards the end, played a decisive if somewhat ambiguous rôle something must be said about him.

It is not definitely known when Welcker entered the Royal service except that it was (as usual) in the rapturous month of May, but by 1878, he was definitely a person of consequence in Ludwig's most intimate entourage.

On January 23rd, from Linderhof, he, on behalf of Ludwig, wrote to Zeigler about an important matter. Whether Hornig was away or temporarily in disgrace, is unknown ; but it is the first recorded occasion on which the King communicated with his most trusted and confidential official through a domestic servant.

Properly speaking, Zeigler's rôle was that of liaison officer between the King and the Cabinet ; but as Ludwig's disinclination to see and confer with his Ministers became stronger, and as he visited Munich more and more infrequently, Zeigler's power and influence increased so that in a short time he became virtually Prime Minister. In refusing to play his proper rôle in the Constitution, Ludwig forgot his grandfather's wise injunction : ' A function that remains unexercised is soon lost altogether.'

Welcker's language was always perfectly correct and suggests a man of some education and talent not entirely

ignorant of social etiquette.   Nevertheless, had Zeigler from
the moment he became Cabinet Secretary in January,
respectfully and firmly declined to receive his Sovereign's
orders through Hornig, Welcker, or any other unauthorized
person, he would have done himself honour and rendered
his King an incalculable service.   Ludwig knew well
enough when to avoid forcing an issue and, had their
baroque senility not prevented his entourage from promptly
resenting unwarranted humiliations, Ludwig's imperiousness
might never have developed into monomania and his reign
ended in disaster.

Bürkel to Zeigler :

October 4th, 1878.

Hornig has to talk to the King for three hours daily,
and Hesselschwerdt goes on lying bravely.   Immediately
after my second bow the King noticed that I was cross—
which, by the way, was the case ; as a reason I gave the
financial situation ; the many unsolved problems ; and
so on.   He would not listen . . .

At the end of the year Otto was finally declared insane.
He was the one person to whom Ludwig clung throughout
his life ; he admired him, looked to him to marry and continue the succession in the direct line.   His grief was heart-
rending and touched all who witnessed it.   As for Otto—
he was indifferent.

Linderhof was at last finished ; Chiemsee and Neuschwanstein begun : but of what use was that ?   Otto
was gone.

The tragic death of Princess Alice of Great Britain, Grand
Duchess of Hesse-Darmstadt, touched the general public
in both England and Germany.   Her child had diphtheria
and she was forbidden to kiss it.   The child asked for a kiss ;
she gave it, and died.

On December 27th Ludwig, recalling happier days, wrote
from Hohenschwangau to his Mother :

How beautiful it was three years ago when Otto was
with us under the Christmas Tree.   Alice's death is a
great loss for all in Hesse and in England.   Everywhere
people are sincerely sorry.   I only knew her a little, but

felt great sympathy for her ; she was always extremely charming to me.

1879

The last seven years of Ludwig's life were filled with such overmastering horror as must condone his worst faults in the eyes of all humanely-minded people. He knew quite definitely that, as he had long dreaded, he was going mad, saw, as inevitable for himself, the terrible fate that had gradually, but surely, overtaken Otto. From that hour Ludwig's misanthropy, his excesses, his loneliness, steadily increased. He was a man beset. Obsessed or, in the older and better word, possessed. In illegitimate gratifications, he vainly sought some assuagement of his very real physical, mental and emotional agony and his dread of insanity.

Between April and December, 1879, he was always in the mountains ; he continued to communicate with Zeigler through Welcker, mostly from almost inaccessible mountain hideouts.

On May 10th, sending Zeigler a curl of his hair, he wrote :

As Don Carlos said to his friend Roderick, so I say to you : ' I throw myself into your arms, Friedrich, I embrace thee firmly and remain faithful to you for ever.'

An immoral relationship is not in question ; it is merely that by now even his Chef de cabinet was to him but a character in a play. A little later he signed himself to Zeigler ' Tibi in aeternum '. Apart from his childish love of charades there was in Ludwig the child's sly intention to profit by flattery. These, and similar expressions, were later on wrongfully used at Ludwig's secret trial to discredit Zeigler.

At the end of October Bürkel made a long report to the King about golden countries far away. Ideal Otherlands, to which Ludwig now wanted to emigrate because reality had become finally intolerable and Bavaria and the Bavarians were hateful.

Bürkel, who had been sent in search of El Dorado, claimed to have travelled almost everywhere, including places as unlikely as the ' Mosquito coast ' and the territory of Angostura in Venezuela, taking in his giant stride Egypt, Afghanistan, the Philippines, Colombia, Costa Rica, the islands of Mallorca, Chiloé off the coast of Chile, Samos and, nearer home, Rügen on the Baltic.   Bürkel, however, was not optimistic and declared to Ludwig that there was ' no doubt about it but that, without one exception, Bavarians were by nature the most faithful and devoted people ' ; he ended his unwelcome report with a generous dose of baroque flattery.

Throughout the year Ludwig saw practically no one who by virtue of birth or official status might be presumed to have the entrée to his presence.   Welcker, acting as his private, confidential secretary, was employed to transmit the Sovereign's orders to all and sundry.

CHAPTER TWELVE

JOSEF KAINZ : THE POOR UNKNOWN : 1880–1882

1881

A MERE recital of the outward facts in a man's life can be grossly misleading : indeed, as they are practically all we have concerning Ludwig II, they can (if taken solely at their surface value) amount to distortion. It is therefore the biographer's duty to pause now and again and try honestly to peer beneath the surface ; gently insinuate a scalpel beneath the surface. For several reasons 1881 is particularly suitable for this purpose. It was the year of climax in the final lustrum of Ludwig's inner and outer life ; Wagner paid his farewell visit to Munich ; Ludwig found and lost his last and most sincere friend and the Diary is more detailed, more coherent, and less cryptic than for any other period.

At the beginning of the year Ludwig placed the orchestra and chorus of the large and handsome Munich Court Theatre at the disposal of the Great Friend for a period of two months. In January *Lohengrin* was given and King and Composer heard together the opera that first drew them to one another, and the magical purity theme of which, like a Wagner leitmotif, runs, somewhat fitfully, through the secret Diary, redeeming its adolescent smuttishness. Practically the whole month was joyfully given up by Ludwig to his distinguished guest, and its high moments duly recorded.

On Tuesday the 11th Wagner and Ludwig dined alone in the Winter Garden at five o'clock and they enjoyed ' intimate precious hours ' ; at eight o'clock they sat together in the lovely little Residenz Theatre, which could be reached direct from the Royal apartments and the Royal box entered unseen. The duality and disjointedness of Ludwig's mental processes are forcibly illustrated by his odd manner of making entries in the Diary. To illustrate this the following passages are set out exactly as written :

News.   Richard Wagner here.   Considered certain special
things for Schloss Chiemsee.
Was present with Richard Wagner at the performance of
Lohengrin, very successful and beautiful.   He present,
with Him in the apartment, sup-
ped in the Wintergarten, a long time together.
On the 11th at 5 o'clock he came to dine (Wintergarten)
intimate, precious hours.   8 o'clock.   I Residenz Theatre.
'Aus dem Stegreif.'   Precious remembrances of the
Queen Marie Antoinette !   To the Royal
France of the Lilies !   On the 12. in the afternoon twice
heard the miraculous
and glorious prelude to Parsifal conducted by the creator
himself.   Profoundly significant.
Also the Prelude to Lohengrin.   Present with Him in the
evening at 'Aus dem Stegreif', very successful performance.   I have always heard it said that there is no
friendship possible between
Prince and subject.   We will prove that at
supper in the Wintergarten—3 o'clock—Saturday
the 13th at 3.30 with him at the Opera Aida . . .
magnificent performance, happy with Him, about 6.30
o'clock left, with Him via Nymphenburg to the Railway
Station, the beloved Lake, looked in the direction of Berg
(May) Staltach departure.   Cordial and sad.   Happiness
and blessings on His beloved head—
Last fall after the double date of 18 (majority) and, by the
greatest luck, another nearly one and a half years of twice
the number
of years of my life as 'King' 19.   No more, no more, no
more.
Sworn anew in the octave of Good Friday.

The Friends never met again.
It is perhaps not obvious from the concluding lines of the
foregoing that what really happened was this :—Making
a detour from the Residenz in order to pass Nymphenberg
they drove to Staltach railway station just south of Starnberg
and, passing 'the beloved lake', Ludwig looked towards
Berg and thought nostalgically of May 'the month of rapture' of seventeen years before.
The words after 'beloved head' have nothing to do with
that occasion, and are left as written in order further to

illustrate the incoherent style used throughout the Diary : having in its two handsome volumes ample room there was no reason why Ludwig should so often run one entry into another, or avoid dating them in normal fashion. The urge to confess was imperative ; he wanted for himself a record of his lapses and vows and childishly imagined that his involved and cabalistic style would preserve his secret. There are many examples of this sort of thing in auto-biography and literature, notably the Gondal diaries of the Brontës.

In the spring of this year, for reasons best known to himself, Ernst von Possart, Director of the Court Theatres, sent Ludwig a photograph of a hard-working Austrian actor of Hungarian extraction aged twenty-three, Josef Kainz who, after tasting the beginnings of success in his own country, had recently joined the Munich Court Theatre in order to gain further professional experience. The photograph showed a boyish, wistful face, with beautiful eyes and sensitive mouth. It pleased Ludwig. Swallowing the bait, he ordered Baron von Perfall, the Intendant, who had no great opinion of Kainz as an actor, to put Hugo's *Marion de Lorme* into rehearsal at once with Kainz in the part of Didier. Ludwig was a great admirer of Hugo, knew many of his plays almost by heart, and his febrile imagination was immediately aflame with a vision of himself as the Marquess de Saverny and Kainz as Didier—with all that their relationships implied.

On Friday, April 29, Ludwig heard *Tristan and Isolde* : ' Imperishably beloved and glorious ; it sounds so old and yet so new like the song of the birds in lovely May.' Next day (Saturday) he saw the eagerly awaited production of *Marion de Lorme* and recorded its impact in three words: 'Didier deep impression.' He immediately sent 'Didier' a ring.

It was at once acknowledged in the following letter, the first of fifty-five from Kainz to Ludwig preserved in the secret Archives :

MUNICH, *May 1st, 1881.*

Most Gracious, Most Powerful King !
Most Gracious King and Master !
In profound humility I take the liberty of laying at

Your Most Gracious Majesty's feet my profound thanks for the precious ring which Your Most Gracious Majesty did me the honour of sending to me.

Your Most Gracious Majesty may be convinced that I shall do my best to prove worthy of the gift with which Your Most Gracious Majesty has honoured me and that I shall always try to earn Your Majesty's satisfaction.

Dying in profoundest humility,
Your most exalted Majesty's
Most humble and faithfully devoted servant,
JOSEF KAINZ,
Kgl. bayr. Hofschauspieler.
(Royal Bavarian Court actor).

On Wednesday, May 4th, *Marion de Lorme* was repeated by command and Ludwig recorded : ' Marvellous ! (The May, the May has come !) ' and sent ' Didier ' a gold chain with (of course) a swan attached. Even after receiving Kainz's first letter Ludwig was incapable of thinking of him as a human being. He was still—perhaps indeed always—only a mummer who by means of a quick intelligence, fascinating personality, pliant body, and a marvellously sensitive and creatively responsive imagination, seemed to Ludwig to make his secret dreams come true.

On Monday, May 9th, Ludwig saw his friend Frau Lewinsky in a ' rather successful performance ' of *La Marquise de Pompadour*—' actor who played Didier present '. This was indeed a signal honour for Kainz, one rarely, if ever, granted to the highest in the land. Ludwig, almost invisible in the great Royal box in the centre of the circle, sent an equerry with a copy of the libretto and a pair of opera glasses to his lonely guest. Links were being forged : instinctively or stealthily, who can say ?

Then came the decisive day, Tuesday, May 10th, and once again, as when he sent Paul Taxis to Wagner in August 1866, Ludwig was considering abdication, ready to abandon the substance for the shadow. Only for Wagner and Kainz did he plan to make this sacrifice, and it is significant that both were artists, and to him both well worth while. The Diary records :

On the 10th of May farewell to the
Reich Zimmer and to the Throne—

and, apparently without any sense of incongruity, the announced performance of the *Meistersinger* was countermanded and *Marion de Lorme* substituted : Kainz had dethroned Wagner ; Didier replaced the Knight of the Swan. The Reich Zimmer, a magnificent eighteenth-century suite of state rooms, exemplified late rococo style at its best and purest, vying in loveliness with the Amalienburg. Including the Throne room where he took his oath to the Constitution, these stately apartments represented to Ludwig his crown, his sceptre, his kingly office. He often mentioned them, and they were not only the inspiration for the decoration of his private apartment in the Residenz, but for much of the decorations of Linderhof and Schloss Chiemsee. Now, for a phantom friendship, his starved soul and hungry heart urged him to abandon everything that normally he held dear. Ludwig, like all men, was slain by his dream.

Of this, to him epoch-making, performance the Diary says :

Instead of Meistersinger Marion de Lorme was given, emotional, deeply touching impression ! ' Shall I more shiningly glorify your life ? '

Next day he quoted :

' 11 May—so unseparated we died, eternally united.'

Then he left for Berg, and little Kainz, overcome with the strangeness of this living play into which he had been so suddenly tumbled, wrote to the King. A simple-minded, lower middle-class Hungarian, his bewilderment is understandable ; yet it was as nothing compared with what was to come. It is almost possible to overhear his feverish breathing as he composed the following letter to Ludwig :

Great psychic emotions make a man speechless. In vain he wrestles with words in order to give the feelings of his heart some shape—but does not find them. And when at last he has found the word and imagines that the feelings of his heart are expressed in sound, they appear cold, stiff and desecrated. ' The word kills ' it says in the Bible.

And so I feel to-day as I take up my pen in order to lay before Your Most Gracious Majesty my very humble thanks for the two most gracious rounds of applause which Your Most Gracious Majesty did me the favour of giving me last night—also for the beautifully-made watch covered with brilliants and the picture representing Poesy. Joy, happiness and enchantment threaten to burst my bosom. Oh, could I do a great deed in order to give Your Most Gracious Majesty a proof of how profoundly I am penetrated by the feelings of gratitude towards Your Most Gracious Majesty—oh, could I die for Your Majesty !

The Diary recorded the arrival of this letter. On Thursday, May 18th, Ludwig had luncheon and tea at Seeleiten, Richard Hornig's home on Lake Starnberg and, with an unnamed friend, enjoyed a walk along the lakeside. On Friday, the 19th, the Diary implored : ' Good fortune and blessings on the actor of Didier ', and he was sent a copy of Hugo's *Hernani*. In thanking him for it on the 19th the actor wrote :

Should Your Most Gracious Majesty be pleased to entrust me with the title rôle I shall try to fulfil the task with the greatest love and diligence in order that Your Most Gracious Majesty may be pleased with my representation of that magnificent part.

Meanwhile in Munich, Kainz, industrious and ambitious, and who afterwards became one of the greatest actors that Germany has produced, was eager to grasp a unique opportunity.

Before he met Kainz, spoke to him, touched his hand and looked into his eyes, Ludwig was casting him for a visionary part that no human being could possibly sustain, dooming their relationships to frustration. All he knew of the man Kainz was what could be discerned through his disguise as Didier—and the greater the actor the more complete the disguise : the mere glimpse vouchsafed by his short-sighted eyes in an auditorium which his aesthetic discernment insisted on being dark cannot have told Ludwig much.

On May 30th the Diary records : ' In the night arrived

the actor of Didier. ' For Ludwig, Kainz was not, even yet, quite a human being ; he was still the character in the play. After his long and tiring journey from Munich to Linderhof the poor devil scrambled into an evening coat and white tie and was conducted through the midsummer night by Bürkel to the Blue Grotto with its small lake and waterfall illuminated—like the rococo sleigh—with brilliant light. The King was disappointed. He had so completely identified Kainz with the heroic fictitious lover of the play ' and was so worked up emotionally ' that he could not at first stomach this slim, unimposing little man whose ductile body, it must be admitted, looked when in mufti something not unlike that of an inferior haberdasher's assistant.

However, it was to everyone's interest to keep Ludwig in a good humour. Bürkel whispered to Kainz : ' Act man, act ! '

He acted ; in fact he ranted and, as he did so, Ludwig thawed. They were ' together until the morning '. The 31st was spent in and around the Schloss.

With him to Kiosk then Hundings
Hütte . . . rowboat on the lake . . . much
talk . . . into the Moroccan house . . . Magic
of the marvellous voice.

Kainz had to read aloud for hours without stopping. It was Ludwig's holiday—not Kainz's ! They read Byron, and Calderon's *Phaeton* ; Kainz, in fact, read till he nearly dropped dead with fatigue. He was well accustomed to sustaining the long, verbose rôles of Victor Hugo and his kind but, in doing so, he had the help of association, costume, scenery, colleagues and audience. Now it had all to be done in cold blood for a solitary listener who was a King. Nor was subterfuge of any sort possible. Had Kainz cut a tedious passage, skipped a boring scene, or misread a line Ludwig, with his prodigious verbal memory, would at once have jumped on him.

Wednesday, June 1st.

Drove to the Plansee, walked, then
went by steamer, Kaiserbrunnen, meal,
works of Byron . . . precious, glorious hours.

Thursday, June 2nd.

Drove to Graswang-thal,
meal under the lindens . . . to the
Moroccan house, coffee, etc.   Again
heard the heavenly voice.   Studied
Don Carlos, illumination of the
grotto.   Kiosk.

Friday, June 3rd.

To the Brunnenkopf (Phaeton
by Calderon) together to the
Purschling (Tell) Remembrance
of ' Marion de Lorme '—Didier . . .
Down arm in arm . . .

Saturday, June 4th.

He with me to Oberammergau . . . precious
hours, back in the dawn Admonishment :
arrange better divisions of the day.

Sunday, June 5th.

Whitsunday, little walks, Kiosk, meal,
very intimate and beautiful hours.
drove to Graswang-thal (very serene),
Decamerone.   Grotto (presented chalice
of dream)

Monday, June 6th.

Whitmonday.   He with me to Partenkirchen,
Partnach-klamm, meal, temple of
Venus [1] (Medea, Grillparzer),
Coffee, Kiosk,
drove as far as the turning point
in the Ammerwald.

The word serene only occurs in the Diary a few times ;
its use to describe events on that Whitsunday is significant,
especially in view of what was to happen (unrecorded by
Ludwig) on the following day.   A well-known student of
Palmistry examined in 1951 a photograph of Ludwig's
right hand and, without knowing who he was, ended an

---

[1] A small temple high up with a figure of Venus and the best view
of the Schloss and gardens.

acute delineation with : ' I should not be surprised to learn that he lived his life in a continuous state of conflict.'

Ludwig is a perfect example of arrested development. All his friendships had in them the impulses that drive love-sick adolescents to suicide—the weak way out. Indeed, suicide was never far from his thoughts. Then, like most adolescents, he had a high ideal of love and friendship ; his letters to Paul of Taxis, Wagner, Richard Hornig, Vari-court and Kainz prove that the beings to whom he addressed them never existed—were mere figments of his pulsating fantasy, as were his idealized vision of Marie Antoinette, Elizabeth of Austria and Sophie, all, by the way, as German as Wagner's Elsa, Brünhilde or Isolde.

Ludwig's two favourite English authors were Shakespeare and Byron and, like them, he lived half in a sordid world of reality, and half in an ideal world of imagination, without their power to find release and purification in a vast creative-ness. The limitations of his own temperament enabled him to appreciate with extraordinary clarity the bi-sexuality in both ; Byron, being nearer to him in time and richly documented, was the greater favourite and although he never spoke English well, he read it with ease and pleasure. Led by Goethe, all cultivated Germans had a profound admiration for Byron.

The biographical hints in the *Sonnets* would not have been lost on Ludwig, and he would have clearly grasped the implications in Byron's *Thyrza*, his poems to his Harrow School friends, and his friendships for lovely, younger boys such as Lords De la Warr and Clare which, he said, ' were with me passions '. Ludwig's liking for the ' gardener's nice boy Peter ' and his admiration for the young wood-cutter of the valley of the Watzmann were of the same texture as Byron's devotion to Robert Rushton, the farmer's boy of Newstead. Ludwig's friendship for Paul of Taxis may well have had at its onset something of the quality of Byron's love for John Edleston, the fifteen-year-old chorister of Trinity College chapel, which he declared was ' violent though pure ', and whom he immortalized as ' the hero of my Cornelian '. Ludwig would have perfectly understood Byron's lifelong need for masculine friends and masculine friendship—so frankly and lavishly indulged. The poet's devotion to the Greek boy Nicolo Giraud to whom he wanted to leave in his will seven thousand pounds, and his love for his last boy friend Lukas whom, at Missilonghi, he said he would rather see dead than falling into the hands of the Turks, who had a way of their own with good-looking boys. All Ludwig's friends were, as Byron said of his, ' spoiled by indulgence '.

This, it is certain, was ever Ludwig's prevision of all his friendships, and he undoubtedly looked upon that first holiday spent with Kainz at beloved Linderhof as only a little less rapturous than the first one he and Wagner had spent together on Lake Starnberg in May 1864 and the discovering of Richard Hornig in May 1867 : May—the ' month of rapture '. It is psychologically significant that what Ludwig always sought, in drama, poetry, music, nature, love and friendship was to be rapt, snatched away in spirit and body, swept upwards, transported from a passing world of unreality to one elsewhere that was real, authentic, eternal. It was this quenchless urge that made him towards the close of his short life send emissaries scouring the earth for El Dorado which he hoped to find poised on a lofty peak in Darien.

Ludwig's reading, within his chosen limits, was incredibly wide and thorough. He loved Greek, and Greek beauty and reticence held him until it was swamped in the turgid mass of Wagner's romanticism. He built up a magnificent library, notably rich in historical, biographical and dramatic works because all knowledge and understanding came to him through human beings, real or imagined, and, like a child, he always confused one with the other. His letters repeatedly tell of how he escaped to the world of imagination oblivious of the truth that an anodine tends by its nature to become obsessive.

Ludwig's nature, if undeveloped, was complex. An incurable strain of infantilism made him long to submit himself to Wagner and Varicourt as to a father or king ; while its opposite, an equally potent strain of Royal paternalism, made him ache to be as a father—even as a god— to anyone he greatly loved or admired, showering upon them sumptuous gifts.   In love and friendship obsessive and demanding, Ludwig needed to give as much as to take.

With his nostalgia for Spain, Ludwig had not failed to note the celebration in Madrid in May in honour of the two hundredth anniversary of the death of Calderon in May—hence the reading of *Phaeton*.   He therefore proposed that Kainz should accompany him on a pilgrimage which he had long secretly contemplated.   Upon his return to Munich Kainz was to do his utmost to win over Bürkel ; but Bürkel, as it turned out, was not to be either wooed or won.

Didier, like Pygmalion's ivory statue was, at last, endowed by Ludwig with life and became (more or less) a human being.   Duty called Kainz back to his work and on June 12th Ludwig allowed him to return to Munich and soon received the following ' glowing ' missive, dated the 14th :

. . . The time from the 31st May to the 11th of June was the most beautiful of my whole life and could anything belittle the joy and all the favours which Your Most Gracious Majesty heaped upon me, it is the thought that my fortune rather than my merit helped me.   I still cannot quite believe that everything really happened ; I feel as if I had awakened to dry cold prosaic reality after dreaming a beautiful dream.

I went to Herr Ministerialrat von Bürkel and tried with all my ' glowing eloquence ', as Your Majesty was pleased to describe it, to disperse his doubts with regard to the journey to Spain.   Yes ;   I did speak very glowingly, but still more glowing is the terrible heat in Spain, which is more than 36 degrees Celsius in the shade, and so all my words were burnt to ashes . . .   My colleagues received me very amiably—though I could not look into their hearts.   To explain my absence by saying that I had been to Vienna was quite impossible ;   the ladies and gentlemen knew almost more about the Grotto, Hundings Hütte and all the marvels of the Linderhof than I did ;   they also knew all about the excursion to Plansee.   I do not know who told them.

But this was by no means the whole story.   Ludwig did not, after all, put everything in the Diary ;   there is no hint there that on their ninth day together, quite unknown at the time to the sensitive Kainz, something happened—or did not happen—something was said or left unsaid—that Ludwig found unforgivable.   Unfortunately Ludwig's letter of complaint has been destroyed.

Kainz to Ludwig :

MUNICH, *June 16th, 1881.*

. . . I am very sorry indeed that Your Majesty has not yet forgiven me for the words I said on the 9th of June.   Your Majesty shall always punish me by recalling that unhappy day . . . if I only knew by what I hurt Your Majesty so much !

As a visit to Spain in June was thought to be unseasonable, besides being very costly, Ludwig, recalling his boyhood's hero, Tell, decided upon another visit to Switzerland and wrote to Kainz telling him to be ready to start on the 27th. Kainz replied that he was ' looking forward to it like a child ' ; therefore as the visit was being made incognito, they set out by special train for Lucerne accompanied by a staff of eight servants, composed of cooks, valets, the indispensable hairdresser, and Forage-Quartermaster Karl Hesselschwerdt, who of late had also become indispensable. After a short stay at the Hotel Axenstein Benzinger in Lucerne a friendly publisher placed the Villa Cautenberg at Ludwig's disposal.   There he was in the cradle of the Tell legend—the leap, the chapel, the background, and the whole inspiration of Schiller's play.

As a friend Ludwig was even more exacting than as a Sovereign.   The visit was not entirely a success.   As with Paul, Varicourt and the others, Kainz somehow mortally offended Ludwig's ultra-sensitive soul and without a word of explanation he suddenly started for home, leaving the humiliated actor to follow as best he could.   On July 16th Kainz wrote from Munich :

I would like to lay before Your Most Gracious Majesty's feet my very humble, heartfelt and profoundest thanks for all I enjoyed by the favour of Your Most Gracious Majesty during the last sixteen days, and if there be anything that darkens the memory of those happy times it is the thought of that unhappy evening on the Rutli.[1]   This frank admission of my guilt may show Your Most Gracious Majesty how profoundly I feel that I offended Your Majesty in a most shameful way.   I do not even consider myself worthy of playing before Your Majesty again . . .

Five days later, when thanking the King for lending him his own saloon carriage for a journey to Austria, he wrote from Kloster Neuberg, his home near Vienna :

> I wish I could destroy the memory of the unhappy day with all its roots, because my guilty conscience tortures me like hell.

It is eternally to the honour of Kainz that, apart from using in his letters the baroque Royal language customary at that time, being an artist, he, from the beginning, declined to be as subservient to Ludwig's idiosyncrasies as were the more highly placed favourites who had preceded him.

Ludwig, too, had a bit of a bad conscience about the rude, unkingly manner in which he had abandoned Kainz in Switzerland ; therefore, after Kainz had got back and had eaten the dust, to make it up he decided that they were to be photographed together—and they were ! Ludwig, who since he had grown big, hated being photographed at all—and never sitting—was taken standing in a majestic attitude behind Kainz, who squirmed on a chair.   Kainz's own account of the incident, also written from Kloster Neuberg, and dated August 2nd, has been preserved :

> Your Most Gracious Majesty is excellent, and my enchantment at now having original photographs of Your Majesty is unlimited.   I am less satisfied with the picture of my own unimportant person ; in one of the photographs where I am with Your Majesty I look as though I were Your Most Gracious Majesty's *Leibmohr*— my face is black and my carriage and expression are so ' mid-African '.   Nevertheless, these photographs shall always be my most precious souvenir of the journey to

[1] Wolf, Georg Jacob, in *König Ludwig II und sein Welt* (Munich, 1922), gives in great detail what exactly took place ; as neither Ludwig nor Kainz did so, and as Wolf was not present, his account is unacceptable.

Switzerland—they shall be the sanctuary and the palla-
dium of my future family . . .

It has not remained unnoticed that I travelled from
Munich to Vienna in Your Most Gracious Majesty's
saloon carriage, and it has caused a great sensation. All
the Viennese newspapers are full of it ! From Breslau,
Trieste, Leipzig and elsewhere I receive letters, mostly
petitions, asking whether I would say a word for the
several ladies and gentlemen with Your Majesty. Some
want their debts paid ; one writes from ' Furth in the
woods ' ; another wants the post of bailiff ; another one
wants my photograph in order to find out whether I am
really more beautiful than he. He says he knows quite well
that he is beautiful, but that does not satisfy him, and he
wants to find out whether he is incomparable . . .

For some time ' Didier ' the actor retained Ludwig's
interest ; but Kainz, the man, had lost it. There is no
human anger more relentless than that aroused by wounded
vanity, or by passion unrequited or spurned. The ' glowing ' summer had gone never to return.

CHAPTER THIRTEEN

DEATH OF WAGNER : BUILDING MONOMANIA : DEGENERATION : 1883–1885

IN January 1883 Prince Ludwig Ferdinand (elder son of Prince Adalbert, the youngest brother of Maximilian II), went to Madrid to bring home an Infanta of Spain as his bride. As we know, Ludwig had always liked ' the Adalberts ' as they were, and still are, affectionately known in Bavaria. The Infanta was the third daughter of Queen Isabella II, a sister of Alfonso XII, and aunt of Alfonso XIII. Reports of her beauty, grace and charm had reached Munich, and Ludwig, with his nostalgia for Spain and his penchant for the House of Bourbon, was predisposed to welcome her warmly. As it turned out, the coming of the young Princess brought a glimpse of warm Spanish sunshine into what had been, so far, the saddest year of Ludwig's thirty-eight years of life.

On February 13th, thirteen months after he had finished *Parsifal* at Palermo, Wagner, who had been ailing for a long time, died in Venice at about two o'clock in the afternoon. He was seized with a heart attack seated at his desk in his apartment at the Palazzo Vendramin-Calenzi on the Grand Canal—a worker to the end. And what a worker ! It was as if an eruption of Vesuvius, lasting seventy years, had suddenly gone out.

Ludwig was deeply grieved. Any shadows that may have fallen between him and Wagner were banished by the clarity and finality of death. He never again heard music in any of his palaces ; all the pianos that the Great Friend and Master had used were covered with crape.

Judging only by his letters to Wagner and his fulsome expressions of admiration, it would be possible to conclude quite erroneously that Ludwig was blind to the shortcomings of genius. That was not so. He clearly realized all Wagner's defects and, in spite of them, never abated his

229

love or curtailed his support.   From the outset he disliked
Wagner's interference in affairs of state and, whenever the
Great Friend insisted on talking politics to him, he would
gaze at the ceiling and whistle.   When Ludwig got angry
he became ungracious, forbidding—he closed up ;   when
Wagner got angry he shouted the most appallingly vulgar
language, even to Cosima—he opened up.   Ludwig complained to Kainz that when Wagner spoke of his enemies
he hammered the table with his fists ; this he considered very
unseemly in his presence.   And no one was more exactly
aware than Ludwig of what he had done for Wagner :

> I have rescued him, and now hope that I have preserved
> for the world, in him, one of my best works.

The Queen Mother wrote to Ludwig her condolences
and he replied :

> For your dear sympathy on the death of R. Wagner,
> which happened so suddenly and unexpectedly, I thank
> you from the bottom of my heart.   I also thank you for
> the beautiful flowers that you sent me.   Wishing you a
> very good night, and again thanking you most heartily,
> I kiss your hand, dear Mother, and remain, with inner-
> most love, your grateful son,
>
> LUDWIG.

Ludwig sent Bürkel to Venice to accompany the cortège
to Bayreuth and represent him at the funeral.

Bürkel's account of Wagner's last illness, death, and
funeral gives at first hand a very full, fresh, and in some
ways new history of what was, and must remain, a poignant
hour in musical history.   As a contribution to knowledge
it must be given in full.   It was dated from Munich on
February the 20th :

> The undersigned left by order of Your Majesty on
> Friday the 16th in the afternoon for Venice, but at Rosen-
> heim he was informed that the hearse had already left
> Venice, and that it was only possible to meet it at the
> frontier at Kufstein.
>
> On Saturday morning at ten o'clock the train arrived

at Kufstein and the most humble undersigned was able to carry out Your Majesty's commands.

While listening to the most gracious message of Your Majesty the widow of the Master, who was scarcely alive, as thin as a skeleton, and completely lost to the outer world, collapsed in a sleeping compartment, and for the first time in five days, opened gratefully her eyes—reawakened to a new life by the Royal sun of Grace.

On Tuesday the 13th of February at 2.30 in the afternoon the whole family were together ready for their meal when the Master sent word that he felt unwell and that the family was to begin without him.

The Master always had a presentiment before his heart attacks came on and liked to be alone until they were over. But, as this time the attack was unusually severe, he rang the bell for the servant who then went to the room where the family were and said to Frau Wagner : ' Please go *at once* to the Master (gnädiger Herr).'   The words ' at once ' terrified them all.

Frau Cosima hurried to the Master's room and found him desperately struggling for breath. She tried to help him in every way, and sent for the doctor. When the convulsions were over the Master seemed to fall asleep ; he sat in an armchair, the lady next to him on a bench. Then, suddenly, an artery must have burst, because he lent on his wife's shoulder—who absorbed his last look and breath—and died.

The doctor who came soon afterwards could only state the cause of death.

Frau Cosima sank down by the side of the dead Master and embraced his feet. There she remained for hours.

Towards evening the Master was laid on a bed and the poor woman wanted to be left alone with him. She threw herself on the precious corpse and spent twenty-five hours in convulsive embracement of the dead body, without moving, without a sound, and without shedding a tear.

The next night she had almost collapsed and the body had to be taken from her in order to be embalmed.

During this procedure the body is painted with arsenic and it is death-giving to remain near it. Therefore Frau Cosima was only allowed to go in for one minute. Thereupon Herr Gross and Dr. Keppler led, or rather carried,

the completely-broken woman into another room and
laid her on a couch.   Three or four hours later, when
Dr. Keppler went to see how Frau Cosima was, he found
the room empty and hurried into the death chamber
where he discovered her in a faint by the side of the
corpse.

Next morning the coffin was soldered in the presence
of Frau Cosima who did not leave it during the process
which lasted five hours.   Before it was finally closed she
cut off her beautiful long hair and gave it to her dead
husband as a remembrance.

The Venice doctor who had to seal the coffin and write
out the official certificate of death as he left said to the
banker, Herr Gross : ' I do not know these people ; but
I do know that no man was ever so loved by his wife.'

When the coffin was closed Frau Cosima, with the cap
of the Master on her head, threw herself on the coffin
with the intention of travelling so to Bayreuth.   She had
completely finished with this life and bewailed the tough-
ness of her constitution which prevented Isolde following
her Tristan : she reproached herself because the pain of
her grief did not kill her, whereas she knew that the
Master would never have survived her death for so
long.

Overwhelmed with grief, she was met by Your Majesty's
sympathy ; her daughter read out to her Your Majesty's
letter, and, touched by Your Majesty's kindness, her will
to live awoke again.

She whispered to her daughter (Daniela) her feelings
of thankfulness and gratitude couched in the most touching language, and begged me to lay them before the feet
of Your Majesty.

Thanks to the united prayers of her family and friends
she was at last induced to take a glass of milk, having
had nothing at all for four days.

MUNICH, *February 20th 1883.*

The obsequies in Bayreuth were very dignified and
one could hear from Englishmen, Frenchmen and
Germans the most enthusiastic praise for Your Majesty
—which indeed fills the hearts of all the Master's disciples
for having been pleased to inspire this Genius for the
creation of his greatest and most mature works.

During the last few days before his death the Master was much pre-occupied with the thought of how it might be possible to give a private performance of *Parsifal* before Your Majesty, and said to Kapellmeister Levi how unhappy he was not to have been able to fulfil Your Majesty's commands.

A few days later Ludwig went secretly to Bayreuth and at night stood alone by the newly-made grave in the garden and made his farewell to the Great Friend. Behind stood the square, rather squat, stone house built by Wölfel nine years earlier. Wagner had chosen his grave himself and had it ready for his forthfaring ; on the façade of the house he had placed a relief representing Wotan the Wanderer, and the inscription : ' I call my house Wahnfried because here my longings first found peace ' : in the forecourt a bust of Ludwig on a tall pedestal was surrounded by growing flowers.

Near to Wagner's grave were the little mounds under which lay the remains of dogs that Wagner had particularly loved : Fuss-Frisch ' Wahnfried's faithful home companion ' ; Erda ; Wolf ; Gremmie ; Froh and—perhaps in memory of one of Ludwig's favourite spots in the Bavarian mountains—' Kochel ', W.'s house companion for twenty years ; ' our dear Faf-Frisch ' and, longest epitaph of all : ' Here rests W.'s faithful guard and friend the good and beautiful Marka '.

But Ludwig, who loved horses and all wild animals, did not care for dogs.

With Wagner's death began to recede Ludwig's dearest and most fantastic dream.

He had written to Wagner at Triebschen that he had a great urge to reconstruct the ruins of the ancient Castle of Falkenstein on the edge of the deep Pollat gorge near Kufstein with a ravishing panorama including Simm See, Chiem See, the Watzmann, the Kaiser Schirze, the Tauern ranges, and the Karwendel and Wetterstein ranges. Ludwig's description is perfect :

The situation is of the finest . . . inaccessible . . . inviolable . . . a temple worthy of the godlike friend

. . . in every way finer and more commodious than Hohenschwangau . . .

Now the godlike friend had joined the gods in Valhalla and this magical earthly shrine was to remain unbuilt.

Another friendship was to be finally broken ; another bar irrevocably added to the cage in which Ludwig had, step by step, been immured by fate. In March Kainz wrote to Ludwig :

> Before long I shall have to say goodbye to the kindly walls of Munich ; fresh developments call me to Berlin ; a great project is going to be realized in which all the first-class German artists are engaged, and I have been considered worthy to take part in this work which some day will stand by the side of the Théâtre français. I am deeply sorry to leave Munich where I became what I am, where the King's grace shone upon me, and where the beams of the gracious sun of Ludwig von Bayern warmed and strengthened the modest plant in the garden of art. . . . I shall never forget What he did for me *the poor unknown* ; and I shall eternally remember with loving gratefulness the benevolence and love that were poured upon me. With burning letters the days of the 30th of April and the 4th and 10th of May 1881, and that of the 29th of April and the 10th and 11th of May 1883, are engraved in my memory. Never shall I again play as I did then, because the stupid noisy mass—on which we actors so completely depend—can never inspire the artist with such enthusiasm as did the only man who follows every finesse of the play and the acting with such extraordinary understanding, who gives himself up completely to the impression of the work, and who considers the Theatre as a Temple.

Wagner and (in a lesser degree) Kainz and their creative work, leavening as they do the arts of music and acting to this day, are Ludwig's finest and most enduring monuments and his chief claims to human gratitude and remembrance.

The full nature and extent of Ludwig's passionate intimacies and the manner in which they found physical expression and liberation are difficult to assess with any degree of exactitude. His first recorded friendship with his cousin Gackl was brief, romantic and, knowing Gackl, quite certainly blameless. They nominally remained friends, although, after the inconsiderate way Ludwig treated his sister Sophie, they inevitably drifted apart. With Paul of Taxis there was, without question, an ardent friendship of an emotional nature. The friendship of Ludwig and Wagner did not break up and remained unbroken in spite of many ups and downs. Sooner or later all Ludwig's highly emotional attachments ended in a quarrel. Whatever Wagner's purpose in putting on record the statement that he could in no wise understand such masculine attachments, or that of his family and heirs in preserving it, it is, as has been suggested, arrant nonsense. Long before he became famous, during the early, poverty-stricken, sordid years at Magdeberg, Königsberg and Riga he had met perverts, who were well known as such, nor had he disdained their help when fighting for himself and Minna Planer both before and after he had regularized their connection by marriage.

Wagner's libretti, indeed his music itself, are textured with powerful passions in many shapes and forms. The blend of emotionalism is so strong and so vivid that Ludwig, amongst so many others, felt its appeal, amplified and lifted up by the strength of the music itself. Again Wagner's theme of 'splendid unrestraint', which has an eternal appeal to the many suffering from repressions, drew the King out of his loneliness to share with the composer his magnificent conceptions on their grand scale. Ludwig could appreciate and lose himself in the Wagnerian world, where the beings are over life-size and in which their abundant vitality finds ample and satisfying expression in the powerful music. Wagner's grandeur and his passion alike were Ludwig's enchantment.

A repudiation of the unsupported statement of Pourtalès that there was an invidious relationship between Liszt and Wagner does not contradict the fact that, sexually speaking, Wagner had an uncanny attraction for both men and women. The extravagantly affectionate terms in which Ludwig and Wagner addressed each other in writing and, it may be presumed, personally, may well be disregarded as largely a form of emotional make-believe and blarney. Wagner, like many artists, was bi-sexual. The latest scientific theory is that everyone is, which sounds reasonable enough when we remember that everyone has a father and a mother : like everything human, it is all a matter of a just equilibrium.

However, when we consider Ludwig's friendship with such men as Paul of Taxis, Varicourt, and Hirschberg we are at once on a different plane. All three were men of but moderate intelligence, in no way mentally, physically, or emotionally notable for charm ; they were in fact what is often intended when a youngish man is described as a ' good soldier ', which means that while he will never fall to the bottom or climb to the top he will always behave decently within his somewhat narrow conventional code. It is remarkable that both Varicourt and Hirschberg were of similar type and appearance ; indeed, glancing at them carelessly, the photograph of one might easily be mistaken for a photograph of the other. All three found fulfilment and happiness in their wives, families and surroundings, and were only ambitious of advancement in their careers as soldiers.

With Varicourt and Hirschberg can be classed Hornig, who, except that he was not nobly born and was never commissioned, was, in every way, essentially the same type. He could truthfully be described as one of Nature's gentlemen. Faithful, discreet, abnormally patient, devoted, a good sportsman and lover of the open air, an admirer of Wagner's music, in every way reliable and efficient ; as a loving husband and father and head of a united and affectionate family, the peculiar tie that bound him to Ludwig is inexplicable. That his love for Ludwig was genuine, and all things considered disinterested, is undoubted.

With Kainz we are back with Wagner on the emotional plane. An artist and unquestionably a great actor, he would be subject to emotional responses and reactions, esoteric, varied, and intangible such as are totally outside the rigid personalities and simple characters of men like Paul of Taxis, Varicourt, Hirschberg, and Hornig. The

manly and legitimate aggressive tone of the two letters
Kainz addressed to Ludwig over the affair of the miniature proved that he was a real artist who could never
prostitute his art in order to become the plaything of a
king.

Ludwig was but one of the great multitude who fall in
love with people because of what they are not, and fall out
of love with them because of what they are.

It was not until late in his life when decadence had super-
vened that Ludwig, probably as a result of repeated rebuffs
and disappointments, began forcing his will upon the
reluctant. To make doing so easier, he chose menials,
stooping in the end to valets, lackeys and even private
soldiers who, practically speaking, had no option but to
consent.

The marriage early in April of his first cousin Prince
Ludwig Ferdinand to the Infanta Paz in Madrid did something to take Ludwig's mind off his grief for Wagner, and
was the occasion of his resuming for the last time his regal
duties. He followed every item of the ceremonies with
intense interest ; sent the bride a wedding present, and a
letter welcoming her to his capital. He admired Prince
Ludwig Ferdinand because of his vocation as a Doctor, and
now personally entered into the details of the Prince's professional studies with interest. Rarest compliment of all,
to the general astonishment—on a night in rapturous May
he gave a romantic supper-party for the bride and bridegroom in the Winter Garden, was more than gracious to
the Infanta, asked her husband for a German translation
of her poems, and even granted her wish to be allowed to
see Schloss Chiemsee. With brilliant charm he discussed
with his guests Calderon, Lope de Vega and Victor Hugo ;
besought the Prince to try and prevent his mother-in-law
Queen Isabella from fulfilling her intention of visiting
Munich, and asked him if he could not have the Order of
the Spanish Golden Fleece ! Ludwig, in fact, gave up
the whole of May and a good part of the summer to the Prince
and Princess. He came completely out of his shell and a
wave of hope swept over Munich society. The Infanta,

who has included in her Reminiscences an interesting and
authentic account of the whole affair, was as enchanted
with Ludwig as he was with her.   In September Alfonso XII
paid a visit to his newly married sister at Nymphenburg
but, contrary to all Kingly etiquette, was not received by
Ludwig.

As the bride was young, very observant and a Spaniard,
Princess Ludwig Ferdinand's first-hand impressions of
Ludwig in his thirty-eighth year are invaluable.   She had
been warned that when they dined at the Residenz she was
not to forget always to treat Ludwig as a King, upon which
she plaintively asked : ' But how does one treat a King ?
The only King I know is my brother.'   She need not have
worried.   Ludwig met his guests at the head of the Emperor's
staircase, gave her his arm and conducted her to her seat.
Being small and slight the Infanta looked like a child beside
him ; he spoke excellent French and walked with his head
held high so that she could hardly hear him.   His dreamy,
dark-blue eyes, pale complexion, jet-black curly hair and
perfect courtesy made an ineffable impression on the young
Princess and while talking to him she could not understand
why people found him stand-offish and unapproachable.
They discussed Victor Hugo and Ludwig mentioned having
first seen Kainz in *Marion de Lorme*.   ' This man ', the
Princess afterwards wrote of Ludwig, ' has something great
and poetic about him, and has powers of imagination such
as one rarely finds in any one '—in fact ' a mute, inglorious
Milton '.   Ludwig was much taken by the Princess and let
her know through the Baroness von Reichlin that he found
her charming, but wished her to make a deeper curtsy on
meeting him, as the other cousins did.   Sending him her
thanks and apologies (through the Baroness) the Princess
modestly said that as the only Monarchs she knew were her
mother and brother she was quite unaware of the etiquette
to be observed in the presence of Majesty !

As Ludwig adored the Winter Garden and throughout
his reign received all his intimate guests there a description
of what it was like towards the end of his reign will give his
favourite background—so familiar to Queen Marie, Otto,
Sophie, Wagner, Paul, Varicourt, Hirschberg and Kainz.

The Princess's description was written at the time in a letter to her mother, Queen Isabella :

At eight o'clock in the evening a messenger brought the King's invitation. We were to be at the Residenz at ten o'clock, Ludwig in a dress suit and I in evening dress. When we arrived the King was waiting for us ; he kissed my hand and led me up one of those stone staircases one sees in all palaces, and which without being particularly handsome, give an imposing impression. A man-servant with a torch walked backward before us and stopped at the door of the King's apartment. We entered a small room hung with red velvet. In the centre a gold embroidered canopy trimmed with ermine overhung a Louis XIV armchair ; a table before it was covered with an equally rich embroidered cloth ; on the mantelpiece was a marble statuette of Marie Antoinette and other works of art, Chinese and alabaster vases and similar ornaments. We next passed into his study— also in Versailles style ; over the doors were bas-reliefs in marble, with medallions supported by Cupids, on which were the portraits of different Kings ; all was in the baroque style, even to the inkstand. Before a window was a flower-stand filled with plants in the midst of which reposed a bust of Richard Wagner. His bedroom was also in Louis XIV style, with extremely rich bed-canopy and curtains. The overwhelming, almost oppressive impression, is indescribable. After passing through yet another equally overloaded room we came to a door hidden by a curtain. The King smilingly drew the curtain aside. I could not believe my eyes. There before me was an enormous garden, illuminated in Venetian style, with palms, a lake, bridges, huts and castellated buildings. ' Come in,' said the King, and I followed him fascinated as Dante followed Virgil in Paradise. A parrot was swinging on a gold ring and shouted ' Guten Abend ' to me, while a peacock gravely and proudly strutted by. We crossed a primitive wooden bridge over a small illuminated pond and saw before us under a chestnut tree an Indian village. When at that moment a hidden military band struck up my *Marcha de Infantas*, I turned to the King and told him in all sincerity that this was perfection of thoughtful kindness.

' By and by you will hear more Spanish music,' he

answered. We now came to a blue silk tent decorated
with roses, inside which a chair supported by two carved
elephants rested on a lion skin. The King took us on
further, down a narrow path to the pond, in which an
artificial moon was reflected, softly lighting up the water
lilies and other aquatic plants. A boat, such as trouba-
dours used in olden times, was fastened to a tree. We
reached an Indian hut ; fans and weapons of the country
hung down from the ceiling. I stopped mechanically,
until the King moved on again. Suddenly I thought I
had been magically spirited to the Alhambra. A little
Moorish room we now entered, with a fountain in the
middle surrounded with flowers, had in a moment transported me back to my own country. Round the walls
were two magnificent divans. In an adjoining circular
pavilion divided from us by a Moorish arch supper was
laid. The King motioned me to take the place in the
middle, and rang a little hand-bell softly. As if from
the void a lackey appeared and bowed low. He only
came to fetch and carry away dishes, or when the King
rang the bell. I could see from where I was sitting,
behind the arch, masses of beautiful plants lit up by many
coloured lamps, while an unseen choir sang softly. Suddenly a rainbow appeared. ' Oh ! ' I cried involuntarily,
' this must be a dream.' ' Ah ! ' but you must see my
Schloss Chiemsee,' said the King. So I was not dreaming
then, and the man who sat beside me was the King of
Bavaria before whom everybody trembled ! And he was
actually inviting me to see the new Castle which he kept
so carefully hidden away from everyone !
    The band then played a Habanera, and we spoke of
Cuba, which with Spain gave scope enough for conversation. After supper the King asked me very politely if
I objected to smoking. Later he took us to a stalactite
grotto ; a tiny cascade trickled mysteriously, and through
a cleft in the roof one could see the moon. After a while
we went to the Indian hut near the lake, so as to hear the
music better, and as we passed the Hindu towers the
orchestra played *Aida*. Next we went back to the tent
with the elephant chair, through a kind of gallery lit
by innumerable coloured lamps. Seated in the tent I
had to repeat some of my Spanish verses for the King ;
even though he did not understand the words he wished

to hear how they sounded.   I translated them into French
and he listened attentively, his large eyes fixed on me.
When I finished saying my *Adieu to my brother Alfonso*
he said the ideas pleased him very much, and that there
was a strain of melancholy throughout it that appealed
to him.   He then stood up and handed me an enormous
bunch of roses.   He was leaving Munich that morning,
he said, but would first accompany us to Nymphenburg ;
we therefore told them to send away our carriage and he
ordered his own.   Just as we were leaving this fairyland
the King threw aside the curtain and exclaimed ' Aurora
has arrived '.   Together we stood and watched the first
faint shimmer of sunrise in the sky.

A carriage and four, harnessed à la grande daumont,
was waiting at the foot of the stone staircase.   I got in
quickly in order to take the seat at the left, but the King
would not allow it.   We drove like a lightning flash from
the Residenz, a groom riding before us with a lantern.
Although suffering from a cold the King refused to put
on his hat in my presence.   It was quite daylight by the
time we arrived at Nymphenburg where nearly thirty-
eight years before the King was born.   He accompanied
us to our apartment and when I tried to thank him for
the fairy-like evening he had given us, he would not let
me speak, but thanked *us* for having come to him, kissed
my hand, and drove away to his mountains . . .[1]

After much confabulation, and on condition of the greatest
secrecy, the visit of the Infanta and the Prince to Schloss
Chiemsee took place.   The Baroness von Reichlin, one of
the few ladies of Munich Court society for whom Ludwig
had a liking, and who was to have been Mistress of the
Robes had he married Sophie, was sent there to receive the
visitors and the indefatigable Bürkel was instructed to act
as cicerone.

One of Ludwig's huge nosegays tied with the silver and
blue of the Bavarian Royal Arms was presented to the
Princess, not only on her arrival, but daily.   These con-
fections varied in size according to the rank of the recipient.
In the case of an Infanta of Spain they would not be less

[1] *Through Four Revolutions*: by H.R.H. Princess Ludwig Ferdinand
of Bavaria, Infanta of Spain, London, John Murray, 1933, pp. 117–124.

than a foot in circumference—therefore the young bride was glad to have the Baroness in attendance.

The empty Hall of Mirrors was opened, illuminated at night by thirty-odd chandeliers and forty-odd candelabra standing on the floor which, between them, held well over two thousand candles. It is said that this undoubtedly magnificent coup-d'œil Ludwig himself only saw once—and saw it alone.

Disliking garish splendour combined with discomfort the Prince and Princess chose to stay at the simple old Schloss where, at least, there was a properly equipped kitchen.

To anyone who knew as intimately as the Infanta did the many Royal palaces of France and Spain, including of course Versailles, the Chiemsee Salle des Gardes, Salon de l'Œil de Bœuf, Chambre de Parade, Salle du Conseil, the King's bedchamber and study, and (copying Louis XIV) the dining-room with its table ascending and descending through the floor, were, like all copies and imitations of works of art and architecture, merely boring.

Bürkel duly reported to Ludwig that the visitors were overcome with the magnificence of the unfinished Schloss (as indeed they were).

Like Wagner, Ludwig loved sumptuously embroidered curtains, cushions, upholstery and portières. Each one of the three Castles he built is overdone with them. He did not worry much about the beauty of the design (which any-how he could not see) so long as it was boldly carried out in gold or silver. At the end of October Bürkel informed him that he now owed two hundred thousand Marks to four embroidery workshops in Munich. The owners had unanimously declared that they could only go on with the work on condition that they were paid something on account early in the following year. But there was worse to follow.

Dollmann now declared that he must have larger sums for current weekly payments and, if he did not get them, that his men Brandl, Ehrengut, Leiss, Dethman, Perrin and Maratelli, all skilled craftsmen, ' who have sunk their whole fortune in the Royal buildings ', will certainly go on strike next year. The painting of the ceiling of the Salle du Conseil at Herren Chiemsee had at last been finished ; the furnishing of the smaller rooms and the imitations of articles and pictures in the Hertford Collection would cost a million Marks, additional to the cost of the needlework. A sum of four million Marks would therefore be essential, and only one million was available. In fact, financially speaking, 1884 was going to be a very uncomfortable year.

What the courtiers and officials who criticized Ludwig for using domestic servants for confidential work forgot was that he had no one else available for the purpose. He could not keep a Court in a mountain hut and, in those days, his castles were difficult to get to. He did not want courtiers around him and when he occasionally summoned some of them, although they did not disdain complaining, avoided resigning. Members of Queen Victoria's family, her Ministers and courtiers used to complain loudly enough about having to journey to, or stay at, Balmoral during the early years of her widowhood ; they objected to receiving verbal or written messages through John Brown. What all courtiers like to forget is that, to the Sovereign, they too are merely flunkeys. Holnstein, as Bavarian Master of the Horse, had no doubt a finer uniform than Hornig, but it was Hornig who did all the work, saw continuously to his master's safety and comfort ; moreover, intercourse with these minor officials could be conducted, not officially, but on the basis of humanity and friendship. Although towards the end Ludwig came to dislike him because of his inability to raise loans, Zeigler, of all Ludwig's permanent officials, was the only one who, as Cabinet Secretary, stuck to him for years and accompanied him from Berg to Linderhof, to Hohenschwangau, to Neuschwanstein, or waited on him at his mountain or forest huts. But that was what he was paid for and after all there were Royal horses, carriages, sleighs and servants in plenty. Of course Zeigler had the advantage of being a minor poet, an amateur painter in water-colours, and a reader : men such as Holnstein, Varicourt, Hirschberg and Dürckheim-Montmartin, it is pretty safe to assume, had no such resources.

Under the strain Bürkel, at last, collapsed. At the end
of January Franz von Pfistermeister became Court Secretary,
and had to face the now quite desperate financial chaos as
best he could. Negotiations undertaken with a banking
firm in Berlin came to nothing ; for the second time Baring
Brothers of London offered a loan of six million Marks—
but, of course, on conditions. On March 24th Malsen and
Pranck, trustees of the entailed estate of Maximilian II,
definitely refused to help ; on March 31st the workmen
said quite definitely that if they were not paid at once they
would stop work. By that time the debts on the King's
various building projects amounted to eight million Marks.
After all, it was not so much for a King, even if his Privy
Purse income was modest. George IV was said to have
spent the equivalent of five million Marks on the Brighton
Pavilion alone ; then there was Carlton House with its
lavish and costly furniture and decorations.

From the beginning of the year Ludwig suffered increasingly frantic agony with what he, in his ignorance, described
as toothache, and Dr. Franz Karl, a mental specialist, was
sent to examine him under pretence of treating it. The
King, taking a liking to him, belatedly admitted that he
was also anxious about his eyes ; however, there was nothing
the matter with his tongue and he talked incessantly for
four hours ! He did not seem to suspect a ruse, and so
greatly astonished and delighted his visitor by the eloquence,
brilliance and logic of his conversation that Karl was completely hoodwinked and reported that not only was there
nothing wrong with the King's brain, but that it was brilliant
and functioned perfectly !

Useful light is thrown on Ludwig's state of mind and
health at that time by a letter which he wrote to his Mother
in Munich on February 12th, and which also serves to show
once again that the relationships between Mother and son
were much more normal, cordial and understanding than
has usually been stated. At a meeting he got ' excited ',
and—as all highly-strung people do—' said things ', and
immediately felt that he owed her an explanation and

apology. The iron hand constricting his brain was stealthily contracting :

I feel urged to thank you once more for the wonderful presents with which you made me very happy. I admire them very much and offer you my innermost thanks for them. Because of a very bad night at Partenkirchen—I went to bed late—I was rather excited this morning. I talked over the plan of Herrenworth (about which I very seldom talk) which, unfortunately, will not be ready for a long time ; I beseech you not to tell anybody anything about what I discussed with you this morning. Thanking you again, dear Mother, and with the best wishes for a good night, I am always in innermost love,

Your grateful son,
LUDWIG.

At the end of April, Pfistermeister having already retired in defeat, one Hermann Gresser, a retired Captain, was appointed Court Secretary. In July he assured Ludwig that he would give the strictest orders that the plumbing installations were to be seen to most carefully : ' the sanitary conveniences in all the rooms of His Majesty will from now on be perfect '. In August, armed with a special order in the King's own handwriting, Gresser went to the Royal Treasury in the Residenz to remove diamonds and precious stones. Count Castell-Castell, who was the official responsible, kept the Treasury locked and in true bureaucratic fashion told Gresser that : ' by the time the permit had got through all the necessary formalities it will be too late to decorate the crown with diamonds '.

As we know, when Ludwig felt overborne by people, the perplexities of kingship, the pertinacities of officials or, above all, by loneliness, he was accustomed to take refuge with Hornig and his family at Seelieten their delightfully-placed villa on Lake Starnberg—the home he had himself caused to be built for ' Richard, Beloved of my Soul '. In February he had lost Wagner ; in March Kainz ; the valet Mayr, loyal enough, and perhaps even affectionate, was still about him ; but, one by one, his intimates were beginning rapidly to fall away.

During the second week in his favourite month of May Ludwig made one of his sudden descents on the Hornig family. As was customary, when he made a stay of any length he was accompanied by a valet—possibly Mayr—and a chef and his assistant who came well supplied with food and wine. This was Ludwig's last visit to the home of his friend in which, for years, he had passed one night weekly. After dinner they ascended the steep pine-covered hill behind the house, and in the little wooden hideout at the top, sat, talked and smoked. Ludwig, who never took to the pipe so popular in Bavaria, smoked cigarettes in moderation and on special occasions after a particularly good dinner, a cigar. Ludwig has been reputed as a glutton and drunkard ; he was neither. He liked good, rather plain, fare and never considered the culinary arrangements at his palaces of any great importance. As for wine, his brain disease was of such a nature that even a small quantity was disastrous.

The following letter from Ludwig to Hornig throws a bright light on one side of the writer's mind and character, and underlines the position and influence of Mayr :

17 May, 1884.

Dear Richard !—From what you have recently told me, it is plain to see that those wretched people who had the arrangements in hand, i.e. Effner, Dollmann, Bürkel and, worst of all, Pfister, were and still are a *drag* on all that is ordered ; I now order you to get rid of this rabble ; Dollmann at the end of the summer, and Pfister definitely next month. Speak with Brantl and the Regensburg architects . . . Talk the matter over with Mayr . . . A few days ago I commissioned you to inform Pfister that he is forbidden to get into direct touch with me, give him that order. He is not in the least reliable. He is *very much* to blame for the delay, because he did not begin months ago. *Someone else* must take up the matter. You announced on the 21st that Gresser has had time to consider the question (of money), see about this . . . According to your statements about the pictures over the doors, it appears that the *quite useless* Pfister declared that certain pictures were decayed which were not so ; do *not* put your trust in him ! ! ! . . . Hurry up with getting a Court Secretary ; I must have one who is submissive and entirely obedient ; (which goes without saying) ; someone who is to notify me personally. Pfister has sunk too low for this . . .

LUDWIG.

Writing from the Royal Palace in Madrid, Prince Ludwig Ferdinand said something that elicited a significant confession from Ludwig. Describing a spot in the demesne of the lovely old Royal Castle of El Pardo, famous for its Goyas, some nine or ten miles north-west of the capital, the Prince said that it reminded him of *Parsifal*. Ludwig replied :

BERG, *July 22nd*.

The first time I saw and heard this wonderful work was in Spring, and it moved me in an extraordinary way. Truly it is uniquely beautiful. It has a purifying effect, and one is carried away in wonder and admiration.

It is worth noting that, of course subconsciously, Ludwig puts seeing before hearing, thus supporting the conclusion that he had no profound understanding of music. *Parsifal*, as a matter of fact, is considered by some musicians to be far more impressive in the concert hall than on the stage. On August 25th Ludwig wrote to his Mother from Sachen:

HERREN CHIEMSEE.

I intended to spend my birthday at Herrenworth this year, but everything there was still so backward that I left after a very short stay. I am very happy that Otto is fairly well.

Traitors, like rats, have an uncanny knowledge of when to leave the sinking ship. Holnstein, who had always been disloyal to Ludwig personally, and who in 1870 became Bismarck's stooge for a ribbon to wear on his coat, openly joined his Sovereign's enemies in the beginning of the year.

At the end of February, after making sure that they would not be there, Ludwig went unannounced one evening to the apartment of Prince and Princess Ludwig Ferdinand in the west wing of Schloss Nymphenburg and asked to be shown their new-born eldest son. After gazing long and earnestly

at the ten-months-old slumbering baby he went away.
Next morning he wrote to the Prince apologizing for his
unceremonious visit, saying that he had never before seen
a new-born infant close at hand, and inviting the Prince
and Princess to a family dinner-party at the Residenz—
the last he ever gave. His apology was disingenuous
because, whatever inward impulse drove this childless man
to go alone to gaze upon the innocence and purity of childhood, it was not ignorance because he had always asked to
see Hornig's children soon after they were born. Perhaps
in all children he saw mirrored Otto's unborn sons.

In the spring of the year Elizabeth of Austria took a villa
at Zandvoort on the North Sea while she was doing a cure
for sciatica. For hours she would watch the flight of the
slender, graceful gulls, and developed a fanciful idea that,
in her whole nature and type of mind, she really resembled
a sea-gull, thirsting for liberty on the broad ocean. She
remembered how frequently Ludwig had compared himself to the eagle which loves to make its home high on the
steepest crag and is king of the mountains, just as the sea-gull
is queen of the seas.

By June Elizabeth was on Lake Starnberg and one day
with her daughters Gisela and Valerie was rowed across the
lake to Ludwig's Isle of Roses. She took with her a verse
which she had written to him while at Zandvoort, copied
it, placed it in a sealed envelope addressed to him, and
left it in one of the rooms of the chalet. It was her last
farewell to him, unavoidably made in writing because he
was now completely inaccessible. If its poetic merit is
modest the quatrain at least expresses their common
unassuaged thirst for freedom :

> Thou eagle high-throned on the mountains
>   The sea-gull swift-circling below
> Sends greetings from foam-crested billows
>   To thee in thy kingdom of snow.

However good the wretched Gresser may have been at
sanitation, he was as poor a hand at raising large sums of
money without security as were any of his predecessors ;
therefore Ludwig, ruthless because he was desperate, got rid

of him and appointed Councillor von Klug in his place. In order to keep him in the dark about the bankruptcy of the Privy Purse, and because his suspicions now amounted to monomania, Ludwig only allowed von Klug less than an hour with Gresser ; consequently he took over with but the faintest knowledge of the many subterranean negotiations that had been going on with bankers and others.

As a brother Sovereign, the official head of the Empire, and a relative, the old Emperor Wilhelm I had been seriously perturbed by reports concerning Ludwig, his health, and his finances which he had received from Bismarck and others. He therefore now made a fine gesture by offering to come to his nephew's rescue on generous terms and conditions. The handsome loan of ten million Marks was declined by Ludwig because the main condition was that the money was to be used for paying his debts, and not for further building.

In the early morning of October 15th Ludwig, in a beautiful state carriage drawn by four white horses with postilions, outriders and equerries, set off from Linderhof to Hohenschwangau, where he arrived at ten o'clock. His purpose was to congratulate his Mother on the sixtieth anniversary of her birth. They had a happy day together in the beloved old castle where she had first taken him in October 1845 when he was not two months old. He spent the night there and the next morning returned to Linderhof.

They never met again.

On December 10th Klug, through Mayr, let Ludwig know that he had found a banker or moneylender, a certain Herr Sohulein, who was prepared at once to advance privately a loan of four hundred thousand Marks towards the building of Herren Chiemsee and Neuschwanstein on condition that he was given a title.

Reluctant to pollute the fountain of honour, Ludwig hesitated. But the situation was desperate. Ludwig's Christmas presents for the previous year, bestowed as lavishly as usual, had not yet been paid for, and presents for the approaching Christmas were almost due ; nor had the many presents bestowed upon officials and servants during the current year been paid for. Klug must have ready money for these purposes. With hands uplifted in prayer he besought Ludwig to grant the title, and Ludwig despairingly agreed.

It is well to recall the successive stages by which Ludwig cut himself off from the world of realities. First he banished all high Court officials, and offended them past redemption in doing so ; next he refused to see his Ministers, thus outraging their conscientiousness in performing their duties, injuring their pride and wounding their vanity ; last, and worst, he discarded his personal and private secretarial staff, and sought to conduct the highest affairs of state through menials such as Welcker, Mayr, Hesselschwert, or some anonymous valet, lackey or private soldier. Reaching the final stage of isolation from humanity he, towards the end, refused to be looked at even by his body servants.

There exists a water-colour drawing in one of his castles showing Ludwig in the early part of his reign leaving the house at night to go for one of his long drives. The elaborate rococo sleigh, with its gleaming light inside the crown on the top, drawn by richly harnessed horses, is waiting ; on either side of the entrance steps to the castle are three footmen in the gorgeous full-dress light blue and silver Royal liveries, their bent right arms raised and held across their eyes as the King descends. This early hatred of being stared at had finally become an obsession.

To give an accurate idea of the strange manner in which Ludwig lived during the last months of his life it is only necessary to quote the written instructions he sent to his servants. These, on all sorts of odds and ends of paper, were sometimes handed to a specially favoured valet or lackey, sometimes left about where they could find them, sometimes pushed out to them underneath closed doors and, as some of the dates show, were often written at night. Servants whose duties made it essential to enter his rooms had to scratch at the door, await an answer and, if admitted, had to remain bent double and never under any circumstances even glance at His Majesty.

To understand Ludwig's incessant complaints against his clumsy amateur attendants it must be borne in mind that he had always been accustomed to perfect service, and that in exalted Continental families most of the housework was always carried out by male domestics.

The many spies around Ludwig's person saw to it that these pathetic scraps of paper showing the workings of a hopelessly diseased brain were carefully retrieved and pre-served for the purpose of self-condemning the writer at some form of projected secret trial; that immediate purpose served, they were sent by his self-elected judges to condemn him before posterity and exculpate themselves. They may now provide material of value for the disinterested curiosity of the alienist.

Notes by Ludwig :

December 13th–14th.

Cutlets, beer, ham bad, the latter cooked badly. When I come back from Mass : one bottle of champagne, one dish *foie gras* and five hundred Marks.

December 14th–15th.
LINDERHOF.

Order another work by Falke about the aesthetics of Art-Industry. Write urgently to Klug saying that I insist that the stoppages by the banks cease. A hundred needle-workers must resume their work in the bedroom here ; it is a real scandal that Klug shouldn't succeed by bestowing orders and titles. I *want* it and therefore it *must* be done. Write very urgently ; he must succeed *at once* and then must report to me urgently. If I give orders to clear my room doing so must not be postponed as has happened. Pencils must be pointed without special orders. The day after to-morrow a thousand Marks. How is Häusler now ? I want to know whether he looks happy. How often have I said that the coffee must not come up boiling hot . . . so that it can only be drunk after standing an hour. I thank Häusler very much for what he wrote. His letter made me very happy.

December 15th–16th.
LINDERHOF.

I send my congratulations to Chamberlain Gross-Jockau on the birth of a daughter. Let Count Rechberg know that H.M. is very glad he is better. Express my

sympathy with Count [1] Hirschberg on his accident.   Write
Baron Varicourt reminding him that he has several
letters from H.M. which I want back in case he still has
them.

December 16th–17th.
LINDERHOF.

How is Häusler to-day ?   Will Ulrich come to-morrow ?
To-morrow drive out one hour earlier, that is at four ;
then every day one hour earlier.   Write it down and be
sure to come.   As Ulrich cannot come to-day Brüller is
to be on duty instead.   The disgraceful Gresser has
behaved like a mean scoundrel.

December 17th–18th.
LINDERHOF.

Häusler is to be told that, as an exception, he may write
a letter for me to-day ; but he must come alone, and the
others are not to be told, as it has nothing to do with them.
His writing is so particularly beautiful that I want to see
more of it ; he may write what he likes—now before
driving out—he has the time.

Why is Ulrich always pushed on to be on duty first ?

December 18th–19th.
LINDERHOF.

Every day get up earlier, for certain.   See to that *very
particularly.   Write it down.*   Is Häusler happy and all
right ?

December 20th–21st.
LINDERHOF.

Every time I have to retie my tie, so badly, so *impossibly*
has the fellow done it.   It is scandal ; the assurance
that it will be done better next time is completely value-
less if it is not *fulfilled.*   Speak to him about it and show
him how to do it *better.*   The point is not the tying itself,
but that he should at least *keep* his promise.

December 23rd–24th.
HOHENSCHWANGAU.

Thierry must be told exactly how I want the new tea-
set so that there shall be no confusion.   It is not to be

---

[1] Anton Hirschberg had succeeded his father Ernest Count Hirschberg (1826–1878).

Chinese and not Japanese. The blue must be *purer* and more *radiating* as on the vase. The cups are to be big and round, the upper edges to be very broad and all in *gold* with relief work only, then the blue is to begin. On the blue ground are to be the gold relief figures from China, buildings, landscapes, birds and dragons.

December 26th–27th.
HOHENSCHWANGAU.

Books which are lying on the little table to go up to the Castle.[1] He ties my tie very badly, show him how to do it better. For this time I have forgiven Häusler. How is he now?

December 27th–28th.

The aigrette to be put carefully on my hat. Papers into the drawer while I have my bath. Lock up Brüller immediately. Write Herr von Schneider that he is to get me another work about China ; the illustrations were not at all good in the last one.

December 28th–29th.
NEUSCHWANSTEIN.

Bath an hour and a half earlier. Write Ministerialrat that I do not want to give the orders to Wollenleben and Zeigler this time, but perhaps the next. That I accept the (New Year) wishes from Baron von Rechern, and that the President of the Landrat of Schwaben is to be thanked in my name. Write Adjutant Count Lerchenfeld saying that the holiday for Dürckheim is granted, but that he is first to talk to Hofmann. That I express my sympathy with Count Otto von Rechberg on the death of his father. Thanks for Christmas presents. To-morrow to bed at half-past nine. Häusler is not to be treated kindly again. The dishes must come more quickly. It was very impudent of Häusler not to report the arrival of the Reports. Treat him harshly.

On December the 30th in the secret Diary Ludwig once again recorded a ' last fall '.

---

[1] i.e. Neuschwanstein.

CHAPTER FOURTEEN

THE BEGINNING OF THE END :
JANUARY–MAY : 1886

January

ON Tuesday, the 19th, Ludwig made the first entry
in the second volume of the Diary :

January 19th.

It is in the name of God, and thinking of the great
King, of the immortal King, that I begin this book, and
may the Almighty God give me the power, may the
memory of the King sanctify me, so that I may conquer
the evil, subdue the senses, so that not once can there be
any question in this book of a relapse (the last in the
fortieth year). Given at Hohenschwangau January 19th
1886 before the portrait of the King.

Did he know that Byron wrote : ' I am thus wasting the
best part of my life, daily repenting and never amending ' ?

On the 21st of January, anniversary of the assassination
of King Louis XVI, day for ever melancholy and terrible.
And at the dread Requiem Mass. Sworn anew before
the image of the Holy Virgin and the Child Jesus. And
before that of the Saintly King Louis IX (White banner)
kissing the crucifix, swearing likewise before the picture
of the King Louis XIV, the Great, to subdue the evil, to
conquer the senses. May God, as well as the memory
of these illustrious Kings, give me power to keep my oath.
The remembrance of the royal blood of Christ and of
the martyr King ought to contribute greatly towards
strengthening me in my projects of wisdom and virtue.
Given at Hohenschwangau, January 21st, 1886.

On the 25th Ludwig addressed a long letter to Klug, the
first half of which was written by a scribe, the second half
and a long postcript by himself. In it he threatened to
commit suicide, or leave the country, if the Royal property
were sequestered, and threw the whole blame for either
possibility on those who did nothing to prevent such a
catastrophe.

By the end of January the last redecoration of the private apartment in the Residenz was finished in exact accord with his detailed instructions ; undoubtedly he inspected the completed work, but there is no record of him having slept there, even for a night.   Until destroyed by a bomb during the Second World War it was, because of its personal associations, the mecca annually of thousands of tourists who—unless forcibly prevented—sat on the blue velvet chair before his desk, fingered the blue leather blotter bearing his cypher and crown, examined the circular piece of floor that covered the access to Sophie's unused staircase, gaped at the bricked-up portion of wall on the left of his desk that once led to the Winter Garden.   The rooms being low the blue and gold canopy of the great bed behind the heavy, gilded balustrade, and the crimson and gold canopy over the chair of state in which he sat in the room which was at once ante-chamber, audience-chamber, and dining-room were overpowering.   Yet, in spite of all its aesthetic short-comings, there remained some feeling, some atmosphere, some lingering aura of the human being behind the King, the dreamer and the madman who occupied it.   Once he dropped in his bedroom and smashed a precious reliquary ; in expiation he had a small ivory cross let into the spot in the beautiful parquet floor.   Linderhof, Schloss Chiemsee, Neuschwanstein are empty unrealities, never giving the impression of having been designed for or lived in by human beings ; Hohenschwangau was the family home, but there, and at Berg, his Mother having a suite of rooms, those two houses were not entirely his own.   But the Residenz apartment was absolutely his own creation, its pictures, busts and objets d'art being purely personal.   Ludwig, like all Royalties, longed for a home of his own.

On the 27th he made the third and last Diary entry of the month :

To the senses mortal hatred ! No more kisses : the day before. Sworn on the day of January 27th.—Abolished in remembrance of the august death of King Charles I of England and of King Louis XVI of France and of Navarre.

February

It had been for some time increasingly difficult to induce men servants to enter the King's household, therefore the help of the Army was invoked and the Colonel of the 4th Chevaux-Léger, Ludwig's favourite light cavalry regiment, then stationed at Augsburg, sent specially selected private soldiers for duty as required. For over a year Holnstein had been in disgrace and Hornig nearly always away, therefore the stables were controlled by Hesselschwert who, unknown to Ludwig, was Holnstein's spy and tool ; the Master of the Household had for many months been on enforced leave ; Ludwig was thus entirely in the hands of his amateur lackeys, almost indeed at their mercy. Naturally most of them disliked the isolation, work to which they were unaccustomed, a background to which nothing in their history or experience gave them a clue and a pervading atmosphere of violence and mystery. Added to this was the Bavarian peasants' deeply-rooted awe of kingship, love for the Wittelsbachs, and terror of madness. Some of the following group of orders were written by Ludwig and dated and signed with an L. ; others dictated to a valet or soldier and additions and corrections made in the Royal scrawl. Collectively they are an absorbing pathological study and tell an extraordinary story :

(NEUSCHWANSTEIN)

February 18th–19th.
It is my express wish that letters are to be written to the Stallmeister [Hornig] and to Klug during the course of the day saying that I assure them with my Royal word that they will both fall into disgrace if the October and November promises are not kept ; that is, if the Throne room here, and the S. Hubertus pavilion and the bedroom in Linderhof, are not finished. This has been promised to Me more than once in the most definite terms and it must be kept. I want it so. Both have the strictest orders to see that the works shall be resumed without delay and that the arrears to the men be paid off by instalments. L : This shall be written—I order it— more strict, more severely, more exact, than ever.

I hope that I can rely on it and that the useless canaille is really treated more severely when I order it. Therefore get others. With the present lot it cannot go on. They are ripe for a mad house.

This is the first definite indication that the break with Hornig (the Stallmeister) was imminent.

On February 19th Ludwig wrote from Neuschwanstein to Prince Ludwig Ferdinand :

> . . . I am infinitely concerned that, as I was always promised, the new Castle here, as well as the Castle and gardens on Herrenwörth, should be finished by 1889. For the Castle of Neuschwanstein the architect assures me he will require five, and, for Herrenwörth, six million Marks. My bedroom in Linderhof—which is as sumptuous as the Reich Zimmer in the Residenz, and which they promised to have finished by November 1885 is, alas, also still very far behind. The painting on the ceiling is, however, nearly completed ; it is an apotheosis of Louis XIV after Le Brun.
>
> I herewith send you a description of the paintings in the Throne room here (in the Byzantine style) which, fortunately, are now finished, thinking it will interest you. The room itself is unhappily not yet completed although it also was promised for December 1885. In my study here, from which I am writing to you, are pictures from the Tannhäuser saga ; in the dining-room the pictures are of the Wartburg in its florescence ; in my bedroom are episodes from Tristan and Isolde and, at the head of the bed is a painting of the Blessed Mother of God after a picture in the Church of S. Sophia in Constantinople ; on the bedstead is a representation, in relief, of the Ascension of Our Saviour. Next to this room is a small Oratory with a picture of S. Ludwig as altarpiece. In the dressing-room are depicted events from the life and writings of Walther von der Vogelweide and Hans Sachs. The sitting-room is adorned with representations from the Saga of the Knights of the Swan ; and the large Sängersaal, on the fourth storey, with paintings illustrating the poetic version of *Parsifal* by Wolfram von Eschenbach . . .

Thus Ludwig himself describes for us, with exactitude

and vividness, the surroundings it gave him such satisfaction to create, and amidst which he was to pass his last hectic hours of freedom.

The only part of the great castle in which it could be said that Ludwig ever lived was the gatehouse. Designed for a lodge-keeper, it is approached by a winding stone staircase and contains accommodation suited to its purpose. Never shown to visitors, it was until a few years ago just as when Ludwig used it. Consisting of a living-room furnished very simply in Bavarian peasant style with the customary fixed wooden seat around two sides of a wall, a heavy table in front, and two small bedrooms, one used by Ludwig and the other by his equerry. The floors were covered with brown coconut matting, and the mattresses and eiderdowns with red Turkey-cotton beloved of the early Victorians. There, in cosy peasant comfort and contentment, Ludwig would frequently stay watching the progress of the building, climbing ladders, talking to all the workmen, winning their love as only he knew how to do, and encouraging their work just as his great-grandfather, grandfather and father used to do when creating modern Munich.

Note by Ludwig:

February 19th–20th.

Will the Ministerial Council please inform Me, with detailed notes, about the behaviour of the Minister of Foreign Affairs, the Minister of the Interior, the Minister of Culture and the Minister of Justice. L : Show them what their duty is. That includes also that the servants know how the shutters and curtains of the windows are opened. Show—not just tell them.

The Stallmeister is not to propose just anyone. He must assure himself beforehand as to how they will behave. Grohe was very talkative. Whether he is to be only temporary remains to be seen. Are the ten days penalty over for his W. Every day, every day, every day, regularly two hours earlier to bed. That is to say, to-morrow at 8 o'clock. Write it down.

The foregoing shows that towards the end of February Hornig was still occasionally exercising functions as acting Master of the Household ; it is the last time but one that he was referred to in writing by Ludwig, and the use of the official title Stallmeister, tells the whole story.

Whatever the nature of their personal relations since their first meeting on Saturday, May 11th, 1867, so many years earlier, Hornig was ever a man of high character, considerable ability, loyal and devoted to his master. He never gossiped, and bore current gossip about himself and the King with a simple dignity. He had an iron nerve, great composure and self-control—and needed both. His patience had to be, and was, almost inexhaustible. When on duty as outrider he had often to dismount seven times in an hour to adjust Ludwig's hot-water bottle. After long journeys on horseback he would return home exhausted and frozen and the devoted and efficient Frau Hornig would wrap him in hot blankets in bed and apply massage. He was sent all over Europe to interview artists and architects and make reports about buildings.

Hornig knew only too well that his Royal Friend and Master who loved him could be cruel, as love often can ; could not brook contradiction, and flew into a rage about trivial matters, as love too often does ; in this he closely resembled Wagner. On the occasion at Schloss Chiemsee while the two thousand five hundred candles burned, Ludwig (who never seemed to want to go to bed) walked up and down the mirror gallery from nine o'clock at night until six in the morning discussing plans for Falkenstein which, had it been built, would have had faults but, being unbuilt, is perfect. All the time Hornig had perforce to stand until he nearly dropped dead and almost went out of his mind because of the insensate manner in which Ludwig kept repeating himself. On another occasion, arguing about finding money for his buildings, the King kept Hornig standing from nine o'clock in the morning until ten in the evening while he himself walked about, lay down, or had his meals. No wonder Hornig's unassailable poise and good manners pleased the King. Ludwig's manners in keeping Hornig on his feet for hours seem inexcusable until we remember that, inheriting the rigid German tradition, Queen Victoria receiving Tennyson in his old age kept him standing throughout a long audience ; for him she

stood herself in homage to his unique eminence ; with
Gladstone, however, because he was one of her servants,
she remained seated while he adroitly compensated himself
and retaliated by addressing her ' as if she were a public
meeting '.

Neuschwanstein, on the south side, rises direct from the
rocky gorge three hundred feet deep and which is, at that
point, the bed of the river Pölatt.   This gorge is spanned by
a narrow suspension footbridge (the Marien Brücke) made of
steel cabling.   Ludwig once took it into his head to make
Hornig ride across this on horseback while he watched the
frail structure swing perilously to and fro getting, presumably, a thrill out of his friend's danger !

Nor was Ludwig's habit of sending through servants to his
Ministers and senior members of his Household so unusual
as it may seem now.   Telephoning was then impossible,
telegraphing slow and public, interior distances in palaces
are considerable, therefore for centuries human beings were
the connecting links.   Lord Ponsonby of Skulkeade in his
Life of his father Sir Henry Ponsonby, who was Private
Secretary to Queen Victoria, records that it was Her
Majesty's custom to send messages through footmen.   She
even sent verbal messages to her sons and members of
the Royal Family in this way.   How else was she to do it ?
Go herself—or send a lady-in-waiting or an equerry !   Sir
Thomas Biddulph complained that the Queen would talk as
if she were Mrs. Jones and could live where and how she
pleased.   He bemoaned the fact that at Balmoral she liked
to be still more alone and to see no one at all, governing the
country by means of messages through footmen to us.
Members of the Enquiry into Ludwig's health were particularly incensed at his treatment of high Court and
Ministerial personages.   Their little vanities were inevitably hurt.   He was the All Highest and that is how they
wrote and spoke of him, but he must never forget that they
were the All Highs.

Ludwig had full need of the reassurances of kingly state
and grandeur and, equally, the need of simple, unrestrained
relations with human beings.   A palace or a hut—no
mediocrities.   It is certain that the weekly dinners at

Seeleiten and the many hours spent there almost as one
of the family were the most peace-filled, serene and enjoy-
able of Ludwig's whole life. He liked Frau Hornig, played
with and nursed the children and continuously gave them
toys and presents. There, as in mountain huts, singing,
romping and drinking beer with groups of peasants, he felt
that he was amongst friends and at home with himself and
his surroundings. As Hornig said, Ludwig ' felt a great
need for human intercourse '.

Now at last, after many quarrels and many reconciliations,
the friendship with Richard was finally broken. Perhaps
Hornig could have borne to the end the futile, humiliating
hunt for money. What he could not stomach was to see
all his influence and power pass into the hands of such men
as Quartermaster Hesselschwerdt (in whom Ludwig had
great and unmerited confidence), and into the hands of a
pack of dirty, lazy, lying varlets—and terrified private
soldiers. The daily increasing deterioration of the King
in his personal habits and his relations with his body servants
—and he would have no one else near him—was to Hornig's
simple, loyal soul cruelly devastating, and when the King
threw objects at his lackeys, and insisted on all servants
practising the kow-tow, approaching him at the crouch
and lying on their bellies on the ground before him to
receive corporal punishment, Hornig, disgusted, at last
declared that he could no longer continue the search for
money. The King flew into a rage, ordered him out of the
house.

The friends never met again.

The written scrawls continued. They are, as far as
possible, given in the exact form and order in which they
were written. Ludwig's literary style is as execrable as his
handwriting and combined they make accurate translation
almost an impossibility. Nevertheless they show, as nothing
else could, how the tottering mind functioned. The next
Note is undated and is given partly in the original as an
example of Ludwig's German towards the end of his life :

The Brüller canaille has not yet fulfilled the order to
catch the big humble bee . . . The awful Brüller shall be

punished severely.   This capital fool and careless swine
. . . Mit der grossten Schärfe auf diesen Schandbrüller
losziehen,   diesen   Capital   Ochsen   und   nachlässigen
Saubengel.

The next note concerns one Hiedl whom Ludwig liked
because he had a good voice.

Undated.

Hiedl must rub oil on his neck to keep it warm, and
take care of himself.
Mulled wine for Hiedl.   I send it to him.   Tell him.
I want to know when he gets his voice back.
I want to know how the face, voice and manners of
Hanizel are?   What age is he?

He would not allow Hornig or anyone else to choose the
most suitable servants to wait on him personally, yet
grumbled incessantly when they did so clumsily.

Undated.

Balcony door has to be shut.   Nobody does anything
by themselves.
It is My own affair whom I want to be on duty with me.

February 21/22.

The Schneider scribble shall be burnt by the Stallmeister.

Undated.

Osterholzer shall be told that he has not to grow a
moustache ;   shall not shorten it either.   Not to be
irritated by the Master of the Horse.   I expect it so.
It never has to be that when my room is got ready for
the night the window is left open.   Horrible nonsense.
More necessary than anything, Brüller to be kept away.
Want one who can not only write fluently but also *well.*
No fresh water for washing !
Write Hesselschwerdt once more that that accident can
never be forgiven, he deserves to be sent away like that
execrable Weclker.
The Brüller canaille once more to be ordered to catch
the big humble bee.
It is too bad that Hiedl lost his agreeable voice yester-
day so that I thought he was somebody quite different.

He shall take care of himself; he *must* know *how* it happened, one surely *feels* that.

Sent Hiedl some of the raspberry sauce ; perhaps it brings back his voice.

Klug's report on his mission to Berlin to implore Bismarck's help was dated February 25th (1886) :

> I have just come back from Berlin—one day earlier than I expected because Bleichroeder had an opportunity of talking to Prince Bismarck yesterday. According to Bleichroeder he (Prince Bismarck) said : ' Without any guarantee it is impossible to raise one million in Germany. Even if His Majesty the King of Bavaria wrote to me personally I should not be able to give any other advice than this : Stop this building and go to the Ministers. Bleichroeder added that under such circumstances His Bavarian Majesty would get the money cheaper (in Berlin) than anywhere in Europe.
>
> All my hopes of being able to get the money which is necessary for the continuation of the buildings have gone since my return from Berlin. I am deeply grieved that Destiny has chosen me to break this sad news to His Majesty.

Following Bismarck's wise advice to lay the whole matter before two Houses of Parliament Ludwig ordered Lutz to do so at once ; but for his own reasons, the Minister-President procrastinated, contenting himself with mentioning the matter privately to a few members. Crailsheim was behind Lutz and both were hand in glove with the traitorous Holnstein who did not consider it beneath his knightly dignity to scurry around like a private detective collecting evidence through servants—as Bismarck put it—' from the King's waste-paper basket '. Bismarck (whose sources of information were unrivalled) said to Lerchinfeld, the Bavarian Envoy to Prussia, that the Bavarian Ministers were ' butchering their King to maintain themselves in office '.

An undated note by Mayr suggests that Ludwig thought of appealing to Clodwig of Hohenlohe :

> Where is Prince Hohenlohe to be on the 31st? Ask Klug when the rooms in Linderhof will be ready. Hesselschwerdt shall not do any more.

Undated Notes by Ludwig.

The door to the balcony is always to be shut when I have passed it. Again left undone. *Write it down.* Nothing is done ·spontaneously.

Only the other day I ordered that the water for the sponge-down has to be *fresher* ! *Horrible.* Very badly done !

It is a shame that the temperature is not looked after.

I want to know how many brothers and sisters Hiedl has. Whether he could not be taught how to behave when on duty.

Paper into the water closet and another pencil.

As soon as I have gone lock up Brüller for $1\frac{1}{2}$ hour.

More than 19 degrees above was forbidden long ago !

From now onwards supper much earlier.

Welcker fell for a time into serious disgrace because he failed to raise a loan of only twenty-five million Marks. An undated Note says :

The pension of the infamous Welcker shall not be diminished ; but he would have got more had he behaved well ; not now. He is infamous.

These awful soldiers can do nothing but give bad service and grouse. Horrible pants, both buttons have gone. Better look after my clothes.

It is a shame not to have been taught how to tie a tie. Four times all wrong. How infamous to keep me waiting like that.

A gigantic bouquet of particularly beautiful flowers shall be sent in My name to the Archduchess Elizabeth the day after to-morrow.

I don't want to write myself ; it's bad for my eyes.

Bad milk ; investigate bed room because of vermin.

Everybody who comes into my room has to bow at the door, and again (immediately) before me. The same on going out.

The command to send flowers on her birthday to the Archduchess Elizabeth, mother of the Queen Regent Christine of Spain, is, as far as is known, the last occasion on which Ludwig concerned himself with the performance of a regal courtesy.

March

As mentally and politically the clouds thickened around Ludwig he instinctively turned more and more towards his Mother ; this tendency, first noticeable after the death of Frau von Leonrod in 1881, became very marked during the last three months of his life :

Ludwig to the Queen Mother :

HOHENSCHWANGAU, *March 9, 1886.*

In remembrance of to-morrow's anniversary of Father's death, and because I am not in Munich as usual at this time of the year, I feel urged to get in touch with you in this way. During the near future I shall remain here anyhow, as what ought to have happened, has not yet happened. Because of profoundly sad experiences I am unhappy and in a bad temper and must wait until the reason for it (the earlier the better) disappears. It is disagreeable to write or say more about it, and I beseech you do not say anything to anybody—even about these pointers. I very much enjoyed the magnificent winter here and would rather like to go to town as usual now . . . The Throne room of the new Castle is not quite finished yet, but the pictures, which are very beautiful, are finished . . . Just now the high mountains are reflecting the morning sun. I am sending you a little Russian altar ; I shall remember you in my prayers. In inmost love I kiss your hand, dear Mother,

Your grateful son,

LUDWIG.

Ludwig to the Queen Mother :

March 11, 1886.

I do hope that you found Otto rather well. To-day I dreamt I spoke to him for a long time. It is deplorable that it isn't possible in reality. I thank you heartily for your dear wishes that I should be happy. That I have not been happy for months has to do with the buildings.

Note by Ludwig :

March 22, 1886.

Hesselschwerdt to speak with Count Dürckheim . . . Count Dürckheim is to come here.

The Queen Mother wrote to Ludwig offering to place at his disposal all the money over which she had any control : he replied :

March 23, 1886.

I feel urged to send you my warmest thanks for your charming offer, which is too kind of you ; but I would like to ask you to allow me to decline.   Through some sort of manipulation the head of the Sekretäriat must succeed in adjusting this matter in time . . .   For some days I have been suffering from a heavy catarrh and pains in my eyes, which I got from reading too much . . .   I should be very glad, dear Mother, to see you here when you leave town . . . especially if I need not see any of your suite (except Countess Du Moulin).

On the same day that Ludwig wrote the above letter Gudden officially told Lutz, the Prime Minister, that the King was mad.   This was exactly what Lutz wanted.

Note by Ludwig :

Even with the tea the milk was bad.
Brüller to be bound.
It strains my eyes too much if I have to write everything myself.   Must be changed.
Don't like Gillitzer ; not agreeable enough.
After getting up, bath ;   I write it down—as an exception.

April

Dürckheim, in the congenial rôle of the King's first favourite, was as careless and indiscreet as he was faithful. The letter of the Emperor Wilhelm I offering Ludwig a loan on conditions had been mislaid and rumours about it had appeared in the *Frankfurter Zeitung*.   There can be no doubt but that at this time, if not indeed much earlier, spies, as Bismarck knew, were smuggled by Ministerial authority into Ludwig's immediate entourage.   Some of the soldiers sent to him may even have been required to play the part of special spies.   Of all this underhand chicanery Prince Luitpold (the King's uncle and Regent Elect) was of course entirely ignorant.

Ludwig, obscurely feeling that he was surrounded by

untrustworthy people, and that the cage he always dreaded and resented was, somehow, closing in around him, naturally enough blamed the wretched Ludwig von Klug—or anyone else at hand.

Notes by Ludwig :

HOHENSCHWANGAU, *April 1st–5th.*

Lock up Nagel for two hours. Tell him that I am dissatisfied with him.

Write Klug that he is an infamous creature ; for the last time write to that infamous one, directly from here, that he must beware of behaving badly. It is his duty to behave well. *Write* once more, and repeat it to him at Steingaden on Monday, that he must not give up trying to get back what I wanted. In October (last) he did not doubt at all that he would get it, nor did he doubt it during the winter. Now I want a proof that he can do more than just make a fool of himself by getting nothing but small things done. For the *last time I order him* to bring back the [Emperor's] lost letter. If he does not do it he shall never be forgiven, and shall always be in disgrace which he has such a talent for throwing himself into.

Undated.

My room has been done *very badly.* I do not want to repeat it *ever.* How often was I told that it should never happen again. It should be *true. Write it down.*

Write Klug that it is the culmination of infamy that that letter got into strange hands.

Want a description of what Gilliger looks like. I didn't see the face properly. When does Prince Ludwig Ferdinand receive the letter ?

Hesselschwerdt shall hurry up to get well.

When I get up I want it to be 17 degrees in the dressing-room. *Note* and *write it down.*

Eberholz must keep himself cleaner and better and wash his shirts ; of the three new ones he has the best movements ; bows his head badly.

When I come it always has to be 15 degrees.

Two loud slaps for the execrable Brüller. Again everything done wrong.

In my dressing-room no fresh toothbrushes. They are used too much.

It has been repeatedly stated by his biographers and others that Ludwig was completely isolated from, and deserted by, every member of the Royal Family during the last months of his life.   This was not so.   True, he was suspicious of his uncle Prince Luitpold, and had never been intimate with him or his children ; but, as was well known, he had always been fond of and intimate with ' the Adalberts '.

Uncle Adalbert had died in 1875, but Ludwig kept him in happy memory and liked all his five children, especially Ludwig Ferdinand the eldest, whom for some time he had been bombarding with letters imploring his help in obtaining money for the castles.   The Prince had done all he could, approaching for a loan, amongst others, his mother-in-law Queen Isabella of Spain.

Ludwig II to Prince Ludwig Ferdinand :

HOHENSCHWANGAU, *April 5th–6th, 1886.*

. . . I am truly sorry to have to trouble you so often with letters, particularly during the last few days . . . up to this it seems you quite hoped that a loan could be raised.   Urgently I beg you to exert yourself to the utmost to prevent above all the sequestration of my Castles . . .

On April 7 Princess Ludwig Ferdinand wrote to her mother Queen Isabella :

Ludwig [Ferdinand] cannot write to you as he is absolutely nearly out of his mind with the daily letters from the King.

Towards mid-April, Marie the Queen Mother went to her mountain villa at Elbingenalp where she planned to stay until December.

About this time at Hohenschwangau Ludwig made an undated entry in the Diary :

. . . Never again (sensual kisses) the morning of the 15th of April 1886 definitively the last fall (which I deplore with all my heart and of which I repent sincerely four months and ten days before the 41st has struck ! . . . oath given before the image of the Holy Immaculate Virgin near the bed, oath.

Notes by Ludwig :

April 22.

Illuminate the Grotto and bring champagne and cigars.

April 24.

Clear the Grotto—Remind me to look happier to-morrow. Write it down. Häussler also.

Häussler and Nagel shall be scolded because they did not bring the vegetables in time.

Ludwig to the Queen Mother :

HOHENSCHWANGAU, *April 26, 1886.*

(Very early in the morning at 5 o'clock)

I spent Easter week very quietly but, unfortunately, like the whole period since August last year, it has been intermixed with bad news., What you write about the love of the Müncheners makes me very glad. I do not doubt that there are many good ones but, unfortunately, they are mixed up with numberless bad ones. Everything could be done—but in an unbearable way !

The same :

HOHENSCHWANGAU, *April 28, 1886.*

I thank you heartily for your loving thought of having Masses said for this unhappy affair.

On April 11th, still at Hohenschwangau, he again wrote to his Mother :

A few days ago the dentist was here and, instead of putting everything right, I have more toothache than before. Please forgive the bad writing, but in consequence of a sleepless night, and the medicines, I am very excited.

Queen Marie offered to come and see him, but he asked her not to do so, saying :

I regret it very much, but you would not enjoy it when I have all these pains . . . it is better so . . .

Note by Ludwig :

April 14.

Serve better and quicker. I don't want to be kept waiting.

Train the canaille better and strictly order them to pay more attention.

Ludwig to his Mother :

HOHENSCHWANGAU, *April 21st, 1886.*

My toothache is gone ; unfortunately not the cause of my melancholy because, instead of getting better, the matter has become worse and worse. Perfectly wonderful are the moonlit nights just now and the view from here is magnificent.

May

In May, the month of rapture which Ludwig so particularly loved, the air in the Bavarian highlands can be like nectar, the sunshine warm, the skies a deep turquoise blue, the lower slopes of the mountains begin to show their endlessly variegated colours while the higher peaks are still in snow. Birds return. Exquisite little spring flowers star the meadows. The larches are already fully clad in their shrill green, contrasting joyously with the deep green masses of the evergreen pine forests. Everywhere beauty and hope abound. Once more Ludwig opened his Diary.

He must make confession somewhere : he cannot do so to his Priest and obtain absolution without solemnly promising to abandon his secret sins, and that he is not yet prepared to do. So reluctant was he to be seen in Church in public, or to face a Priest, that because there was no room for an oratory inside, he had a small, ugly chapel erected in the hillside above Berg and there he went at times to read Mass . . . alone.

Diary :

On the 6th of May, at 7 o'clock in the morning, three months and seventeen days (number of the Royal Lilies in the Great Age). Before the 41st year. Last sensual trespass and kisses—In the name of the Great King, the end for ever, definitely for the last time.

HOHENSCHWANGAU, *the 8th May, 1886.*   LOUIS.

On the 11th Ludwig made a journey from Hohenschwangau to Berg, and a lovely journey it is at any time of the

year. He knew intimately every yard of the road, had seen
it all repeatedly in every season of the year, and never
without joy that at times climbed to rapture.   There were
wayside trees he loved so much that he would stop, remove
his hat, and greet them as personal friends.   He would travel
that road only once again.

Except for too much gilding and a monotonous use of the
colour blue, there is nothing in or about the little Schloss
Berg to suggest that it was the favourite residence of the
King of Bavaria.   When Ludwig was in residence the
Bavarian standard, lozengy silver and azure, flew from the
squat tower over the main entrance ; otherwise the exterior
differed little from thousands of upper middle-class homes
throughout Bavaria.   Inside the walls were mostly blue
with a pattern of gold fleurs-de-lis, and gold stars sprinkled
on the ceilings.   The curtains, portières and upholstery
were of figured blue velvet or silk with a superabundance of
fringing.   Busts of Maximilian II, of Ludwig himself, and
of Wagner stood on circular marble pedestals ; there was
a statuette of Lohengrin drawing his sword, and one of Tell
with his bow in his right hand.   The walls were adorned
with richly-framed rather poor water-colours of scenes from
Wagner's operas.   Ludwig's sitting-room and bedroom and
the dining-room were lit by ugly gas chandeliers of ornate
metal suspended from the centre of the ceilings.   The Queen
Mother's sitting-room and her bedroom—in which Ludwig
was so soon to sleep—were lit by lamps and candlesticks.
The china used by the family, although all made in the
Royal porcelain factory at Nymphenburg, was massive and
useful rather than beautiful.

Ludwig's favourite cup and saucer was of deep Bavarian
blue with heavy gold ornament, an outsize such as big men
like.

The little towers added by Maximilian II are gone ;
inside everything is changed, there being almost nothing to
recall Ludwig II or Queen Marie.   What was in its way a
perfect little period piece laden with historic memories has
disappeared in the sacred cause of progress.

A reversal of all normally accepted values is a commonplace of paranoia.   Ludwig may never have loved or had

entire trust in his father, but he respected him as parent and King. The lay mind was therefore naturally shocked when it was reported that Ludwig exclaimed : ' I was just now in my mind's eye in the vault in the Theatiner Kirche, tore King Max out of his coffin and boxed his ears.' He outraged his own exalted sense of the Kingly office, his habitual courtesy and his shrewd common sense when he sent Hesselschwerdt to the stately father of Paul of Taxis to demand a huge loan ; worse still, he sent him to the King of Sweden and Norway on a similar errand—and was promptly snubbed from Stockholm for doing so.

Towards the end of his life every consideration of every kind was sacrificed by Ludwig to his maniacal obsession for building : ' I must build, or die.' Lack of money was preventing him from continuing to build, therefore, whatever the cost, whatever the loss of Royal dignity amounting to humiliation, money must be found. From Holnstein his Master of the House and Zeigler his principal private secretary down to valets like Mayr ; from Richard, Beloved of my Soul to Welcker of the last fall they, one and all, fell into disgrace because they failed to borrow, beg, or even steal, money ! Because the Bavarian people did not rush to his aid he wished : ' That they had only one head so that he might cut it off ' ; the Chambers were to be dissolved and the Ministry dismissed, and replaced by others more amenable ; individuals unable or unwilling to help to raise money were to be imprisoned or executed.

What very few knew was the pitiable truth that practically all his adult life Ludwig suffered agonizingly from pressure and pain at the back of his head and from chronic sleeplessness. To alleviate these paralysing symptoms for years he took chloral two or three times weekly, later changing to other soporifics. His immeasurable agony may be judged by the fact that he had frequently to have ice packs applied to his head, occasionally even during meals. Until after the post-mortem even those closest to Ludwig did not realize how terrible and continuous were his sufferings : That is his absolution.

CHAPTER FIFTEEN

THE INEVITABLE END : JUNE : 1886

Which built desolate places for themselves.

JOB.

IN formulating a plan for forcing the King to abdicate, the Bavarian Government held several strong cards : Ludwig's prolonged neglect of his Regal duties ; the large sums he had over a period of twenty years lavished on Wagner personally and on the production of his Operas ; his extravagance in building three great unnecessary castles and having had fantastically beautiful plans made for a fourth, Falkenstein, in the Chinese tradition, which in size and cost was to outvie the others and have an even more enchanting site than Neuschwanstein.

The cardinal fact that all the money expended came from Ludwig's Privy purse, or from his patrimony, was ignored. Obviously none of the cost of helping Wagner, commanding private performances in the Residenz Theatre, building his castles and so on fell upon public funds because there had been no government grant for any such purposes throughout the reign. The financial score worked up by Lutz and his camarilla to discredit the King was largely anticipatory. Bavarians were not once reminded by any one in authority that they owed almost every fine and beautiful thing they possessed to the artistic flair and personal munificence of the long line of Wittelsbach Dukes, the seven Wittelsbach Electors and the four Wittelsbach Kings. Moreover, the populace had always criticized ; had indeed actively opposed Maximilian I, Ludwig I, and Maximilian II for all they did in a thousand ways to advance Bavarian art, architecture, culture and prestige. After all, Ludwig II was employing nothing but native artists and craftsmen : had he gone abroad the artistic results might well have been more admirable.

Ludwig himself was quite clear on all this, and it was

one of the rankling causes of his dislike and distrust of the Bavarian people in general and the Müncheners in particular. On the night of April 5–6, recalling his grandfather's abdication, and the revolutionary upsurge throughout Europe of which it was one of the symptoms, he wrote to Prince Ludwig Ferdinand :

> Now the people understand what our grandfather did for them—while he was still reigning King they behaved shamefully to him, opposing him particularly for his artistic aspirations, and not only on that account, until finally, in the year 1848, they all turned against him . . .

On the abdication question the Government's best card was the clause in the Constitution which provided that a Sovereign who became incapable of exercising his proper functions could be set aside and a Regency proclaimed ; but there was silence as to how this should be done. It was under this clause that, driven by Lutz, the Government and Prince Luitpold (the nearest male capable of ascending the throne) acted. The legal dilemma was that according to the basic law of the Constitution the executive power resided in the King, and the responsibility for the government of the Kingdom in his Ministers : therefore, in the absence of Ludwig's acquiescence, one half of the Constitutional power was, in fact, acting without the other.

Many informed and responsible people, including his uncle, the second Prince of the Blood Royal Luitpold, Heir Presumptive, Councillor of State, Inspector-General of the Army and, after Otto, the highest personage in the realm, were reluctant to make use of the only valid right they had, the state of the Sovereign's mental health.

There was mental instability on both sides of the Royal Family. Princess Alexandra, Luitpold's own sister, had spent her life under restraint and, from his earliest years until her death, her health was a matter of deep concern to her nephew Ludwig. His mother's uncle, King Friedrich Wilhelm IV of Prussia, became insane in 1857 when Ludwig was aged twelve and old enough to be severely shocked and frightened by the event. When Otto's case was pronounced hopeless Ludwig was heart-stricken. He then realized in his inmost soul that now there could be for him no reprieve ; that he would himself be the next victim in this terrifying succession.

But it was one thing for such tragic facts to be vaguely known ; it would be quite another thing, and a serious one, to blazon them to the world by an official act of the Bavarian Government branding the King and his brother as lunatics. Moreover, the Bavarian Royal Family was not only closely related to almost every Royal House in Europe, Catholic and Protestant, but was deeply entrenched in the hearts of the Bavarian people as in spite of—perhaps because of—his vagaries and temporary phases of unpopularity was Ludwig himself. In justice to the country the Government had no option but to remove Ludwig from the active functions of kingship. If it did no wrong it did what was right in the wrong way. Every agent it employed was inept, stupid and unbelievably clumsy. That the whole problem was never objectively considered, and that it was poisoned with personal considerations and secret, unavowable ambitions, is proved by the fact that no provision was made for simultaneously removing Otto from the succession ; therefore the procedure adopted simply removed one lunatic from the Throne in order to substitute another.

It will make not only for clarity and convenience, but for a better understanding of the working of Ludwig's mentality if, from now on, we follow the happenings of the last thirteen days of his life strictly in chronological order.

The creaking legal machinery was set going by the following letter from Prince Luitpold :

MUNICH, *June 1st, 1886* [*Tuesday*].
My dear Ministerial Councillor Dr. von Zeigler :
The obvious illness of His Majesty the King has, as you know, put the country in a very sad predicament so that I consider it my duty to consider taking measures which—within the Constitution—would guarantee the continuity of the Government. For this purpose it is absolutely necessary to get as exact a picture as possible of the mental state of His Majesty the King. As you have been in the immediate surroundings of His Majesty

for a long time, you should be in a position to give trust-worthy facts which would be valuable as psychological evidence, and I therefore request you to let me have a memorandum with the observations which you have made in that direction.   With the assurance of my esteem, I am,

Your gracious

LUITPOLD

Prince of Bavaria.

While his uncle was composing this difficult letter Ludwig —although neither knew it—was writing to his Mother for the last time.

LINDERHOF, *June 1st, 1886.*

Dear Mother !
Heartfelt thanks for your dear letter and the news which it contained.   As I have been exceptionally long this year at Hohenschwangau, having only left there on the 11th of May, I did not go back there during that month—as I usually do—but only to-day the 1st of June.   I shall be there for a few weeks, and then probably for the end of July or beginning of August as usual.   That you are glad not to be in Munich I can well understand ; it is horrid there, especially in the summer.   It was very beautiful on the Hochkopf with splendid moonshine, and also *here* at *Linderhof.*   I hope you will have some nice summer days at Elbingenalp ; I can quite understand that you do not wish to go to town during the visit of Queen Isabella, but I think she will leave soon after the delivery of her daughter.[1]   I kiss your hand, dear Mother, and am always, in innermost love,

Your grateful son,

LUDWIG.

That Ludwig had lost none of his gracious courtesy towards women or that, even now, he was entirely divorced from a sense of his Regal duties, is proved by the following letter to Prince Ludwig Ferdinand.   It is one more example of the complete duality with which his mind functioned :

[1] Major H.R.H. Prince Adalbert of Bavaria was born at Schloss Nymphenburg on June 3rd, 1886. He m. in 1919 Princess Agusta, great-granddaughter of the Emperor Franz Josef and the Empress Elizabeth ; they have two sons, the Princes Konstantine and Alexander.

HOHENSCHWANGAU, *June 4, 1886. Friday.*

Beloved Cousin !

Receive first of all my heartfelt thanks for your last two letters. My heart is illumined with pleasure by the pure gold of your friendship, faithful and firm as a rock. I know that I can always count not only on you but on my beloved cousin your brother.[1] Greet him affectionately for me, please, and thank him heartily in my name.

To the proposed visit of inspection by Queen Isabella to the unfortunately still unfinished Schloss Chiemsee I, of course, cordially agree. I pray you, however, to beg the Queen to be so kind as not to speak of it. I am also very anxious that Her Majesty should through you know beforehand that, so far, there is very little to see ; moreover, the paintings on the ceilings have become very faded and require renovation. Please lay me at the Queen's feet—and try to prevent her expectations being too high.

Receive at the same time my warmest congratulations on the birth of your son.

Embracing you, with heartfelt love,

Your faithful Cousin,

LUDWIG

Monday, June 7th

In Munich the plot against the Sovereign was being relentlessly, if not very skilfully, developed ; the cross-examination of Hesselschwerdt and Welcker, which had begun on May 18th, was continued.

Pitiable human document though the Diary be, its use is justifiable, indeed here imperative, because it proves that, from beginning to end, Ludwig fought the sin that did so easily beset him, and ' in his innermost heart ' never *assented* to sin. If tempted to judgment it would be well to remember that, if not in words on paper, Everyman keeps perforce some sort of secret diary in the hidden recesses of his life. Ludwig's Diary is one more proof (were such needed) that what man needs is not so much a doctor to repair his body as a physician to heal his soul.

However it may appear, no human happening is really

---

[1] Prince Alfonso (1862–1893) married Sophie's daughter, Princess Louise d'Orleans.

sudden.   Life is incontestably continuous and the outward manifestation has long been prepared for by foreshadowings unnoted, unseen, perhaps, as they arrived, almost unseeable. An event, often quite trivial, occurs and the secret, long-nourished heroisms or abasements suddenly stand forth in stark reality.

As far back as his twentieth year Ludwig had, as we know, aroused gossip by an invidious friendship with the valet called Voelk during the period when he was repeatedly exchanging repeated vows of eternal friendship with his cousin Gackl, Paul of Taxis and Wagner.   We now come to his last Diary entry from which there is no evading the fact that Welcker was his minion :

> 1st June definitely the last full 2 months and 3 weeks
>   before the 41st birthday
>   You remember Sire
>   Remember
>   Remember
>   From henceforth never !
>   From henceforth never !
>   From henceforth never ! ! !
>
>   Sworn in the name of the Great King
>   now invoking the puissant aid of the Redeemer.
>
> Linderhof.
>   (Also from kisses strictly to abstain
>   I swear it in the name of the King of
>   Kings.)
>
> Alfonso.   7 June   Ludwig

Sealed with the Royal cypher and Crown, this time Ludwig kept his pledge inviolate.

Welcker, on a basis of equality, added his name to this solemn pledge ; yet, between the day of the act at Linder-hof on Tuesday the 1st which Ludwig described as ' very beautiful, with splendid moonshine ', and its repudiation five days later at Hohenschwangau, Welcker, after giving evidence against his Sovereign, master, and friend before the Commission of Inquiry, returned from Munich and, displaying an amazing combination of acting ability and duplicity, joined in signing the final oath.

Fortunately for the last remnant of his peace of mind Ludwig—deceived and betrayed to the end—went to his grave believing that Alfonso Welcker, at least, was faithful.

The last Diary entry differs from most of the others in not being made in the revulsion of spent passion ' when all animals are sad ', but after several days of remorseful regret.

Tuesday, June 8th

In Munich four doctors sat considering Gudden's evidence from 9.00 a.m. to noon. They agreed that a personal examination of the King was unnecessary, and Gudden signed his report which then became the basis for all further action.

Wednesday, June 9th

A deputation representing the Government and the Commission set out in the afternoon for Hohenschwangau by special train. At its head was Kraft Baron von Crailsheim, Minister of the King's Household and of Foreign Affairs, Count Holnstein, Ludwig's Master of the Horse, Baron von Malsen, Grand Master of his Household, Count Toering, one of the most prominent nobles in his kingdom, Lieutenant-Colonel Baron von Washington, one of his aides-de-camp, Gudden, and Karl von Rumpler who was appointed to act as secretary. Arriving at Hohenschwangau and finding the King not there they decided to rest and confer. As was customary, Ludwig's carriage and horses were ready in case he suddenly decided to take a nocturnal drive. Holnstein, that ' Wolf with a privy paw ', ordered the horses to be unharnessed and the coach put away. Osterholzer, the King's coachman, realizing that something was seriously wrong and his Sovereign in danger, slipped off in the dark and hurriedly crept up to Neuschwanstein by a mountain footpath. Admitted by Weber into the ante-room he warned Ludwig who, at first unbelieving, said : ' It cannot be ; Hesselschwerdt would have warned me.' However, he sent to the villages of Hohenschwangau and Füssen, aroused the local authorities, summoned the police and Fire Brigade, the villagers and the peasantry, all of whom immediately responded.

Thursday, June 10th

When after their rest the deputation eventually reached the new castle gateway about 5.30 a.m. they found it strongly guarded and themselves surrounded by an angry crowd armed with rifles, knives, scythes, axes and cudgels. The officer in charge of the castle guard said that if anyone tried to enter, his men would shoot. Because they insisted upon seeing the King one of the visitors was knocked down and, frightened and discomfited, they all retired to Hohenschwangau. Ludwig, with one of his rare fits of energy, then ordered Dürckheim to send the Master of the Castle Watch and eight men down to Hohenschwangau and arrest Crailsheim, Holnstein and Toering. They resisted arrest by insisting that it was illegal, and that they had their orders from Prince Luitpold, who was now Regent—which was not yet true. However, on the officer showing that he would, if necessary, use force to execute the King's command, the three nobles 'consented' to be arrested, were marched on foot up the hill to Neuschwanstein and imprisoned in the castle gateway. In the confusion Rumpler escaped and posted off to Munich with the news. Ludwig talked wildly of having the lot beheaded—especially Holnstein, his friend of over twenty years' standing, whose open treachery he rightly found unpardonable. However, as the newly-occupied castle was not provisioned for a siege, there was no way of feeding the prisoners and, when his temper cooled, he ordered his enemies to be released and they slunk back to Munich humiliated and—for the time being—demoralized but full of guile. The Government was also frightened, seeing clearly that if Ludwig and his friends and supporters resolutely took command of events it could result in Civil War.

During the absence of the Commission the Government Proclamation announcing that King Ludwig was unfit to govern and that a Regency under Prince Luitpold had been established was posted in Munich, and a meeting of the Landtag or Lower House called for the 15th.

At Neuschwanstein Ludwig held a Council of war. Dürckheim and Welcker advised him to escape across the Austrian frontier, an hour's drive away, and, upon his refusing to leave his kingdom, telegraphed to Kempten for troops to defend the castle and sent telegrams to Bismarck and the Emperors Wilhelm I and Franz Josef. Ludwig and Dürckheim next drew up a Proclamation denouncing all traitors and calling upon all his loyal subjects for their support. It was a clear, well-considered piece of appealing rhetoric and, in terms of law and loyalty, unanswerable. Dürckheim managed somehow to have ten thousand copies printed. They were confiscated by the Government.

Ludwig had now no one near him but domestics, most of whom, although as yet he knew it not, were traitors. He sat down at his ornate desk in his study or workroom from the walls of which brilliant frescoes illustrating the Tannhäuser legend with scenes showing the Sängerkrieg in the Wartburg looked down. There, hurriedly but clearly, using a pencil, he wrote to his faithful cousin Prince Ludwig Ferdinand whom he told that an astonishing thing had happened. One of his servants had come to him privately and told him that a Court official and some others had arrived from Munich to seize his horses and carriages secretly in order to make him a prisoner. He was to be forced to abdicate on the ground of illness. Can you, he exclaimed, credit such infamy? He besought the Prince to try and find out what it all meant and throw some light on ' this abyss of treachery '. ' I cannot think who is behind it. Someone must be. Can you discover? For some time I have known that people have been paid for going about saying that I am ill and unfit to reign. Such infamy.' That—any more than his Proclamation—is not the letter of a lunatic. The conditions under which both were written would have more than excused mental confusion of which there is not a trace. The servant who was sent with the last letter Ludwig wrote did not manage to deliver it at Nymphenburg in time to do any good. When it reached Prince Ludwig Ferdinand the King was already a prisoner at Berg. Upon her husband telling the Infanta Paz the tragic news she burst into a storm of tears.

Could this admittedly very perplexing situation have been dealt with less clumsily? Differently inspired, yes : Prince Luitpold himself might have gone to see his nephew and, in an affectionate talk, perhaps have persuaded him to abdicate. Should this have looked too like self-interest to be dignified, he could have sent his eldest son, Ludwig's first cousin, who afterwards reigned as Ludwig III, or he could have sent Prince Ludwig Ferdinand (who, as he must have known, was in constant touch with the King), or the Queen Mother, or Elizabeth of Austria (who was nearby), the Crown Prince Rudolf of Austria, or even the Emperor Franz Josef himself, all closely bound to the Wittelsbachs by blood and marriage, could fittingly have been asked to intervene ; Clodwig von Hohenlohe, if only because he was related to Queen Victoria, would have been acceptable to Ludwig. Best of all would have been the Queen Mother who may not have been politically brilliant by Bismarckian standards but who by her power to soothe Otto and her incomparable patience towards him proved that she was richly endowed with the priceless wisdom of the heart.

As it was, a pack of the most obtuse alienists that ever assembled was entrusted with what was after all a highly delicate historic task. Gudden's brutality can perhaps be palliated on the ground that it was at the time mental specialists still considered it desirable to treat lunatics with harshness often amounting to cruelty. There is, however, little or no excuse for the others. Gudden's obtuseness was monumental. As Ludwig loved Linderhof some kindly person suggested it as a suitable and congenial retreat ; but it was reputed that the population was so incensed by rumours of what was happening to the King at Neuschwanstein that the idea was dismissed. Whereupon Gudden, backed by Holnstein, advised Fürstenried as convenient for himself and others, asserting that he could so arrange matters that Ludwig and Otto would never meet. It did not occur to him that the dreadful proximity would have a most demoralizing effect on both patients. Finally Berg was decided upon and Grashey was sent there to have Ludwig's private apartment turned into a prison.

NEUSCHWANSTEIN, *night of Wednesday, June 9th*

During that night and the day of the 10th (Thursday) Ludwig at Neuschwanstein was exposed to the utmost mental and emotional strain. Dürckheim recalled to Munich by a telegram from the Minister of War, Holnstein was absent and so Ludwig was alone except for a few frightened domestics. Overcome with irresolution, he seemed unable or unwilling to tear himself away from the castle which seemed somehow to be concrete evidence that he still had a will and an existence of his own.

Ludwig spent the night of the 10th wandering from room to room of the almost completed new and greater Wartburg of his dreams. Isolated, beset by foes from within and without, he, as usual, escaped into fantasy. He was still King of Dreams. The great house that he had against all obstacles created was peopled only by ghosts : by the ghosts, so vividly pictured on its walls, of Sigurd, Tannhäuser, Walter von der Vogelweide, Hans Sachs, the heroes of the Wartburg, of S. Louis himself. They, and the huge castle in which he had tried to re-endow them with a semblance of life, were shrouded in an uncanny silence. Ludwig's foreboding and intuitive soul waited for its oncoming destiny. With no man or woman to help him in his agony he wandered in dishevelled thought from empty room to empty room.

A few dozen yards away was the great, cold Byzantine Throne room two storeys high with magnificent views all over the High Country of the Swan. The enormous dais, reached by some twenty semi-circular steps, was placed in an imposing apse like the chancel of a Romanesque Church. True, there was as yet no Praetorian Seat—but cunning craftsmen far away were engaged in making a Byzantine Throne of solid gold. Then upstairs, just over his own private apartment, was the great new Sängersaal, ninety feet long, which he had planned as a fitting temple in which the Master, the Great Friend, would himself fill its arches with his own glorious, incomparable music . . . The Royal dais in the new Throne room was empty . . . An empty niche mocking him, for he had no money now for his golden throne—and neither his children nor those of Otto would ever occupy that phantom seat. The Great Friend would never make music in the New Castle of the Swan : nevertheless, while he was King, no lesser musician should ever desecrate its dedicated silences. The whole of the Romanesque palace was created for, and dedicated to, artists and art. Courtiers, sycophants, the obtuse, war-mongers, money-grubbers, decoration-scroungers like Holnstein, and such as bought with money spurious titles of nobility, would be for ever excluded. But crusaders, knights, poets, lovers, peasants and simple people ; all the worshippers of beauty, the musicians and singers from all over the world, would be welcomed in fitting, regal surroundings, by a King. As he had once said to the Great Friend :

> The artist and the king, being of the heights,
> Should always walk hand in hand.

Friday, June 11th

While Ludwig was lost in fantasy his enemies were active.

The second delegation set out from Munich for Neuschwanstein. No longer making any pretence of negotiations, it consisted only of doctors, policemen, five mental keepers and one of Ludwig's traitorous servants. This time Gudden was in sole command—he had charge of all the lunatics in Bavaria—and had as his assistants Dr. Grashey, his son-in-law, and Dr. Müller, both of whom were also mental specialists. Horn, Captain of the Gendarmes at Schwanstein, assured the connivance of the local police and Leefield, Richard Hornig's deputy, ensured control of all the Royal horses and carriages. The castle guard was superseded by soldiers from Munich.

Arriving at Neuschwanstein about midnight the party was surreptitiously admitted by Ludwig's own valet, Mayr, who was awaiting them. He implored the doctors to go at once to the King, who was threatening suicide.

During the earlier part of the night Ludwig had kept demanding the key of the main tower, nearly two hundred feet high, but was told that it was mislaid or lost and that

the servants were looking for it. Mayr advised Gudden
not to enter the private apartment lest the King should
jump from the balcony. Gudden therefore placed his men,
armed with strait-jackets, in strategic positions in the long
wide corridor and staircase, sent Mayr to give the King the
key, and himself hid near the principal staircase which
Ludwig must use in order to ascend to the roof of the
tower, two storeys higher up.

It would seem that when, a few minutes later, Ludwig
approached the staircase, he had definitely determined to
commit suicide. However, two stalwart warders stepped
forward and he was seized by each arm. The strait-
jacket carried by one of them did the rest.

Gudden revealed himself and, incredibly, immediately
made a speech reminding Ludwig that they had already met
on one occasion when he was honoured with an audience for
the purpose of personally presenting a report on Otto's
condition ! Ludwig, outraged to the depths of his soul,
miraculously composed himself, and Gudden suggested that
he should go back quietly to his apartment, which he did.
Warders were posted at the windows and the balcony doors.

All Ludwig said was :

'Without examining me, how can you pronounce on the
state of my health ? '

To this pertinent question Gudden pontifically replied :

'An examination is unnecessary ! '

An examination was 'unnecessary' because the Commission now held not only the ace, but the trump. There
was no longer any need to rely exclusively on medical
evidence ; or, as Bismarck put it, upon the scroungings of
the King's wastepaper basket ; one of the spies around
Ludwig's person had purloined the secret Diary and, the
ink on the last entry hardly dry, it was in the possession of
his enemies.

Having first seated himself without permission—an
impertinence for which Ludwig made him pay—Gudden
then proceeded to harangue his Sovereign for three hours !
However, it gave Ludwig what he wanted most—time to
mature his plan of escape. Every atom of his mind con-
centrated on that ; his dangerous quietude hoodwinked

Gudden completely and, when the harangue at last ended, knowing exactly what he intended, Ludwig agreed to go quietly to Berg, every blade of grass of which he knew as friendly. There, in the beloved castle with its precious memories of Wagner, Paul, Richard, Varicourt, Hirschberg, Kainz and Alfonso the faithful, he would say good-bye to life.

Whit Saturday, June 12th

At four o'clock in the morning, Ludwig entered his coach alone because Gudden, in order to avoid exasperating him, had—with unusual delicacy—arranged for him to travel without a strange companion. However, every precaution had been taken. The head nurse, as he was euphemistically described, seated himself on the box beside the coachman, the door handles of the carriage had been removed so that it could not be opened from the inside. A groom rode alongside.

What were Ludwig's thoughts ? His plans ? His hopes ?

He was locked into the centre one of the three carriages, the little procession looking not unlike a modest country funeral except that the vehicles were in Royal colours and the horses perfect ; four to each carriage, they carried Royal silver and blue harness and trappings. In the carriage immediately behind were Gudden, the traitorous Captain Horn, and Gudden's assistant, Dr. Müller.

As Dürckheim and Welcker had sensibly emphasized, Ludwig could easily have crossed the frontier and claimed the protection of Franz Josef, Elizabeth and his friend the Crown Prince Rudolf. His Mother was living on Austrian soil. Escaped ? Escaped from Bavaria, yes ; but could he at the age of forty ever have escaped from himself?

We know what Gudden thought on that journey because Grashey has told us.[1] As the account was set down before the events had lost colour in his mind, it may, all things considered, be taken as the fairest, most complete and most accurate we have.

Three carriages cannot travel as fast as one ; relays of horses had been arranged ; there was a brief pause at

---

[1] *Nekrolog auf Dr. Bernhard von Gudden*, von H. Grashey, Archiv für Psychiatrie, Bd. xvii (Berlin, 1886).

Weilheim, in order that the men might obtain relief and refreshment. The King, however, was not allowed to leave his carriage. He had inside the small travelling commode he usually carried strapped in a stout leather case not unlike a much enlarged old-fashioned leather travelling case used in Victorian days for carrying silk hats. At Weilheim, Mayr, who was in the first carriage with two of the keepers, left the party, and the last man who had an opportunity of betraying Ludwig vanished from the shadier outskirts of history into a disgraceful obscurity.

Travelling via Peitring, Weilheim and Seeshaupt, the party covered the eighty-four kilometres in some eight hours, arriving at Berg just before noon.

The King, who had not been in bed the night before, and who could not have had any solid food for some fifteen or sixteen hours, was very quiet, conversed with Gudden as he went to his apartment, followed his advice to eat something and then go to bed at once in his own bedroom. Watched by a keeper after having been served by keepers, and with two others posted in the ante-room, he slept for some hours, at first quietly, then grew restless and talked in his sleep.

Whit Sunday, June 13th

On the morning of the Feast of Pentecost, Ludwig awoke about 2 a.m. and wanted to get up, but was persuaded to stay in bed until six o'clock. He then had, as was his morning custom, a cup of soup and asked for his valet Mayr and his hairdresser Hoppe. He was much distressed when told that they were not there to wait on him ; reluctantly he suffered Alexander, one of the keepers, to act as valet, but would not allow him to shave him.

Meanwhile downstairs men from Munich had arrived and were measuring all the windows in order that they might be fitted with iron bars. Like Charles I he could listen to his scaffold being built. Hammering was going on everywhere, and the texture of Ludwig's skull was so thin that all his life noise drove him frantic.

At 8 o'clock Gudden asked for an audience ; this was granted at 8.15, he was allowed to present Grashey who conversed for half an hour, answering his Sovereign's questions, and tactfully putting some of his own.   Inferior in professional rank to Gudden, he was superior to him in every other way.   As neither Gudden nor Grashey left any record of these questions and answers it is only possible to infer what was in Ludwig's mind.   He remained dangerously quiet ; completely self-controlled ; courteous ; kind.   He asked that it should be arranged for him to hear Mass, and his request was refused.   Had this last wish been granted, Ludwig might well have opened his heart, disclosed his intentions to his Confessor, and murder and suicide been prevented.   Gudden, being a Protestant, acted ignorantly. It was not Ludwig's fault that he went to his death unshriven.

At ten o'clock, at Gudden's suggestion, he and his prisoner went for a walk.   It was raining a little so Ludwig took his overcoat and umbrella—the large untidy umbrella and thick, ill-fitting double-breasted overcoat with a velvet collar that he affected in his later years.   In front went a policeman, followed by Ludwig and Gudden quietly con- versing side by side ; about thirty paces behind them walked two keepers.   Grashey watched the tragic proces- sion from the window of the King's ante-room.   After a little Gudden looked back, making a gesture which clearly conveyed that the two warders following were to keep a good distance.

Ludwig, noticing the policeman ahead, asked uneasily if there was any danger.   For some time he had been so afraid of assassination that he had ordered a chain-mail waistcoat to be made, but seldom wore it.   During the walk Gudden arranged for another walk after dinner, which was to be served at four o'clock.

When they got back to the Schloss Gudden instructed Grashey that it would be better to do without the police- man as his presence excited the King ; he, however, said nothing about the advisability of going without the keepers.

At four forty-five Grashey left Berg for Munich to report to the Regent and Government that all was well !

The King dined alone attended by Bruno Mauder, one of the keepers, whom, later, he sent to find Gudden in order to go for the promised walk.   He went to Gudden's room, told him the King was ready, got the King's hat, overcoat and umbrella, and then warned Schneller that it was his turn to accompany him on guard. Mauder helped the King on with his coat and handed him his round felt hat, the wide, silk-bound brim turned up at each side. At six-thirty as the King left the southern or garden entrance to the Schloss he asked Mauder to roll his umbrella which, being damp from the morning stroll, had been left unrolled. Mauder, having done so, turned back to speak to Gudden who was four or five paces behind the King. Gudden, sealing his own fate, said : ' The nurses must not go with the King' (Es darf kein Pfleger mitgehen).

Before this Gudden had told Müller that he and the King would be back by eight o'clock.

At seven-fifteen Müller joined von Washington, the jailer aide-de-camp in-waiting, who was staying at the Villa Poschinger near by, where dinner was to be served at eight o'clock for Washington, Gudden and Müller.

When, at eight o'clock, word was brought to Müller that the King and Gudden had not returned as arranged, he went back to the Schloss and ordered a policeman to search for them. The policeman did not return, and, getting really uneasy, Müller sent out two more policemen and one of the keepers. Presently the whole Schloss was aroused. There had been considerable delay on Müller's part. Searchers were now hurriedly sent out in all directions.

At ten-thirty they found Ludwig's hat, jacket, overcoat and umbrella on the shore of the lake. Then Hubert, the steward at Berg, discovered the two bodies, lying a short distance apart. Gudden's feet were on dry ground with his face downward under the water as if his slight body were forcibly held there by a strong man of six foot three until he drowned. The King's body lay in the water a little farther out, but so shallow that it would not have reached his knees standing up. A boat was sent for ; the bodies were brought ashore and placed on the gently sloping bank and Müller tried artificial respiration. At twelve o'clock he gave it up and declared that the King and Gudden were both dead. Ludwig's watch had stopped at 6.45 p.m.

Bearers were arranged, the bodies taken back to the Schloss and laid out in separate rooms on the first floor.

The Bürgomeister and other officials were summoned from Starnberg and examined the bodies. Gudden's face, especially on the nose and forehead, was badly scratched ; there was a large blue bruise over the right eye ; the nail of the middle finger of the right hand was missing.

Whit Monday, June 14th

At dawn, Philipp Count von Eulenburg, Secretary of the Prussian Legation, who in the absence of his chief was Chargé d'Affaires and who had a summer villa at Starnberg, arrived at the Schloss. He afterwards said that he 'had seen on the heavy neck of the physician the terrible marks of strangulation'. None of the officials or doctors concerned confirmed this.

There was no mark of any sort or kind on Ludwig. His face was once again young and beautiful and filled with peace as if at last, he could truly say : ' to me my rest '.

A messenger was hurried off to the Regent who, when he heard the disastrous news, burst into tears.

Whit Monday, June 14th

About eleven o'clock a messenger brought a small bunch of Jasmine from the Empress Elizabeth, who was at Possenhofen, with the express wish that it should be placed in the King's hand.

A little girl, the daughter of a tailor who was accustomed to reline the King's suits with the white silk lining he insisted on having to every garment, was sent to the Schloss with a message early on the Monday evening. She was taken to the death chamber and, long afterwards, when she was an old woman, told a young Bavarian Princess that she had never been able to forget the dead King's sleeping marble face as white almost as the jasmine blossoms lying on his breast, or his thick, wet, black, wavy hair.

The Bavarian people were indignant, angry, revengeful. What evil had been done to their Fairy King? He had been abstracted, imprisoned, murdered—and so on. Rumour herself became drunk with rumours.

The body was conveyed after midnight on Monday privately to Munich where an autopsy was performed.

Ludwig's body, which was found to be very healthy, was

dressed in the robes of the Grand Master of the Knights of
S. Hubertus, consisting of black silk knee-breeches, black
figured velvet knee-length tunic elaborately trimmed with
silver, short black cloak lined with white silk, white ruff,
deep white turned-back ruffles round the wrists and around
the neck the Collar and badge of the Order. The well-
shaped left hand lay by his side, the fingers on the sheath of
the slender sword ; his right, placed across his breast, held
Elizabeth's Jasmine. Not having been shaved since the
Friday morning the marble face showed a distinct trace of
dark beard growing upwards from the imperial towards the
ears. The hair, brushed upwards and backwards to conceal
the work of the surgeons, gave an elongated, uncharacteristic look to the forehead and head.

For the last time Ludwig slept in the Residenz. He lay
in state on an inclined open bier which was covered with
his ermine robe of State and surrounded by flowers and
lighted candles. The sumptuous Reiche Kapelle, consecrated in 1607, was glorious with its gold and silver
ornaments and lovely wall panels after Dürer's Life of the
Virgin, and adjoined the Reich Zimmer which Ludwig so
subjectively loved.

When Duchess Karl Theodor entered to say good-bye
to the man who, only a few hundred yards from the spot
where he now rested, had first introduced her to the beauties
of Wagner's *Lohengrin*, all the widow of Ludwig's first friend
Gackl could see was a marble profile with closed eyes, a
marble hand holding a white nosegay, and glimpses of a
sixteenth-century dress almost entirely covered with concealing flowers carefully arranged, especially about the head.

Thursday, June 17th

The King was borne to his tomb in the noble Court
Church of S. Michael in the great black hearse still pre-
served in the Marstall Museum. Eight horses drew it and
Ludwig's favourite charger walked behind. Knights of
the Order of S. Hubertus flanked the coffin on each side.
The new Prince Regent walked alone with lowered head,
followed in a body by the Princes of his House, Courtiers,
State officials and notabilities.

The troop-lined route was packed with an enormous crowd of Ludwig's mourning people. To give as many as possible of his bewildered subjects an opportunity of saying farewell the procession followed a circuitous route from the Residenz to the Church ; such a funeral had never been seen in Bavaria ; it took two and a half hours to pass a given spot.

The chief foreign mourner was the Crown Prince Rudolf of Austria-Hungary. Mourner and mourned understood and loved one another, subconsciously recognizing, even as did Rudolf's mother Elizabeth, that they were doomed to share a latent originality, a thwarted genius, a common fate.

Peaceful at last, Ludwig's unhappy heart was laid to rest amongst the twenty-odd hearts of the Rulers and Princes of the House of Wittelsbach preserved in the Votive Chapel of Alt-Otting, watched over from her silver tabernacle by the famous miraculous Black Madonna. His, as he would have liked, was enshrined in an ornate silver-gilt vase of French design bearing his favourite cypher, two reversed L's intertwined. Close to it are the urns containing the hearts of his father Maximilian II, and his grandfather Ludwig I. Otto's heart is a little way off as, when it came, there was not room for it beside the others : these three Kings, each in their appointed way, had to learn the bitter and universal truth that neither men nor nations can subjugate destiny.

If we have any faith in mercy and justice we cannot fail to believe that such prolonged and, seemingly, fore-ordained spiritual, emotional, mental and physical agony as Ludwig the Second suffered will somehow, somewhere, be purged and assuaged. Meanwhile we dare not—will not—judge. Some five hundred and fifty years ago Dame Juliana of Norwich knew well that the Saints are but the sinners who kept on trying ; it is therefore only brotherly to take leave of the Lonely King in the sweet words from her *Revelations of Divine Love* :

> In every soul that shall be saved is a godly will
> that never *assented* to sin . . .

CHAPTER SIXTEEN

WHAT HAPPENED AFTERWARDS

'I CAN bear that they take the Government from me, but not that they declare me insane.' [1]

In this his last recorded saying we have, if anywhere, the secret of Ludwig's end. As for abdication, there is ample evidence, from the date of Wagner's banishment from Munich in 1865, that, much as he loved his kingly dignity, he again and again seriously considered voluntarily leaving the Throne. Moreover, from his late teens the idea of suicide was recurrent. Had the project of abdication been put to him persuasively in 1886, accompanied by an undertaking that he would be given the money with which to finish Schloss Chiemsee and Neuschwanstein and a promise obtained from him not to start Falkenstein—he would, under tactful pressure from some relative like his Cousin Prince Ludwig Ferdinand, in all probability have accepted it. Wagner was dead ; Bayreuth now occupied the pre-eminent position in World Opera that he and the Great Master had together originally designed for Munich. Otto was lost to him ; the cares of monarchy were increasingly distasteful ; public appearances and audiences (especially with officials) were anathema ; dreams had irrevocably usurped reality.

If Ludwig might not live a free man, he could always die. To arrive at a decision as to whether he did, or did not, commit suicide three aspects of the problem must be scrutinized : the physical ; the mental ; and, predominantly, the psychological.

On the physical side there can be no doubt but that Mayr, who had been close to his person for years, and an hourly witness of his last months of deterioration, was terrified out of his wits on the night of Friday, June 11th, and convinced

[1] Reported to have been said to Alfonso, Welcker, Weber, Mayr and Hoppe during the night of Thursday, June 10th.

that, if he handed him the key, Ludwig would have climbed the staircase to the top parapet of the great tower on the north-west corner of the Schloss and flung himself as nearly as might be into the beloved Schwan See on which once Paul had posed for him as Lohengrin. Water had always fascinated Ludwig. If a man is destined to commit suicide he is probably born to do so in a particular way.

Almost exhausted by the ordeal of his examination by the Commission on June 3rd and 10th in Munich, by the responsibility, by the incessant demands of the King, Mayr welcomed Gudden and his armed police and prison wardens with relief, threw open the castle gate and doors, and warned Gudden how best to proceed. It is significant that when, finally, he was given the key, Ludwig at once made for the entrance to the tower. His threat was not bluff and, because it was not, he was trapped.

The moment Ludwig saw Gudden and his colleagues he knew abdication was out of the question, and that, like Otto, he was to be buried alive.

Pathologically sensitive, uniquely intuitive, abnormally proud, he skilfully dissembled. Had he not a few weeks earlier completely deceived a noted alienist sent to him in the disguise of a dentist? Well, he could, and would, outwit the crude, stupid Gudden who, because he had the King's only brother under his control and, because he dealt all the time with lunatics, thought he knew everything—he, who, uninvited, dared to sit in his Sovereign's presence. Well, he would pay for that, and soon. Gudden apparently failed to realize that, because of their reversed sense of values, the mentally afflicted are always swayed, always goaded into action, by apparently trivial things.

It is necessary, as far as is legitimately possible, to reconstruct what happened and how.

At six-thirty in the evening of the Feast of Pentecost, the day upon which, bringing them peace, the Holy Ghost descends upon all sinful men, Ludwig and Gudden left the castle by the garden entrance, passed southward into the woods a few hundred yards away, and were never seen alive again.

The demesne of Berg is quite small, about one hundred

and fifty acres and, banking steeply away from the lakeside, is mostly woodland. The lakeside path ended at a small private gate that led to Seeleiten, Richard Hornig's house.

Some considerable time after eight o'clock—the delay has never been satisfactorily explained—the whole Berg household was alarmed and searching, yet the bodies of the King and Gudden were lying in shallow water in a spot that, were it not for an intervening wooded headland, was within sight of all the south windows of the Schloss and were not discovered until after ten-thirty when the King's body was found by Hubert. What happened between their leaving the castle and the King's watch stopping a quarter of an hour later ?

There would have been just time for them to follow the path to the small demesne and return to where the bodies were found ; on the other hand, the King's watch may not have stopped directly he entered the water.

The probabilities are that Ludwig, having determined that he would never join Otto at Fürstenried, threw down his umbrella, flung off his hat, overcoat and coat and walked into the water to drown himself. Gudden of course intervened, but would have no chance against Ludwig who, bigger, heavier and younger, was temporarily endowed with the strength of a maniac. He thrust Gudden's head, face downward, under the shallow water, then walked a little way, lay down and deliberately drowned himself. In order to fulfil his purpose he was, in fact, forced by Gudden to act as he did. Therefore he was not, in intention, guilty of murder.

A man does not discard his umbrella, hat, overcoat and coat unless he is determined to commit suicide, but inasmuch as such a verdict would have denied Ludwig Christian burial, and been an additional cause of grave scandal, the whole episode was glossed over.

Ludwig was ten weeks and three days short of being forty-one years old ; Gudden, between Monday, June 7th, and Saturday, June 12th, had slept only two nights ; he was sixty-two years old.

On the lakeside there were traces of footsteps and evidence

of a struggle. The wind on that Sunday evening was West South-West, the sky overcast with a tendency to rain, the temperature of the water 12° centigrade.

At the moment of birth Ludwig was greeted by water. All the lofty fountains before and behind Schloss Nymphenburg flung high their silver cascades to greet his first sunrise. As a baby he adored watching the Marmor Kaskade. His tiny feet first walked beside the mile-long waterpieces and the lakes in the Schloss Park adjoining the Pagodenburg and the Badenburg. At sinister Fürstenried he and Otto, leaning over a marble fountain, fed the fish. At Berg all the rooms he used were within sight and sound of water. In his bedroom at Hohenschwangau directly he became King he had a fountain with running water made. Linderhof, with its blue grotto, he made a miracle of fountains and water pieces ; Schloss Chiemsee on its small island is surrounded by water. The loveliest views from Hohenschwangau and Neuschwanstein is that of the eerie, deep-green-blue Schwan See. The Isle of Roses on Lake Starnberg is lapped by the ever-changing waves. A powerful and accomplished swimmer, Ludwig was a complete nympholept ; born under the spell of running water, loving its caresses on his body, its kiss on his eyelids, its music in his ears he, at the end, exultingly embraced it as it drew him home to its eternal quietude, thus keeping for ever inviolate his last secret.

As he walked quietly beside Gudden whose profane intrusive feet were soiling the path consecrated by the Great Master, by Paul his first comrade, by Elizabeth, by Sophie his shimmering dove, by Richard beloved of his soul—by a thousand memories happy and sad—Ludwig made up his mind. The walls of the little castle behind him had been the first in Bavaria to echo to the strains of his sensuous music played by the Master himself—not with notable skill but with ineffable love and perfect understanding.

Lohengrin ! Tristan ! Parsifal ! Had not the Great Master said that he, Ludwig of Bavaria, had inspired and personified them all.

As they sauntered quietly underneath a low cloud-laden

sky, the fine rain and mist silencing and softening everything, Ludwig vividly overheard Isolde's last words :

To be dissipated on the air, among the floods of the
voluptuous sea, in the resonance of the aerial waves, in
the universal breath of the All, drowned, absorbed ; oh,
oblivion, supreme joy . . .

At last the Lonely King had himself found the only possible
answer to his lifelong prayer : ' To me my rest.'

The Queen Mother Marie survived Ludwig by less than
three years. She remained benign and sweet-tempered
looking to the end, dying at the castle of Hohenschwangau
on May 17th, 1889. Like many converts, she was extremely
devout. Her private life was very quiet, utterly simple,
filled with prayer and unostentatious charity. There is
no record of her having seen Ludwig after his death nor, as
far as we know, did she, between Ludwig's death and her
own, ever see Otto. Indeed, such an interview would
have been not only agonizing, but useless.

Immediately after Ludwig's death two tall stakes were
sunk deeply into the ground on the exact spot in Lake
Starnberg where he was drowned. They formed a socket
for a cross which during his mother's lifetime, and for many
years afterwards, always bore a wreath of flowers. On the
lakeside opposite the cross the Queen Mother had a rather
heavy, Romanesque votive chapel built on a space cleared
for the purpose. Until the advent of Hitler the altar rail
was always surrounded by wreaths placed there annually
on S. Ludwig's Day, on All Saints' Day, and on other anniversaries. Invariably they were tied with ribands of the
Bavarian national colours of white and blue and bore an
epigraph and the donors' names in silver or gold. Until
then there was also a King Ludwig's Brotherhood, the chief
objective of which was to keep his name and memory alive,
hold commemorative services, and engage in certain
philanthropic and social activities. It had its headquarters
in Munich and branches throughout Bavaria. People,
young people, who could never have known Ludwig, met
regularly to remember the Fairy King and pray for the

furtherances of his ideals and the repose of his soul.   Until
recently Bavarian peasants wore a medallion of Ludwig on
their gaily coloured neckties.   The Chapel is now beautifully kept and fully restored to its dedicated purpose.

The Queen Mother also had built on a grass mound halfway between the west front of the Chapel and the Memorial
Cross in the water a tall, stone pillar containing a lamp, the
lantern surmounted by a cross, which it was her intention
should bear a light in perpetuity.   The last three years of
her sad and lonely life were filled, and it may be comforted,
by these pious activities.

The lifelong relations between Mother and son were close
and comforting.   He never, in 1870 or at any other time,
refused to meet her ' because she was a Prussian princess '.
His few outbursts of irritability and petulance towards her
were easily accounted for by the brain pressure to which he
was excruciatingly, continuously, and increasingly subject.
To his mother he was, as to all women, consistently kind
and courteous and towards the end of his life their common
concern for Otto, and his mother's intuitive understanding
of his dire inner need to continue building, made them
almost one.   They had it in common that they were a king
and queen of loneliness.   His mother loved Ludwig, but
Otto was her favourite.

Amongst her most sacred possessions Queen Marie
treasured Ludwig's last letter to her which he wrote from
Linderhof on that first of June—the final day at Linderhof,
the day of the ' last fall ', the day Welcker gave evidence
against him in secret, the day of the last journey from
Linderhof to Hohenschwangau.   On it the Queen wrote :
' Died 13th June at Berg.   Whitsunday !   Last letter.'

But it was of 1851, when he was only six years old, that
his mother wrote the authentic epitaph of one who, like
too many others, never laid aside his toys :

Early in life Ludwig was attracted by art, he was fond
of building churches (with toy bricks), monasteries and
similar things, he enjoyed listening to my telling him
Biblical stories and loved seeing the illustrations ;   he
especially liked the story of the Samaritan, and the
Sunday lessons.   He had a predilection for the Cathedral

in Munich, and used to disguise himself as a nun. He enjoyed theatricals, loved pictures and so on, was fond of listening to stories either read or told to him. From his childhood he loved giving away things to others.

Let us hope that this poor Mother was spared the ultimate anguish of realizing it might well have been through her that Ludwig inherited the peculiar temperament of her great-great-uncle Friedrich the Great of Prussia, and which later reappeared in two of the sons of Wilhelm II.

Unlike Ludwig, Otto remained slim to the end. After the fashion set by Napoleon III and by Ludwig himself, he grew a moustache and imperial of thinnish, auburn hair. As far as preventing self-injury permitted, he was always treated as a King, but there is no evidence that he ever realized that he had inherited his brother's crown. Some people held that in their earlier years Otto was handsomer and more winning than Ludwig. He was shorter and lighter, with an attractive bearing and carriage, fine, slim, muscular limbs and auburn-blonde hair. A photograph taken at the age of sixteen in the uniform of a First Lieutenant in the Infantry Life Guards shows that he had a strange, pensive charm. Like many melancholy souls he, at any rate in earlier years, wore so successfully his mask of spurious gaiety that he was known in Munich society as ' the merry Otto '. But timidity lurked behind the deep-set beautiful dark blue eyes with their long dark lashes ; the handsome mouth was nervously held in control ; the fine nose had delicate, sensitive nostrils ; the hands, however, were coarse and were clumsy. Otto escaped into what people call madness ; Ludwig remained imprisoned in his cage. Late photographs of Otto were those of a ghost ; there was nothing there but a shivering apprehension.

He spent countless hours of his life with his face pressed to a window staring out at nothingness.

At the Castle of Fürstenried God released him from this vigil on October 11th, 1916, at eight-fifty in the evening, the cause of death being a haemorrhage of the stomach. The inevitable fluctuations of his health were recorded daily and preserved in forty-odd bound foolscap volumes in the secret House Archives. It is to be hoped that they have not perished ; as a prolonged and detailed case-paper they were probably unique and would have great clinical and pathological value.

Three days after his death Otto was given, in spite of the First World War, a King's funeral. Flags were at half-mast. The crowded streets were lined with troops ; older Members of the Royal Family, Foreign Princes, Envoys and Diplomatists, and many older representatives of the Bavarian nobility, packed the Church of S. Michael ; all the young Princes of the Blood like Prince Adalbert were on active service. The Court went into mourning for three months.

Otto was borne down the stone steps on the Gospel side of the sanctuary—to the Royal tomb below and his coffin placed beside that of Ludwig in the vacant place that had awaited it for thirty years. Both catafalques are very large as if they contained several inner shells and are covered with velvet palls embroidered in silver long since tarnished and both bear full-sized gilt crowns. In death, as in life, Ludwig and Otto are side by side—but not together. Ludwig loved Otto ; whom, or what, Otto loved nobody knows. Ludwig flung his secret at the world. Otto kept his own counsel. He is the most silent King in history.

The uncle of Ludwig and Otto, Prince Regent Luitpold, died in 1912 in his ninety-second year, twenty-six years after Ludwig and four years before Otto, after reigning in their stead for over a quarter of a century, a well-beloved, popular and deeply respected figure. He was succeeded by his son, Ludwig (father of the Crown Prince Rupprecht) who, in 1913, ascended the Throne as Ludwig III. There were then two kings in Bavaria, one at Fürstenried and one at the Residenz !

Ludwig III was a simple, quiet-living man without personal ambition, by choice an admirable farmer. Without doubt, for what at the time seemed to them cogent reasons, his constitutional advisers urged him to don his mad cousin's crown. Strict Legitimists withheld their allegiance ; rigid Catholics said their Rosary ; the superstitious prophesied disaster and declared that, by what amounted to usurpation, the seven hundred and thirty-three year old good luck of the Wittelsbachs had come to an end. It did so five years later.

Ludwig the Second's favourite female cousin and true friend, Anna of Hesse, was born on May 25th, 1843, and was therefore two years and three months his senior. She was married on May 12th, 1864, when Ludwig was feverishly searching for Wagner, to Friedrich Franz II Grand Duke of Mecklenburg-Schwerin and, after eleven months of marriage, died in childbirth on April 16th, 1865, aged twenty-two, about the time Ludwig renamed his steam launch *Maximilian* the *Tristan*. The baby, a girl, died of tuberculosis before she was twenty.[1]

Ludwig's calf love for her mother made it impossible for him even to consider falling in love with and marrying the only daughter of the Tsar Alexander II of Russia and Princess Dagmar of Denmark. Only eleven when her mother brought her to Bavaria to meet Ludwig, the Grand Duchess Marie Alexandrovna afterwards married Queen Victoria's second son, Alfred, Duke of Edinburgh, who in due course became Duke of Saxe-Coburg and Gotha. A woman of strong character and somewhat imperious temper, she became the mother of Queen Marie of Rumania and the Grand Duchess Kyril of Russia, and in all probability she was much happier living in England and Saxe-Coburg than she would ever have been in Bavaria.

The fate of Elizabeth of Austria and her only son the Crown Prince Rudolf is too well known to require much space. He had loved her. Ludwig's death shocked Sisi profoundly, not so much because she loved or admired him, as because she was sore afraid for herself and for Rudolf; both of whom were too like Ludwig, and therefore understood him only too well. Naturally, Elizabeth was furious at the crude treatment meted out to their King

[1] The author is indebted for this and other information to Anna's niece, the late Dowager Marchioness of Milford Haven, e.d. of Ludwig IV Grand Duke of Hesse-Darmstadt and Princess Alice of Great Britain : the Dowager Marchioness was the grandmother of H.R.H. the Duke of Edinburgh.

by the heads of the Bavarian Government and its emissaries, and did not hesitate to say so.   She went to the S. Michael's Church, descended to the crypt, prayed for Ludwig and left flowers above his heart.   She had Masses said for the repose of his soul.   Better still, heartachingly she devoted time, care and money to improving the welfare of the insane in Austria and elsewhere.   Perhaps in one of the mental institutions she founded the lunatic who stabbed her to death on the quay in Geneva in 1898 may eventually have found refuge.

So much has been written about Elizabeth and Rudolf that is conjectural and misleading that two first-hand, authentic impressions are worth rescuing from oblivion. The Archduchess Maria Josefa, a daughter of King Georg of Saxony, wife of the Archduke Otto and mother of the Emperor Karl, of course knew Elizabeth extremely well. In 1938, living in exile in Bavaria, talking to a visitor, she described Elizabeth as ' beautiful, simple and charming ', declaring that she always loved her husband.   Once at Cannes, Franz Josef called on the Archduchess and, some time afterwards, Elizabeth did likewise ; she demanded of her hostess : ' How was he ?   How did he look ?   Show me where he sat that I may sit there too.'   Duchess Karl Theodor (Gackl's widow) who was of course her sister-in-law admired Sisi greatly and considered that she bore her many tragic misfortunes with dignity and Christian resignation ;   adding that she always found Rudolf ' gentle, charming, chivalrous, and devoted to his mother '.

Rudolf, like Ludwig, most probably committed suicide in that shooting-lodge at Mayerling outside Vienna on that night in January 1889, when he and Marie Vetsera died together.   A man of marked ability, he was an expert linguist, a serious student of natural history, a far-seeing politician and a writer of definite promise.   Had he lived l⸗ ger and matured he might well have saved the Austro-Hungarian Empire from rapine and disaster but, like Ludwig, he put himself before his duty.

Elizabeth's younger sister, Sophie, the six months' love of Ludwig, was like him, Elizabeth and Rudolf to die a violent death.   There is no reason to assume that her marriage to the Duc d'Alençon was anything but a success. At any rate, their daughter Princess Louise d'Orleans married in 1891 Prince Alfonso of Bavaria (younger brother of Prince Ludwig Ferdinand), lived happily in Bavaria and had two children, Prince Clemens and Princess Elizabeth. Princess Louise inherited Sophie's beauty and a generous measure of her quiet, pensive charm.

As a leader of Royalist Society in France Sophie was naturally much occupied with charities of all kinds. As one of the Patronesses she was present at the great charity fête held in Paris in May 1897 : a terrible fire broke out and, with many others, Ludwig's one-time affianced wife was burned to death. Survivors said she maintained her presence of mind and died heroically trying to help others to escape.

Paul of Taxis married morganatically, was disowned by his haughty family, resigned from the Bavarian Army, and disappeared into obscurity. His relations with his Sovereign and former best friend remained sufficiently good for him to ask Ludwig to give him a title upon his marriage to a minor actress. What Ludwig replied is unknown, but in the 1875 and 1880 issues the *Almanach de Gotha* stated that Prince Paul had renounced his birthright, his rank, and his name, and had been ' inscribed upon the list of the nobility of Bavaria as Monsieur de Fels '. As he possessed the Order of the Crown this would of itself give him in Bavaria noble status.

Upon his final disagreement with Ludwig in the spring of 1886, Hornig retired to the house he occupied at Rohren-feld-on-Donau as Chief of the Royal Stables and Stud Farms. His evidence before the Government Committee of Inquiry was both damning and conclusive. On that Whit-Sunday night in June 1886 he was at Gastein in Austria taking a cure and was hastily summoned to Seeleiten by his family. The delay in finding the bodies of Ludwig and Gudden was probably caused by the fact that the search party went direct to Seeleiten to look for Ludwig whom they thought would surely have gone to Hornig for help. They scoured the house and grounds of course without success. Hornig always said Ludwig did not commit suicide but, fighting Gudden to escape from his custody, had a heart attack. But the autopsy disclosed no heart trouble and, anyhow, Gudden was forcibly drowned. Two simultaneous heart attacks are incredible.

Ludwig repeatedly offered Hornig dignities which, to his honour, he always refused. Indeed, Ludwig had wanted to create him a noble and send him as his Representative to Versailles in 1870. Perhaps his patient, peasant common sense might have infused a greater measure of foresight into the deliberations.

However, after Ludwig's death Hornig remained in the Royal service and tamely consented to be ennobled by the Government of the Prince Regent Luitpold in 1901 when he was granted the coveted participle Von. He died at Rohrenfeld in August 1911, was cremated in Ulm and buried in Munich. His daughter Helene Frau Von Schroen—to whom the author is greatly indebted for information—survived until after the outbreak of the Second World War.

From an equivocal Court position Varicourt and Hirschberg retired into a self-respecting obscurity from which they had by a Royal whim been almost forced to emerge. Except Wagner, who was great enough to impose his own terms, none of Ludwig's friendships or loves had the ghost of a chance because he saw in each, not a human being, but the embodiment of a fevered dream. Paul was Pythias to his Damon, Sophie the apotheosis of Wagner's Elsa, Sisi that of S. Elizabeth of the Wartburg, Varicourt of Louis XIV, Hirschberg of an adolescent's dream of an heroic man, and Kainz the protean embodiment of half a score of romantic stage heroes. Nevertheless, Kainz, by reason of his manly independence of spirit, emerged from the dangerous position of Royal favourite. He is almost unique in history in doing so with enhanced stature, and lived to be one of the greatest actors Austro-Hungary has produced. He played all the famous classical parts, his Hamlet being among the greatest of them all and died greatly loved and honoured. He treasured every souvenir or gift received from Ludwig and always held the King's name in warm affection and his fame in cherished reverence.

Ludwig's intense and emotional love always turned to hatred when a subject boasted of his friendship with his King. He called it ' becoming haughty '. Very early in their relationships Ludwig had severely to reprimand Dürckheim-Montmartin for this mistake. But Dürckheim was as indiscreet as he was loyal, the type of good, sound, honest soldier with more heart and courage than brains. A worse emissary to send to borrow money without security for a bankrupt monarch could hardly be imagined. That, short of threatening to shoot the German Emperor, Bismarck, the bankers, and everyone uncomplaisant, Dürckheim took every impossible measure to achieve success is, however, certain. He returned to Hohenschwangau during the excitement of the first attempt at Ludwig's arrest and did all he could to defend his master and friend. His telegrams in the King's name to the Emperors Wilhelm I and Franz Josef, to Bismarck and to the Officer Commanding at the Jäger (Chasseurs) Regiment stationed at Kempten to report immediately at Neuschwanstein were all suppressed by the Government. Cut off from the outer world Ludwig was powerless, and was probably the first King in history to be dethroned and imprisoned by means of the telegraph.

It is uncertain if Dürckheim had a hand in drawing up Ludwig's last Proclamation. It is an excellent document, admirably designed to achieve its purpose and, if Ludwig drafted it unaided, is further proof that, in many ways, he was far from being insane.

Some time after Ludwig's death Dürckheim was allowed to resume his Army career, reached the rank of General, and honourably ended his military career in command of the third Bavarian Army Corps at Würzburg. The type of soldier who likes fighting his battles over again, he was given to boring his fellow members of his Munich club by boasting in great detail of his relationships with Ludwig, his financial skirmishes, and his organization of the last defence of the Castle of Neuschwanstein. Some, if not all,

of the members of the Royal Family liked him and in 1906
he was in the suite of Prince and Princess Ludwig Ferdinand
when they represented the Prince Regent and the Bavarian
Royal Family and Government at the wedding of King
Alfonso XIII with Princess Victoria Eugenia, niece of
King Edward VII of Great Britain.

Dürckheim-Montmartin died in Locarno in April 1912,
aged sixty-two.

During, and after, Ludwig's death Holnstein's position
in Bavaria became increasingly ambiguous, largely because
of his political activities in 1870–1871.   He was in fact from
first to last not Ludwig's Master of the Horse, but Bismarck's
supple tool.   His brewery, the Thalhauser Bock, supplied
Bismarck's cellar.   In 1883, at the onset of the financial
crisis, he at last fell out of favour with Ludwig because he
refused to try and raise loans.   He disappeared into a well-
deserved obscurity, eventually becoming blind.   It was
generally believed that he received from Bismarck a large
sum of money for his complicity in 1870.

Of Welcker nothing is known.   As he was only about
two-and-twenty in 1886 it is just possible that, hidden away
in the lovely Bavarian mountains, there is an old, old man
who knew, as few others knew him, the Fairy King and, all
passion spent and purged, treasures, like all the old, idealized
memories in his heart.   As a Royal valet of the Chamber
he must have known Ludwig more intimately than anyone
else in the Household entourage.

Women, in fact, played a considerable part in Ludwig's
life, and nearly all of them considered it their privilege to
give him unasked-for advice as to how best to order his
private and public life and this, oddly enough, he never
resented.   His genuine love for Anna of Hesse and Sibylle
von Leonrod is amply proved by their correspondence.
Ludwig did not meet Cosima Wagner very often ; but
their extensive correspondence is well known ; he liked her
and admired her enormously.   In 1869 he begged her as
' his truly loved friend ' to come with Wagner to Munich
to hear *Tristan*.   Cosima's grasp of affairs, intense devotion

to the Great Master, relentless purpose in shielding him, and forwarding his success at any cost made her to Ludwig, after Wagner, ' the dearest being on earth and one most worthy of veneration '.

Like Cosima, most of the other women in Ludwig's life came into it by way of singing, music and, in the one instance of Elizabeth Ney, sculpture.   It is doubtful if Ludwig would ever have developed even a passing interest in Sophie were it not that she had a charming soprano voice, was an accomplished pianist, possessed of a genuine understanding of music, and was the sister of Gackl and Sisi.   Malwina Schnorr von Carolsfeld interested Ludwig because she was the wife of the great German heroic tenor who created so many Wagner rôles and, on her own account, because of the beautiful performance she gave when together they sang the title rôles in *Tristan und Isolde* in Munich in 1865. Lili von Balyowski he admired because of her re-creations of such parts as Maria Stuart, and his favourite Louis XIV dramatic concoctions.   Lili von Balyowski had a lovely voice but, as she was fat and ugly, he very wisely made her hide behind a screen of flowers when singing for him.   If a nightingale may without indignity do this, why not an ageing prima donna ?   Singers, actresses and actors appealed to Ludwig only in so far as they made his dream world more real.   But, because of his nature, all Ludwig's loves, male or female, were fated to sterility.   Perhaps, of them all, the most potent was his passion for Marie Antoinette, of whom he said : ' I love her better than any woman who ever lived.'

INDEX